# Artificial Intelligence, Computer Vision and 3D Display

# Artificial Intelligence, Computer Vision and 3D Display

Guest Editors

**Yu Zhao**

**Yan-Ling Piao**

**Hui-Ying Wu**

**Xiang Yin**

MDPI

Basel • Beijing • Wuhan • Barcelona • Belgrade • Novi Sad • Cluj • Manchester

*Guest Editors*

Yu Zhao
College of Information Engineering
Yangzhou University
Yangzhou
China

Yan-Ling Piao
Institute of Optoelectronics
West Lake University
Hangzhou
China

Hui-Ying Wu
School of Information and Communications Engineering
Chungbuk National University
Cheongju-si
Republic of Korea

Xiang Yin
College of Information Engineering
Yangzhou University
Yangzhou
China

*Editorial Office*

MDPI AG
Grosspeteranlage 5
4052 Basel, Switzerland

This is a reprint of the Special Issue, published open access by the journal *Electronics* (ISSN 2079-9292), freely accessible at: https://www.mdpi.com/journal/electronics/special_issues/5YK8P8ENTU.

For citation purposes, cite each article independently as indicated on the article page online and as indicated below:

Lastname, A.A.; Lastname, B.B. Article Title. *Journal Name* **Year**, *Volume Number*, Page Range.

**ISBN 978-3-7258-7304-3 (Hbk)**
**ISBN 978-3-7258-7305-0 (PDF)**
**https://doi.org/10.3390/books978-3-7258-7305-0**

# Contents

# About the Editors

**Yu Zhao**

Yu Zhao is affiliated with the College of Information Engineering at Yangzhou University, Yangzhou, China, where he currently serves as an Associate Professor. He received his Ph.D. in Information and Communication Engineering from Chungbuk National University, South Korea, in 2018. His research interests focus on three-dimensional display, computer-generated holography (CGH), and three-dimensional image processing, with an emphasis on real-time color holographic 3D display technologies for real-world objects and AI-driven acceleration algorithms for hologram generation. Dr. Zhao has led or participated in multiple national and provincial research projects, including the National Natural Science Foundation of China, the Jiangsu Provincial Youth Fund, and the China Postdoctoral Science Foundation. He has published over 40 peer-reviewed papers as first author or corresponding author in prominent journals such as *Optics Express*, *Optics* and *Lasers in Engineering*, and *Applied Sciences*, as well as in leading conferences including Digital Holography and 3-D Imaging (DH) and the International Symposium on Display Holography (ISDH). He holds several patents and software copyrights related to holographic display, image processing, and interactive systems. Dr. Zhao serves as a Guest Editor for the journal *Entropy*, *Electronics* and as a reviewer for several international journals in the fields of optics and imaging. He was selected for the Jiangsu Province Science and Technology Vice President Project and the 2019 Yangzhou City "Green Yangzhou Golden Phoenix Plan" Outstanding Doctoral Program. His current work includes the development of full-color holographic systems using RGB-D salient object detection, point cloud gridding methods, and holographic voice-interactive technologies.

**Yan-Ling Piao**

Yan-Ling Piao is affiliated with the Institute of Optoelectronics at Westlake University, Hangzhou, China. Her research interests include holography, computer-generated holography (CGH), integral imaging, and three-dimensional image encryption. She has contributed to advancing digital holographic display systems and phase retrieval algorithms for secure 3D imaging. Dr. Piao has published extensively in internationally renowned journals such as *Applied Optics* and has presented her work at major conferences including SPIE OPTO, OSA Digital Holography and 3-D Imaging (DH), and the International Meeting on Information Display (IMID). She has collaborated on multiple interdisciplinary projects involving holographic optical elements and 3D visualization technologies, and serves as a reviewer for several optics-related journals. Her current research explores the integration of holographic displays with AI-driven imaging techniques for next-generation immersive visual systems.

**Hui-Ying Wu**

Hui-Ying Wu is affiliated with the School of Information and Communications Engineering at Chungbuk National University, Cheongju-si, South Korea, where she currently serves as a postdoctoral researcher. Her research focuses on full-color holography, holographic optical elements (HOEs), holographic waveguide displays, and the optical characterization of photopolymers for augmented reality (AR) and solar concentrator applications. She received her Ph.D. in Information and Communication Engineering from Chungbuk National University in 2022, with a dissertation on high-efficiency full-color holographic optical elements. Dr. Wu has participated in numerous national research projects funded by the National Research Foundation of Korea (NRF) and the

Institute for Information & Communications Technology Planning & Evaluation (IITP), focusing on holographic near-eye displays, HOE-based waveguide systems, and light field microscopy. She has authored or co-authored over 20 peer-reviewed journal articles and conference proceedings in leading optics publications such as *Optics Express*, *Optics* and *Laser Technology*, and *SPIE Proceedings*. Her contributions include the development of time-scheduled exposure methods for full-color holograms and the design of holographic solar concentrators with high diffraction efficiency.

**Xiang Yin**

Xiang Yin is affiliated with the College of Information Engineering at Yangzhou University in Yangzhou, China, and serves as a Guest Editor for the international journal *Electronics*' special issue on Artificial Intelligence, Computer Vision and 3D Display. His core research interests lie in artificial intelligence and optical signal processing, with a research focus on the interdisciplinary integration of AI technologies and optical information processing, exploring the application of artificial intelligence algorithms in optimizing optical signal transmission, processing and analysis for 3D display and computer vision systems. He has conducted in-depth research on AI-driven image processing and optical signal processing technologies, and his research outcomes provide important technical support for the innovation and practical application of intelligent 3D display and computer vision systems. As an academic researcher in the field of information engineering, he is committed to promoting the combination of artificial intelligence and optical engineering, and participates in academic exchanges and research cooperation in the interdisciplinary fields of artificial intelligence, computer vision and 3D display, contributing to the development and technological progress of related research directions.

# Preface

The interdisciplinary convergence of artificial intelligence (AI), computer vision, and three-dimensional (3D) display technologies is reshaping the landscape of intelligent visual perception and human-computer interaction. This Reprint presents a curated collection of peer-reviewed open-access articles from the *Electronics* special issue "Artificial Intelligence, Computer Vision and 3D Display, 2nd Edition," showcasing cutting-edge research that bridges theoretical advances and practical applications in these rapidly evolving fields.

The contributions featured in this volume explore a wide spectrum of topics, including holographic display systems, AI-driven computational imaging, 3D image processing, and edge computer vision. Beyond algorithmic innovations, this Reprint emphasizes the synergistic integration of optical engineering with machine learning and deep learning techniques. It explores how AI enhances hologram generation, optimizes 3D visualization, and enables real-time interactive systems for applications in manufacturing, healthcare, education, and urban planning. The collected works also address critical challenges in image security, data privacy, and system efficiency, reflecting the multidimensional nature of contemporary research in intelligent imaging and display.

We extend our sincere gratitude to all the authors for their valuable contributions, to the reviewers for their rigorous evaluation, and to the editorial and publishing teams at MDPI for their continuous support. It is our hope that this Reprint will serve as a valuable resource for researchers, engineers, and practitioners seeking to advance the frontiers of AI, computer vision, and 3D display technologies, and inspire further interdisciplinary collaboration and innovation.

**Yu Zhao, Yan-Ling Piao, Hui-Ying Wu, and Xiang Yin**
*Guest Editors*

*electronics*

MDPI

*Article*

# Transformer Based on Multi-Domain Feature Fusion for AI-Generated Image Detection

**Qiaoyue Man and Young-Im Cho ***

Department of Computer Engineering, Gachon University, 1342 Seongnamdaero, Sujeong-gu, Seongnam-si 13120, Republic of Korea; manqiaoyue@gachon.ac.kr
* Correspondence: yicho@gachon.ac.kr; Tel.: +82-31-750-5800

**Abstract**

With the rapid advancement of Generative Adversarial Networks (GANs), diffusion models, and other deep generative techniques, AI-generated images have achieved unprecedented levels of visual realism, posing severe challenges to the authenticity, security, and credibility of digital content. This paper proposes a novel hybrid transformer model that integrates spatial and frequency domains. It leverages CLIP to extract semantic inconsistencies in the image's spatial domain while employing wavelet transforms to capture multi-scale frequency anomalies in AI-generated images. After cross-domain feature fusion, global modeling is performed within the Swin-Transformer architecture, enabling robust authenticity detection of AI-generated images. Extensive experiments demonstrate that our detector maintains high accuracy across diverse datasets.

**Keywords:** AI-generated image detection; forged forensics; frequency domain analysis; semantic analysis

## 1. Introduction

Recently, AI-generated content (AIGC) technology has made groundbreaking progress, especially with the widespread application of generative models such as Generative Adversarial Networks (GANs) and Diffusion Models. These advances have enabled AI-generated images to reach a level of visual quality that is nearly indistinguishable from reality. The continuous evolution of diffusion models, in particular, has significantly blurred the boundary between synthetic and real images. Their powerful text-to-image generation systems not only produce works of high artistic value but also demonstrate broad application potential in advertising, entertainment, and education. However, the rapid development of these AI technologies has also introduced serious societal challenges, including security risks such as the spread of misinformation, digital identity forgery, and the erosion of evidentiary credibility. Consequently, accurately and efficiently detecting AI-generated images has become a critical research topic in computer vision, digital forensics, and cybersecurity.

Faced with this pressing challenge, developing reliable and robust detection methods for AI-generated images has emerged as a core issue in multimedia forensics, content security, and AI governance. Early detection approaches primarily relied on convolutional neural networks (CNNs), which distinguished synthetic images by modeling high-frequency artifacts, boundary discontinuities, or spectral anomalies unique to generated content in pixel space. Representative works include Chen et al. [1], who employed an improved Xception model to detect faces generated by local GANs; Darius et al. [2], who proposed MesoNet—an efficient architecture for automatically detecting face tampering in videos;

and Guarnera et al. [3], who utilized the expectation-maximization (EM) algorithm to extract local features and model convolutional traces potentially present in images. These models were largely optimized for specific generative architectures (e.g., ProGAN [4] and StyleGAN [5–7]) and achieved strong performance on data drawn from similar distributions. However, their detection accuracy degrades dramatically in "open-world" scenarios—such as images generated by unknown architectures, cross-domain generation (e.g., from natural photographs to artistic styles), or images subjected to common post-processing operations (e.g., JPEG compression, blurring, cropping, or color dithering). This generalization bottleneck fundamentally stems from CNNs' over-reliance on local textures and low-level statistical cues, which limit their ability to capture high-level semantic inconsistencies or cross-modal logical contradictions inherent in the AI image generation process.

To address this limitation, researchers have begun exploring more generalizable detection paradigms. One promising direction involves integrating frequency-domain analysis into AI-generated image detection, leveraging systematic biases exhibited by synthetic images in the Fourier domain or discrete cosine transform (DCT)—such as periodic artifacts and anomalous high-frequency energy—for authentication. For instance, Li et al. [8] proposed FreqBlender, a frequency analysis network that adaptively segments frequency components associated with forgery traces. Luo et al. [9] employed frequency-domain masking combined with spatial interactions to help models more effectively capture subtle manipulation signatures and enhance generalization. Liu et al. [10] introduced SFANet, a Spatio-Frequency Attention Network based on wavelet transforms, which uses a dual-attention mechanism to adjust frequency-domain weights for deepfake detection dynamically. Nevertheless, approaches that merely combine frequency-domain features with CNNs or standalone frequency classifiers can capture generation-specific fingerprints but often lack robust semantic context modeling, rendering them prone to misclassification in complex, open-world environments.

More recently, Transformer-based detector models have demonstrated superior generalization capabilities due to their global receptive fields and exceptional ability to model long-range dependencies. As a result, they are gradually replacing CNNs as the backbone architecture for forgery detection. Li et al. [11] developed the Detail-Aware Transformer (DAT) to focus on subtle fusion traces arising from inconsistencies in image details. Wang et al. [12] proposed $M^2$TR (Multimodal Multiscale Transformer), which fuses image frequency-domain features with RGB information and processes image patches at multiple scales to detect local inconsistencies across different spatial resolutions. Furthermore, the advent of large-scale pre-trained vision-language models like CLIP offers a powerful tool for assessing high-level semantic consistency in images. Liu et al. [13] introduced FatFormer, a forgery-aware adaptive Transformer that identifies and integrates local forgery traces from both spatial and frequency domains. Yan et al. [14] presented AIDE, an AI-generated image detector based on hybrid features, which employs multiple expert modules to simultaneously extract visual artifacts and noise while leveraging semantic and contextual cues for effective identification.

Existing CLIP/ViT-based methods emphasize semantic generalization but underutilize fine-grained, local frequency artifacts. Conversely, simple wavelet-based CNNs or frequency-domain classifiers can detect generation fingerprints yet lack robust semantic reasoning, leading to performance degradation in complex open-world settings involving diverse categories and environmental variations. To bridge this gap, we propose a hybrid model that jointly leverages spatial and frequency domains. Specifically, our approach utilizes CLIP to extract semantic inconsistencies in the spatial domain, employs discrete wavelet transforms to capture multi-scale frequency anomalies characteristic of AI-

 https://doi.org/10.3390/electronics15030716

generated images, and performs cross-domain feature fusion before feeding the combined representation into a Swin Transformer for robust authenticity verification.

Specifically, this paper makes the following contributions:

1. We propose a multimodal backbone network based on Transformers and CLIP, effectively capturing semantic inconsistencies inherent in AI-generated images.
2. We introduce the discrete wavelet transform for multi-scale frequency analysis, extracting distinctive features across different sub-bands to enhance sensitivity to generation traces.
3. We design an efficient feature fusion mechanism that organically integrates semantic and frequency-domain features into complementary representations. Extensive experiments validate the superior performance and robustness of our method across various generative models and under diverse perturbation conditions.

## 2. Related Works

Spatial Domain-Based Forgery Detection. Deep learning techniques dominate the field of detecting AI-generated images, with convolutional neural networks (CNNs) and vision transformers (ViTs) [15] being particularly effective. Early approaches to deepfake and AI-generated image detection [16,17] primarily relied on CNN architectures, which automatically learn spatial-domain artifacts such as edge blurring, inconsistent textures from upsampling, and local color discrepancies. Much of this work is built upon established backbone networks—such as ResNet [18] and Xception [19]—to perform binary classification on benchmark datasets including FaceForensics++ [20], Celeb-DF [21], and GAN-synthesized image collections [22]. While these methods achieve near-saturated accuracy on their respective training datasets, subsequent studies have revealed significant performance degradation when evaluated across unseen or heterogeneous datasets—a phenomenon often referred to as domain shift or generalization collapse.

Frequency-Based Forensics. Frequency-domain analysis methods transform images into spectral representations (e.g., via Discrete Cosine Transform or wavelet transforms) to examine generation-induced artifacts that are less apparent in the spatial domain. A key advantage of these approaches is their relative insensitivity to semantic content and robustness to common post-processing operations such as resizing and cropping. For instance, Sun et al. [23] proposed a time-frequency convolutional neural network that leverages an Upsampling Artifact Representation Module (UARM) and a Frequency-Assisted Temporal Incoherence Module (FATIM) to detect fake faces by modeling inconsistencies in frequency responses. Zhou et al. [24] introduced the Frequency-based Local and Global (FLAG) Network, which incorporates a Frequency-based Attention Enhancement Module (FAEM) to facilitate synergistic fusion between CNNs and ViTs. By exploiting frequency-domain cues to capture local textural anomalies and global structural inconsistencies jointly, FLAG demonstrates improved cross-dataset generalization. Similarly, Jia et al. [25] developed a frequency-based adversarial attack detection framework for facial forgeries, applying the Discrete Cosine Transform (DCT) and introducing a dedicated fusion module to highlight salient regions of adversarial perturbations in the frequency domain. However, as generative models advance—particularly with the rise of diffusion-based synthesis—the frequency-domain artifacts they produce have become increasingly subtle and model-dependent, limiting the effectiveness of purely frequency-based detection strategies.

Challenges Posed by Generative Model Diversity. A major challenge in current forgery detection lies in the heterogeneity of modern generative models. Common architectures include Generative Adversarial Networks (GANs), Diffusion Models, Variational Autoencoders (VAEs), and Autoregressive Models, each with numerous variants and distinct generation mechanisms. These differences lead to diverse statistical footprints and artifact

 https://doi.org/10.3390/electronics15030716

patterns in synthesized images. For example, GAN-generated images often exhibit grid-like or rasterized artifacts due to transposed convolutions during upsampling, whereas diffusion models may introduce subtle deviations in noise distribution or high-frequency coherence. Consequently, detectors fine-tuned on one class of generative models (e.g., StyleGAN) frequently fail to generalize to others (e.g., Stable Diffusion or DALL·E), highlighting a critical "model gap." This gap is exacerbated by the rapid pace of generative model development, underscoring the need for detection frameworks that identify universal traces of synthetic origin rather than model-specific signatures.

To address these limitations, this paper proposes a hybrid detection architecture that jointly exploits spatial and frequency domains. Specifically, we employ CLIP to capture semantic inconsistencies in the spatial domain—leveraging its strong zero-shot generalization and sensitivity to implausible visual-textual alignments—while simultaneously analyzing multi-scale frequency anomalies through wavelet-based decomposition. The resulting multi-domain features are then fused and globally modeled using a Swin Transformer, enabling robust and generalizable detection of AI-generated imagery across diverse generative paradigms.

## 3. Method

The model we propose is illustrated in Figure 1. It consists of preliminary multi-domain feature extraction, comprising spatial semantic inconsistency detection based on CLIP and frequency-domain feature anomaly detection based on wavelet transform. These complementary features are then fused and input to a Swin Transformer for global contextual modeling, ultimately determining whether the image is AI-generated.

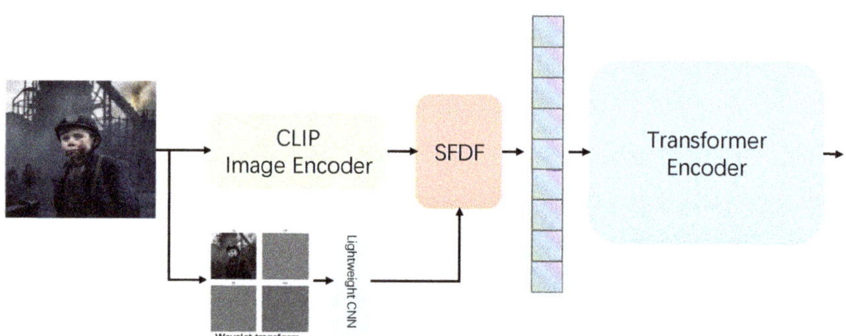


**Figure 1.** Our proposed model framework.

### 3.1. Feature Extraction

This module is responsible for extracting two complementary feature representations from the input image, including spatial domain features based on CLIP deep semantics and frequency domain features based on wavelet transform frequency domain texture.

In spatial-domain feature extraction, the CLIP encoder is used to extract pixel features from images. Considering efficiency and computational complexity, we selected ViT-L/14 as the backbone network. Since the authenticity detection model does not require learning new semantic features from images—only detecting "semantic inconsistencies" using existing prior knowledge—we adopted a frozen CLIP model. First, the input image $I \in \mathbb{R}^{H \times W \times 3}$ is segmented into N = 14 × 14 blocks, and each block is mapped to a $D_p$ dimensional embedding vector through a learnable linear projection layer $E$. The embedding sequence is then fed into CLIP-ViT, which consists of an $L_{clip}$ layer Transformer encoder. Each layer contains a multi-head self-attention (MSA) module and a multilayer perceptron

 https://doi.org/10.3390/electronics15030716

(MLP) module, along with layer normalization (LayerNorm) and residual connections. The spatial domain feature vector $F_s \in \mathbb{R}^{N \times D_p}$ is computed via the Transformer encoder.

In frequency domain feature extraction, to capture the inherent high-frequency inconsistencies in AI-generated images—particularly those arising from upsampling operations in diffusion models and generative adversarial networks (GANs)—while balancing computational efficiency, we employ a multi-level discrete wavelet transform (DWT) based on the Daubechies-4 (db4) wavelet basis, which is more efficient than other wavelet methods. The db4 wavelet was selected due to its four vanishing moments, which enable sparse representation of smooth natural signals while maintaining high sensitivity to unnatural oscillatory artifacts commonly found in synthetic images. First, a single two-dimensional discrete wavelet transform (2D-DWT) is performed independently on each color channel (R, G, B) of the input image $I \in \mathbb{R}^{H \times W \times 3}$. After the transform, each channel yields four sub-bands: a low-frequency approximation component (LL) and high-frequency detail components in three directions: horizontal (LH), vertical (HL), and diagonal (HH). The low-frequency subband LL mainly contains the overall image information and highly overlaps with pixel-domain features. The high-frequency subbands LH, HL, and HH, on the other hand, contain detailed information such as texture and edges, which are precisely the parts where the generative model is prone to distortion. Therefore, we discard the low-frequency LL and concatenate the three high-frequency subbands along the channel dimension. For a three-channel image, we finally obtain a 9-channel high-frequency feature map $\mathrm{W} \in \mathbb{R}^{(\mathrm{H}/2) \times (\mathrm{W}/2) \times 9}$. To encode the high-frequency feature map W into a sequential feature set matching the spatial resolution of the pixel-domain feature Fp, we designed a lightweight CNN encoder. This encoder consists of three convolutional blocks, each containing a 3 × 3 convolutional layer, batch normalization (BatchNorm), and a ReLU activation function. Downsampling is performed through convolutions with a stride of 2. Finally, an adaptive average pooling layer resizes the feature map to match $F_s$ and flattens it into a sequence $F_f$.

### 3.2. Spatial-Frequency Cross-Domain Feature Fusion

To effectively fuse semantic (CLIP) and artifact (Wavelet) information, we designed a two-stage fusion mechanism:

(1) Cross-Attention Alignment. Using spatial feature $F_s$ as the Query, and frequency domain feature $F_f$. as both Key and Value, compute cross-domain attention:

$$\begin{gathered} Q = F_s W_Q, K = F_f W_K, V = F_f W_V \\ A = \mathrm{Softmax}\left(\frac{QK^\top}{\sqrt{D}}\right)V, A \in \mathbb{R}^{N \times D} \end{gathered} \tag{1}$$

where $\mathrm{W_Q}, \mathrm{W_K}, \mathrm{W_V} \in \mathbb{R}^{D \times D}$ are learnable projection matrices.

(2) Gated Feature Integration. Compared to simple addition or concatenation, gating mechanisms can adaptively suppress noise bands or semantically ambiguous regions. Here, we introduce a gating mechanism to dynamically weight information from both domains:

$$\begin{aligned} G &= \sigma(\mathrm{MLP}([F_s; A])) \in \mathbb{R}^{N \times D}, \\ F_{\text{fused}} &= G \odot F_s + (1 - G) \odot A, \end{aligned} \tag{2}$$

where [·;·] represents channel concatenation, the MLP consists of two layers of linear transformation + GELU, and σ is a Sigmoid. The gate value $G$ learns the relative importance of spatial and frequency features for each token.


https://doi.org/10.3390/electronics15030716

### 3.3. Swin Transformer Backbone

The fused features obtained by combining the spatial domain and frequency domain are input into the Swin-Transformer. Through progressive downsampling using a shifted window MSA, multi-scale feature maps are output. As shown in Figure 2.

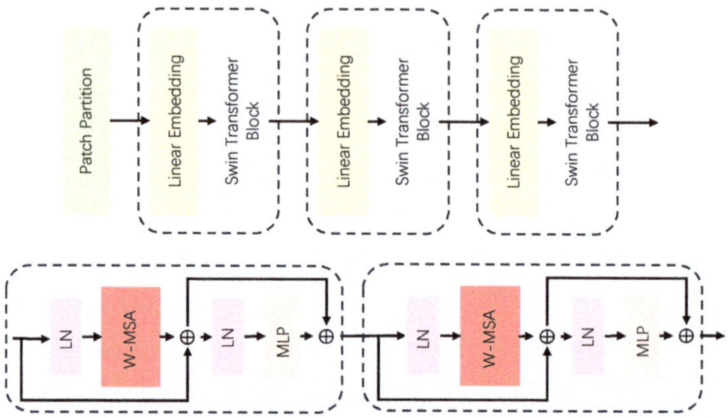


**Figure 2.** Swin-transformer internal main framework.

The fused feature map $F_{fused} \in \mathbb{R}^{H \times W \times C}$ is first projected into non-overlapping patches using a convolutional embedding layer:

$$X_0 = \text{PatchEmbed}\left(F_{fused}\right) \quad (3)$$

where each patch is mapped into a token of dimension $D$. This operation preserves spatial correspondence while enabling efficient Transformer-based processing.

The embedded tokens are processed by a sequence of Tiny Swin Transformer blocks, each consisting of Window-based Multi-Head Self-Attention (W-MSA), Shifted Window Multi-Head Self-Attention (SW-MSA), and Feed-Forward Network (FFN). Formally, the $l$-th Swin block is defined as:

$$\begin{aligned} \hat{X}^{(l)} &= \mathrm{W-MSA}\left(\mathrm{LN}(X^{(l)})\right) + X^{(l)}, \\ X^{(l+1)} &= \mathrm{FFN}\left(\mathrm{LN}(\hat{X}^{(l)})\right) + \hat{X}^{(l)} \end{aligned} \quad (4)$$

where LN denotes Layer Normalization.

We only take the final layer $Z_{\text{final}}$.

$$\begin{aligned} \mathbf{z}_{\text{pool}} &= \text{GlobalAvgPool}(\mathbf{z}_{\text{final}}) \in \mathbb{R}^{768}, \\ \hat{y} &= \text{Sigmoid}\left(\mathbf{w}^{\top}\text{MLP}\left(\mathbf{z}_{\text{pool}}\right) + b\right) \in (0,1) \end{aligned} \quad (5)$$

The main loss function can be expressed as:

$$\mathcal{L}_{\text{cls}} = -\frac{1}{B}\sum_{i=1}^{B}\left[(1-p_i)^{\gamma} y_i \log p_i + p_i^{\gamma}(1-y_i)\log(1-p_i)\right] \quad (6)$$

where $p_i = \hat{y}_i$, $\gamma = 2$ are the focusing parameters, and $y_i \in \{0, 1\}$ are the true labels (0 = real, 1 = AI-generated).

 https://doi.org/10.3390/electronics15030716

# 4. Experiments and Results

## 4.1. Dataset

In terms of dataset selection, to better verify the reliability and robustness of the model and consider the impact of different types of generative models on the detection model, this study used multiple datasets for verification experiments, including the common face dataset DFDC, as well as ForenSynths [26] and GenImage [27], which contain various types of images, as shown in Figure 3. In splitting the dataset, we used 80% for model training and 20% for testing.

**Figure 3.** Images generated by different AI models.

DFDC, the Deepfake Detection Challenge dataset, is a large dataset released by Meta to measure the progress of Deepfake detection technology. This dataset is a deep face detection dataset consisting of more than 100,000 fake videos created from 19,154 real videos and fully considers the diversity of subjects and backgrounds in real scenes (skin color, gender, lighting conditions, etc.).

ForenSynths: This dataset contains fake images generated by 11 different convolutional neural network (CNN)-based image generator models. These models cover commonly used architectures today (ProGAN, StyleGAN, BigGAN, CycleGAN, StarGAN, GauGAN, DeepFakes, etc.).

GenImage is an AI-generated image detection dataset comprising millions of images. It utilizes the same 1000 categories as ImageNet, with synthetic images generated by Midjourney, Stable Diffusion, ADM, GLIDE, Wukong, VQDM, and BigGAN.

## 4.2. Evaluation Metrics and Implementation Details

Before model training, the training images were uniformly resized to $224 \times 224$ pixels and augmented using random flipping, random cropping, and JPEG compression. During training, the lightweight CNN employed the AdamW optimizer with a learning rate of $1 \times 10^{-4}$, while the backbone Swin Transformer network used the AdamW optimizer with a learning rate of $1 \times 10^{-5}$. The batch size was set to 16, and the number of training epochs was 100. We used mean accuracy (AP) and accuracy (ACC) as evaluation metrics to

 https://doi.org/10.3390/electronics15030716

assess the proposed method. All experiments were trained on a server equipped with dual NVIDIA RTX 3090Ti GPUs, an AMD Threadripper 2950× CPU, and 64GB of RAM.

### *4.3. Comparisons with State-of-the-Art Methods*

Among AI-generated fake images, fake facial images dominate. Here, we first analyze model performance using the CFDC dataset based on facial images. Simultaneously, we test the impact of different modules on the overall network architecture. As shown in Table 1, we tested models using Clip alone for spatial feature extraction, models combining Clip-based spatial and frequency-domain feature extraction, and models employing feature fusion methods incorporating cross-domain feature attention and gating. By introducing spatial semantic analysis and frequency-domain features, and focusing on anomalous features through cross-attention and gating, our model demonstrated outstanding performance in both accuracy and average precision.

**Table 1.** Comparison with state-of-the-art models on AI-generated face forgery datasets.

| Models | DFDC | |
|---|---|---|
| | ACC | AP |
| Xception | 66.3 | 68.3 |
| $F^3$-Net [28] | 75.7 | 76.0 |
| TAN-GFD [29] | 84.3 | 85.8 |
| WMamba [30] | 90.5 | 90.0 |
| VIB-Ne [31] | 93.8 | 93.2 |
| Ours (Clip) | 94.1 | 93.8 |
| Ours (Clip + F) | 95.3 | 94.5 |
| Ours (Clip + F+A) | 97.6 | 96.0 |
| Ours (Clip + F+A + G) | 98.1. | 96.8 |

We performed a frequency domain visualization comparison of real and synthetic facial images, as shown in Figure 4. Although current AI generation capabilities have nearly reached the level of fooling the human eye, subtle differences remain detectable in the frequency domain features. Concurrently, we visualized the model's feature attention patterns.

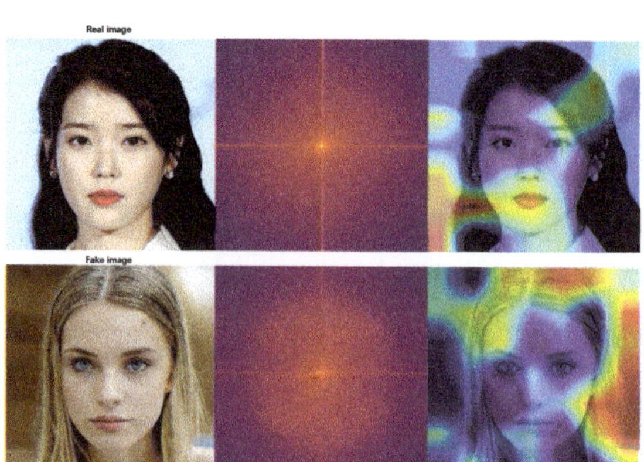


**Figure 4.** Frequency domain features of real and fake facial images and regions of interest for artifact detection.

In model testing experiments designed to detect deepfake images generated by GAN-based models, we utilized the Forensynths dataset to evaluate images produced by various GAN models, as shown in Table 2. Compared to other state-of-the-art models, our model demonstrated superior robustness.

**Table 2.** Performance comparison with other state-of-the-art models on the GANs dataset based on accuracy (ACC)/average precision (AP).

| Methods | ProGAN | StyleGAN | StyleGAN2 | BigGAN | CycleGAN | StarGAN | GauGAN | Deepfake | Mean |
|---|---|---|---|---|---|---|---|---|---|
| Wang | 64.6/92.7 | 52.8/80.8 | 75.7/96.3 | 50.7/70.2 | 58.1/79.3 | 51.2/81.7 | 53.6/84.7 | 50.3/51.5 | 57.1/79.7 |
| Fank [32] | 85.7/81.3 | 73.1/68.5 | 75.0/70.9 | 76.9/70.8 | 86.5/80.8 | 85.0/77.0 | 67.3/65.3 | 50.1/55.3 | 75.0/71.2 |
| F$^3$-Net | 87.8/82.4 | 80.3/84.7 | 82.2/87.9 | 65.5/73.4 | 81.2/89.7 | 87.8/90.4 | 57.0/59.5 | 59.9/83.0 | 75.2/81.4 |
| BiHPF [33] | 87.4/89.3 | 71.5/74.1 | 77.0/81.1 | 82.6/80.6 | 86.0/86.6 | 93.8/95.5 | 75.3/84.7 | 53.5/55.8 | 78.4/81.0 |
| FrePGA [34] | 95.3/97.1 | 82.0/90.9 | 72.2/93.8 | 66.7/69.4 | 69.7/71.1 | 97.3/99.0 | 53.7/55.0 | 62.7/80.1 | 75.0/82.1 |
| UniFD [35] | 98.3/99.8 | 78.5/92.8 | 75.4/96.0 | 89.1/94.7 | 91.9/98.0 | 96.1/99.3 | 92.6/98.3 | 80.8/90.2 | 88.1/96.1 |
| FreqNet [36] | 99.2/99.9 | 90.4/98.0 | 85.8/98.3 | 89.7/96.4 | 96.7/99.1 | 97.5/99.4 | 88.3/98.9 | 81.9/92.7 | 91.2/98.0 |
| FatFormer | 99.6/99.9 | 78.8.7/97.5 | 75.7/97.1 | 96.3/98.9 | 98.1/99.4 | 98.8/99.6 | 95.5/98.7 | 89.3/95.7 | 91.5/98.4 |
| VIB-Ne | 89.4/96.6 | 82.1/94.9 | 89.8/97.2 | 92.5/98.2 | 97.6/98.4 | 95.7/97.6 | 96.6/98.4 | 92.7/93.3 | 92.1/96.8 |
| Ours (C + F) | 97.9/98.1 | 93.2/96.7 | 88.8/97.0 | 96.3/98.4 | 98.2/99.0 | 97.3/98.6 | 96.1/97.9 | 93.3/95.4 | 95.1/97.6 |
| Ours | 98.9/99.0 | 96.3/97.5 | 91.7/99.1 | 98.5/99.1 | 98.5/99.4 | 98.7/99.5 | 97.8/98.9 | 95.3/98.6 | 96.9/98.9 |

Compared to deepfake images generated using Generative Adversarial Networks (GANs), those produced by diffusion models are more difficult to detect. They exhibit more natural edge transitions and more concealed forgery traces, making them challenging for detection models based on a single network. As shown in Table 3, most detection models perform poorly when addressing these challenges. Our proposed multi-domain fusion Transformer network simultaneously searches for forgery traces in both the spatial domain's semantic inconsistencies and the frequency domain's high-frequency features of tampered images, significantly enhancing the model's detection capabilities. Even when compared to other state-of-the-art models, our approach consistently demonstrates superior performance.

**Table 3.** Accuracy and average precision comparisons with state-of-the-art methods on the diffusion model dataset.

| Methods | PNDM | Guided | DALL-E | VQ-Diffusion | Mean |
|---|---|---|---|---|---|
| Wang | 50.8/90.3 | 54.9/66.6 | 51.8/61.3 | 50.0/71.0 | 51.8/72.3 |
| Fank | 44.0/38.2 | 53.4/52.7 | 57.1/62.8 | 52.0/66.3 | 51.6/55.0 |
| F$^3$-Net | 72.8/80.5 | 69.7/72.1 | 72.3/80.0 | 91.8/94.7 | 76.7/81.8 |
| UniFD | 75.3/92.5 | 75.7/85.1 | 89.5/96.8 | 83.5/97.7 | 81.0/93.0 |
| FreqNet | 89.3/97.0 | 81.2/92.0 | 94.8/98.3 | 92.0/97.3 | 89.3/96.2 |
| FatFormer | 92.5/94.2 | 76.8/91.7 | 95.3/99.0 | 95.4/99.1 | 90.0/96.0 |
| VIB-Ne | 94.9/97.1 | 85.1/88.9 | 97.0/98.4 | 96.5/97.8 | 93.4/95.6 |
| Ours (C + F) | 95.7/97.5 | 85.8/90.7 | 97.8/98.8 | 97.3/97.6 | 94.2/96.2 |
| Ours | 96.5/98.3 | 87.3/91.9 | 98.5/99.1 | 98.0/98.3 | 95.1/96.9 |

In AI-generated image authenticity detection tasks, operations such as image file compression, blurring, and resizing can significantly impact the model's performance, even leading to model failure. However, our proposed model, as shown in Figure 5, combines spatial, frequency, and semantic features to detect multi-dimensional features, mitigating these problems to some extent and resulting in more robust model performance.


https://doi.org/10.3390/electronics15030716

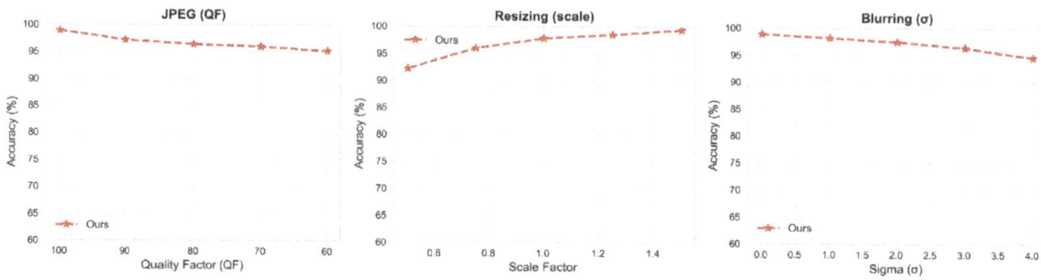


**Figure 5.** Robustness analysis of model performance across different image qualities.

We conducted a visualization analysis of the regions of interest for real and fake images in model detection, especially for AI-generated images based on diffusion models, which are currently more difficult to distinguish from real images, as shown in Figure 6.

**Figure 6.** Visual analysis of model attention focuses for real images and AI-generated fake images (left: real image; right: AI-generated image).

## 5. Conclusions

In this paper, we propose a novel cross-domain AI-generated image detection framework that integrates spatial-semantic information based on CLIP with frequency representations based on wavelets through a cross-attention fusion mechanism. Leveraging the hierarchical modeling capabilities of the Swin Transformer backbone, our method effectively captures the inherent local artifacts and global inconsistencies present in AI-generated images. Extensive experiments demonstrate that our approach outperforms existing methods across multiple benchmarks and generative models, particularly in cross-model generalization scenarios.

**Author Contributions:** Conceptualization, Q.M.; methodology, software, Q.M.; validation, Q.M.; Y.-I.C.; formal analysis, Q.M.; investigation, Q.M.; resources, Q.M. and Y.-I.C.; data curation, Q.M.; writing—original draft preparation, Q.M.; writing—review and editing, Q.M.; visualization, Q.M.; supervision, Q.M. and Y.-I.C.; project administration, Q.M. and Y.-I.C.; funding acquisition, Q.M.; Y.-I.C. All authors have read and agreed to the published version of the manuscript.

 https://doi.org/10.3390/electronics15030716

**Funding:** This research was supported by the Korea Institute of Marine Science & Technology Promotion (KIMST) from 2022 under the project entitled "Development and Demonstration of a Data Platform for AI-Based Safe Fishing Vessel Design" (RS-2022-KS221571). This work was also supported by the Ministry of Trade, Industry and Energy (MOTIE) and implemented by the Korea Institute for Advancement of Technology (KIAT) under the project entitled "Development of an International Standardization and Sustainability Integration Framework for AI Industry Internalization and Global Competitiveness Enhancement" (RS-2025-07372968). In addition, this work was supported by the Gachon University Research Fund in 2021 (GCU-202106340001).

**Institutional Review Board Statement:** All subjects gave their informed consent for inclusion before they participated in the study. Ethics approval is not required for this type of study. The study has been granted exemption by the Creative Commons BY 2.0, Creative Commons BY-NC 2.0, Public Domain Mark 1.0, Public Domain CC0 1.0, or U.S. Government Works license.

**Informed Consent Statement:** Not applicable.

**Data Availability Statement:** All datasets utilized in this article are open-source and publicly available for researchers.

**Conflicts of Interest:** The authors declare no conflicts of interest.

## References

1. Chen, B.; Ju, X.; Xiao, B.; Ding, W.; Zheng, Y.; de Albuquerque, V.H.C. Locally GAN-generated face detection based on an improved Xception. *Inf. Sci.* **2021**, *572*, 16–28. [CrossRef]
2. Afchar, D.; Nozick, V.; Yamagishi, J.; Echizen, I. Mesonet: A compact facial video forgery detection network. In Proceedings of the 2018 IEEE International Workshop on Information Forensics and Security (WIFS), Hong Kong, China, 11–13 December 2018; pp. 1–7.
3. Guarnera, L.; Giudice, O.; Battiato, S. Deepfake detection by analyzing convolutional traces. In Proceedings of the IEEE/CVF Conference on Computer Vision and Pattern Recognition Workshops, Seattle, WA, USA, 16–18 June 2020; pp. 666–667.
4. Gao, H.; Pei, J.; Huang, H. Progan: Network embedding via proximity generative adversarial network. In Proceedings of the 25th ACM SIGKDD International Conference on Knowledge Discovery & Data Mining, Anchorage, AK, USA, 4–8 August 2019; pp. 1308–1316.
5. Karras, T.; Laine, S.; Aila, T. A style-based generator architecture for generative adversarial networks. In Proceedings of the IEEE/CVF Conference on Computer Vision and Pattern Recognition, Beach, CA, USA, 18–20 June 2019; pp. 4401–4410.
6. Karras, T.; Laine, S.; Aittala, M.; Hellsten, J.; Lehtinen, J.; Aila, T. Analyzing and improving the image quality of stylegan. In Proceedings of the IEEE/CVF Conference on Computer Vision and Pattern Recognition, Seattle, WA, USA, 14–19 June 2020; pp. 8110–8119.
7. Karras, T.; Aittala, M.; Laine, S.; Härkönen, E.; Hellsten, J.; Lehtinen, J.; Aila, T. Alias-free generative adversarial networks. *Adv. Neural Inf. Process. Syst.* **2021**, *34*, 852–863.
8. Hanzhe, L.; Zhou, J.; Li, Y.; Wu, B.; Li, B.; Dong, J. FreqBlender: Enhancing DeepFake Detection by Blending Frequency Knowledge. In Proceedings of the Thirty-Eighth Annual Conference on Neural Information Processing Systems, Vancouver, BC, Canada, 10–15 December 2024.
9. Luo, X.; Wang, Y. Frequency-Domain Masking and Spatial Interaction for Generalizable Deepfake Detection. *Electronics* **2025**, *14*, 1302. [CrossRef]
10. Liu, X.; Xiao, W.; Lin, X.; He, S.; Huang, C.; Guo, D. Deepfake Detection via Spatial-Frequency Attention Network. *IEEE Trans. Consum. Electron.* **2025**, *71*, 9832–9841. [CrossRef]
11. Li, J.; Yu, L.; Liu, R.; Xie, H. A Detail-Aware Transformer to Generalisable Face Forgery Detection. *IEEE Trans. Circuits Syst. Video Technol.* **2024**, *35*, 3262–3275. [CrossRef]
12. Wang, J.; Wu, Z.; Ouyang, W.; Han, X.; Chen, J.; Jiang, Y.-G.; Li, S.-N. M2tr: Multi-modal multi-scale transformers for deepfake detection. In Proceedings of the 2022 International Conference on Multimedia Retrieval, Newark, NJ, USA, 27–30 June 2022; pp. 615–623.
13. Liu, H.; Tan, Z.; Tan, C.; Wei, Y.; Wang, J.; Zhao, Y. Forgery-aware adaptive transformer for generalizable synthetic image detection. In Proceedings of the IEEE/CVF Conference on Computer Vision and Pattern Recognition, Seattle, WA, USA, 19–21 June 2024; pp. 10770–10780.
14. Yan, S.; Li, O.; Cai, J.; Hao, Y.; Jiang, X.; Hu, Y.; Xie, W. A sanity check for ai-generated image detection. *arXiv* **2024**, arXiv:2406.19435. [CrossRef]

 https://doi.org/10.3390/electronics15030716

15. Dosovitskiy, A. An image is worth 16x16 words: Transformers for image recognition at scale. *arXiv* **2020**, arXiv:2010.11929.
16. Nguyen, H.H.; Yamagishi, J.; Echizen, I. Capsule-forensics networks for deepfake detection. In *Handbook of Digital Face Manipulation and Detection: From DeepFakes to Morphing Attacks*; Springer International Publishing: Cham, Switzerland, 2022; pp. 275–301.
17. Chen, L.; Zhang, Y.; Song, Y.; Liu, L.; Wang, J. Self-supervised learning of adversarial example: Towards good generaliza-tions for deepfake detection. In Proceedings of the IEEE/CVF Conference on Computer Vision and Pattern Recognition, New Orleans, LA, USA, 21–24 June 2022; pp. 18710–18719.
18. He, K.; Zhang, X.; Ren, S.; Sun, J. Identity mappings in deep residual networks. In Proceedings of the European Conference on Computer Vision, Amsterdam, The Netherlands, 11–14 October 2016; pp. 630–645.
19. Chollet, F. Xception: Deep learning with depthwise separable convolutions. In Proceedings of the IEEE Conference on Computer Vision and Pattern Recognition, Honolulu, HI, USA, 21–26 July 2017; pp. 1251–1258.
20. Rossler, A.; Cozzolino, D.; Verdoliva, L.; Riess, C.; Thies, J.; Nießner, M. Faceforensics++: Learning to detect manipulated facial images. In Proceedings of the IEEE/CVF International Conference on Computer Vision, Seoul, Republic of Korea, 27 October–2 November 2019; pp. 1–11.
21. Li, Y.; Yang, X.; Sun, P.; Qi, H.; Lyu, S. Celeb-df: A large-scale challenging dataset for deepfake forensics. In Proceedings of the IEEE/CVF Conference on Computer Vision and Pattern Recognition, Seattle, WA, USA, 14–19 June 2020; pp. 3207–3216.
22. Ren, H.; Yan, A.; Ren, X.; Ye, P.-G.; Gao, C.-z.; Zhou, Z.; Li, J. Ganfinger: Gan-based fingerprint generation for deep neural network ownership verification. *arXiv* **2023**, arXiv:2312.15617.
23. Sun, R.; Yu, X.; Wang, F.; Da, Z.; Zhang, Y.; Gao, J. Frequency-Assisted Temporal Upsampling Artifacts Representation Learning for Face Forgery Detection. *IEEE Trans. Biom. Behav. Identity Sci.* **2025**, *7*, 728–739. [CrossRef]
24. Zhou, K.; Sun, G.; Wang, J.; Wang, J.; Yu, L. FLAG: Frequency-based local and global network for face forgery detection. *Multimed. Tools Appl.* **2025**, *84*, 647–663. [CrossRef]
25. Jia, S.; Ma, C.; Yao, T.; Yin, B.; Ding, S.; Yang, X. Exploring frequency adversarial attacks for face forgery detection. In Proceedings of the IEEE/CVF Conference on Computer Vision and Pattern Recognition, New Orleans, LA, USA, 19–24 June 2022; pp. 4103–4112.
26. Wang, S.-Y.; Wang, O.; Zhang, R.; Owens, A.; Efros, A.A. CNN-generated images are surprisingly easy to spot… for now. In Proceedings of the IEEE/CVF Conference On Computer Vision and Pattern Recognition, Virtual, 14–19 June 2020; pp. 8695–8704.
27. Zhu, M.; Chen, H.; Yan, Q.; Huang, X.; Lin, G.; Li, W.; Tu, Z.; Hu, H.; Hu, J.; Wang, Y. Genimage: A million-scale benchmark for detecting ai-generated image. *Adv. Neural Inf. Process. Syst.* **2023**, *36*, 77771–77782.
28. Qian, Y.; Yin, G.; Sheng, L.; Chen, Z.; Shao, J. Thinking in frequency: Face forgery detection by mining frequency-aware clues. In Proceedings of the European Conference on Computer Vision, Glasgow, UK, 23–28 August 2020; pp. 86–103.
29. Zhao, Y.; Jin, X.; Gao, S.; Wu, L.; Yao, S.; Jiang, Q. TAN-GFD: Generalizing face forgery detection based on texture infor-mation and adaptive noise mining. *Appl. Intell.* **2023**, *53*, 19007–19027. [CrossRef]
30. Peng, S.; Zhang, T.; Gao, L.; Zhu, X.; Zhang, H.; Pang, K.; Lei, Z. Wmamba: Wavelet-based mamba for face forgery detection. In Proceedings of the 33rd ACM International Conference on Multimedia, Dublin, Ireland, 27–31 October 2025; pp. 4768–4777.
31. Zhang, H.; He, Q.; Bi, X.; Li, W.; Liu, B.; Xiao, B. Towards Universal AI-Generated Image Detection by Variational Information Bottleneck Network. In Proceedings of the Computer Vision and Pattern Recognition Conference, Nashville, TN, USA, 11–15 June 2025; pp. 23828–23837.
32. Frank, J.; Eisenhofer, T.; Schönherr, L.; Fischer, A.; Kolossa, D.; Holz, T. Leveraging frequency analysis for deep fake image recognition. In Proceedings of the International Conference on Machine Learning, Virtual, 13–18 July 2020; pp. 3247–3258.
33. Jeong, Y.; Kim, D.; Min, S.; Joe, S.; Gwon, Y.; Choi, J. Bihpf: Bilateral high-pass filters for robust deepfake detection. In Proceedings of the IEEE/CVF Winter Conference on Applications of Computer Vision, Waikoloa, HI, USA, 4–8 January 2022; pp. 48–57.
34. Jeong, Y.; Kim, D.; Ro, Y.; Choi, J. Frepgan: Robust deepfake detection using frequency-level perturbations. In Proceedings of the AAAI Conference on Artificial Intelligence, Virtual, 22 February–1 March 2022; pp. 1060–1068.
35. Ojha, U.; Li, Y.; Lee, Y.J. Towards universal fake image detectors that generalize across generative models. In Proceedings of the IEEE/CVF Conference on Computer Vision and Pattern Recognition, Vancouver, BC, Canada, 18–22 June 2023; pp. 24480–24489.
36. Tan, C.; Zhao, Y.; Wei, S.; Gu, G.; Liu, P.; Wei, Y. Frequency-aware deepfake detection: Improving generalizability through frequency space domain learning. In Proceedings of the AAAI Conference on Artificial Intelligence, Vancouver, BC, Canada, 20–27 February 2024; pp. 5052–5060.




 https://doi.org/10.3390/electronics15030716

electronics

MDPI

*Article*

# Noise-Resilient Masked Face Detection Using Quantized DnCNN and YOLO

**Rockhyun Choi [1,2], Hyunki Lee [1], Bong-seok Kim [3], Sangdong Kim [3,4] and Min Young Kim [2,*]**

1 Division of Intelligent Robot, ICT Research Institute, Daegu Gyeongbuk Institute of Science and Technology (DGIST), Daegu 42988, Republic of Korea; choimosi@dgist.ac.kr (R.C.); hklee@dgist.ac.kr (H.L.)
2 School of Electronic and Electrical Engineering, Kyungpook National University, Daegu 41566, Republic of Korea
3 Division of Mobility Technology, ICT Research Institute, Daegu Gyeongbuk Institute of Science and Technology (DGIST), Daegu 42988, Republic of Korea; remnant@dgist.ac.kr (B.-s.K.); kimsd728@dgist.ac.kr (S.K.)
4 Interdisciplinary Engineering, and Department of Advanced Technology of Daegu Gyeongbuk Institute of Science and Technology, Daegu 42988, Republic of Korea
* Correspondence: minykim@knu.ac.kr

**Abstract**

This study presents a noise-resilient masked-face detection framework optimized for the NVIDIA Jetson AGX Orin, which improves detection precision by approximately 30% under severe Gaussian noise (variance 0.10) while reducing denoising latency by over 42% and increasing end-to-end throughput by more than 30%. The proposed system integrates a lightweight DnCNN-based denoising stage with the YOLOv11 detector, employing Quantize-Dequantize (QDQ)-based INT8 post-training quantization and a parallel CPU–GPU execution pipeline to maximize edge efficiency. The experimental results demonstrate that denoising preprocessing substantially restores detection accuracy under low signal quality. Furthermore, comparative evaluations confirm that 8-bit quantization achieves a favorable accuracy–efficiency trade-off with only minor precision degradation relative to 16-bit inference, proving the framework's robustness and practicality for real-time, resource-constrained edge AI applications.

**Keywords:** noise reduction; DnCNN; object detection; YOLO; edge AI

## 1. Introduction

Reliable face detection in real-world environments remains challenging due to various image degradations such as illumination changes, motion blur, sensor interference, and low-resolution imaging. These degradations distort facial texture and significantly reduce the performance of conventional detectors, especially when facial regions are partially occluded. Prior studies have shown that noise is one of the most influential factors that deteriorate face-related tasks, particularly under unconstrained conditions where imaging quality cannot be guaranteed [1]. Low-quality or compressed images often fail to preserve key discriminative features, making downstream recognition and detection less reliable [2]. Such degradations are common in many practical deployments such as surveillance systems and low-cost camera platforms [3].

In addition to these challenges, face occlusion caused by mask-wearing has become increasingly relevant in various scenarios. Masks are often worn in medical facilities, industrial environments, public transportation, and crowded indoor locations where health or safety considerations are required; the COVID-19 period is a representative example


https://doi.org/10.3390/electronics15010143

that highlighted the widespread impact of mask usage. The presence of masks further complicates the detection process by covering key facial regions. Previous works have attempted to address masked face detection; however, noise contamination continues to be a major obstacle for achieving stable performance under real-world conditions [4].

Deep learning-based image restoration models have recently shown strong capability in suppressing complex and spatially varying noise. Among them, the Denoising Convolutional Neural Network (DnCNN) has demonstrated high effectiveness due to its residual learning framework and batch normalization mechanism, outperforming classical filtering-based approaches [5]. Nonetheless, integrating such denoising networks with modern object detectors such as YOLOv11 [6] imposes substantial computational overhead. As a result, real-time deployment on resource-constrained edge-AI devices becomes difficult without additional optimization.

To overcome these limitations, this work proposes a noise-resilient masked face detection framework that combines DnCNN-based denoising with YOLOv11 detection, enhanced through neural network quantization techniques. Quantization is widely adopted to reduce memory usage and computational complexity for edge deployment [7]. Furthermore, recent findings indicate that quantization can provide a beneficial regularization effect, improving robustness under noisy conditions [8–10]. Motivated by these insights, this work focuses on both noise resilience and computational efficiency by unifying quantized denoising and high-accuracy object detection within a single edge-friendly architecture.

The key contributions of this paper are summarized as follows:

- End-to-End Noise-Resilient Detection Pipeline for Edge Deployment: We propose an end-to-end denoising–detection pipeline that integrates a lightweight DnCNN-based denoiser with the YOLOv11 detector, enabling robust masked-face detection under noisy imaging conditions on resource-constrained edge devices.
- Systematic Evaluation across Desktop and Embedded Platforms: We perform a comprehensive and controlled evaluation of the proposed pipeline on both a desktop workstation and the NVIDIA Jetson AGX Orin, focusing on detection robustness, quantization stability, and real-time feasibility under multiple noise levels.
- Practical INT8 Deployment via QDQ-Based Post-Training Quantization: We demonstrate that ONNX-compliant QDQ-based post-training quantization enables efficient INT8 acceleration of the denoising stage with minimal accuracy degradation, supporting practical deployment in latency-tolerant edge scenarios.
- Parallelized Edge-AI Execution Pipeline: We implement a parallelized CPU–GPU execution pipeline that overlaps preprocessing, denoising, and detection, significantly improving hardware utilization and increasing end-to-end throughput on the Jetson AGX Orin.
- Comprehensive Validation across Noise Levels and Hardware Settings: Extensive experiments on the FMLD dataset across noise variances from 0.01 to 0.10 confirm consistent detection improvements and demonstrate the robustness and deployability of the proposed system in real-world edge environments.

The remainder of this paper is organized as follows. Section 2 reviews related work on denoising, masked face detection, and model quantization. Section 3 details the architecture and methodology of the proposed model. Section 4 presents experimental results, and Section 5 concludes the paper.

https://doi.org/10.3390/electronics15010143

## 2. Related Work

### 2.1. Image Denoising and Restoration

Image denoising and restoration techniques have traditionally relied on filtering-based approaches due to their computational efficiency and simplicity. Representative methods include BM3D [11], wavelet-based filtering [12], and multiscale or low-rank formulations for structured noise suppression [13–15]. However, these approaches depend on handcrafted transforms and manually designed priors, which limits their generalization to diverse noise characteristics and often leads to over-smoothing or loss of fine details. These limitations motivate the adoption of more expressive, data-driven denoising models.

Deep learning-based methods have thus emerged as powerful alternatives, offering the ability to learn adaptive representations that surpass the capabilities of traditional filtering-based algorithms. Convolutional Neural Network (CNN) models such as DnCNN [5] leverage residual learning and batch normalization to perform robust blind denoising without requiring explicit noise-level information. Transformer-based architectures like SwinIR [16] further enhance restoration quality by modeling long-range dependencies through self-attention mechanisms, achieving state-of-the-art performance across diverse benchmarks. Despite these advantages, deep learning-based denoisers often suffer from substantial computational and memory costs, particularly Transformer-based designs. This limits their suitability for latency-sensitive or resource-constrained environments, such as edge devices or real-time applications. Consequently, lightweight CNN-based models such as DnCNN and FFDNet [17] have been explored to strike a more practical balance between efficiency and performance. Notably, DnCNN functions as a blind denoiser without requiring a noise-level map [18], making it more adaptable to dynamic real-world conditions where noise variance is unknown. Nevertheless, even these CNN-based models can impose non-negligible latency depending on the platform and precision used. These observations motivate the need for further complexity reduction, especially through quantization or model simplification, to enable efficient yet robust denoising pipelines suitable for real-time deployment. To balance representativeness and experimental feasibility under edge deployment constraints, this study restricts the denoising comparison to three representative models: DnCNN as a blind CNN-based denoiser, FFDNet as a lightweight non-blind model, and SwinIR as a Transformer-based state-of-the-art approach.

Several studies have investigated YOLO-based object detection under challenging imaging conditions. Li et al. proposed a YOLO-based ship detection framework for thermal infrared images captured under complex backgrounds, demonstrating the applicability of YOLO detectors in degraded sensing environments [19]. Rodríguez-Rodríguez et al. systematically analyzed the impact of noise and brightness variations on modern object detectors, including YOLO, highlighting robustness degradation induced by input perturbations [20]. More recent works have explored architectural or preprocessing modifications to improve YOLO robustness under adverse conditions, such as DiffuYOLO for small-object detection in remote sensing imagery [21] and Dark-YOLO for low-light object detection [22]. In contrast to these studies, which primarily emphasize detection accuracy under clean or moderately degraded conditions, this work focuses on system-level robustness under severe noise and low-precision inference in resource-constrained edge environments.

### 2.2. Masked Face Detection Under Adverse Conditions

Environments where mask-wearing is unavoidable—such as medical facilities, industrial sites, and pandemic situations like COVID-19—have increased the demand for robust face detection systems capable of handling occlusions. Benchmark datasets such as MAFA and the FMLD dataset [23,24] were introduced to address this challenge. Although state-of-the-art object detectors, including YOLOv10 [25] and the recently released

YOLOv11 [6], have improved occlusion robustness through advanced feature fusion modules (e.g., PANet, BiFPN), their performance degrades sharply when visual degradations are combined—such as a masked face in a noisy, low-light environment [4].

Most existing studies focus on either denoising or masked face detection in isolation. There is limited research on integrated frameworks that simultaneously address occlusion and sensor noise. This study bridges this gap by proposing a unified pipeline that enhances the input quality for YOLOv11 via a lightweight denoiser, ensuring robust detection even under severe noise conditions.

### 2.3. Quantization for Efficient and Robust Edge Deployment

Deploying deep neural networks on resource-constrained edge devices (e.g., NVIDIA Jetson series) requires rigorous optimization. Post-Training Quantization (PTQ) and Quantization-Aware Training (QAT) are essential techniques that reduce model size and inference latency by converting 32-bit floating-point weights to lower-precision formats such as INT8 [7].

Beyond computational efficiency, recent theoretical and empirical studies suggest that quantization can enhance model robustness. Research indicates that the discrete nature of quantized weights can act as a form of implicit regularization, filtering out high-frequency noise perturbations and preventing overfitting to noisy labels [8,9]. For instance, Wang et al. [10] demonstrated that quantization consistency regularization improves generalization in varying domains. Motivated by these findings, this study explores how low-bit quantization (up to 8-bit) of the DnCNN module not only accelerates inference but also contributes to stable detection performance by suppressing minor noise artifacts.

## 3. Proposed Method

### 3.1. System Architecture: Initialization, Validation, and Edge Deployment

This subsection provides an overview of the end-to-end architecture of the proposed noise-robust masked face detection framework. The system is organized into three sequential stages—Initialization, Validation, and Edge Deployment—that together define the full operational pipeline from training to real-time inference on embedded hardware. Figure 1 summarizes this three-stage workflow; panels (a),(b), and (c) correspond to the Initialization, Validation, and Edge Deployment stages, respectively.

As shown in Figure 1a, the initialization step trains the YOLOv11 detector using both masked and unmasked images from the FMLD dataset to establish a baseline for masked-face detection. During this stage, Gaussian noise is added to create noise-augmented datasets that are later used to assess the benefit of denoising within the pipeline. A pre-trained DnCNN model is applied to generate reference denoised outputs. The DnCNN is intentionally not retrained, ensuring that the subsequent evaluation isolates the contribution of denoising itself and avoids dataset leakage or noise-specific overfitting.

Figure 1b illustrates the validation step, where noisy FMLD validation images are restored using 8-bit and 16-bit quantized versions of the DnCNN model. The denoised images are then processed by YOLOv11, which predicts both masked and unmasked face classes. The examples shown in the figure represent typical outcomes, where YOLOv11 correctly labels unmasked subjects as "face" and masked subjects as "mask" after the denoising stage. This step measures how quantization and denoising jointly influence detection robustness prior to deployment.

The complete denoising–detection pipeline is executed on the NVIDIA Jetson AGX Orin, as depicted in Figure 1c. Incoming images, including both masked and unmasked cases, are preprocessed on the CPU and sent to a TensorRT-based DnCNN engine for patch-wise denoising. The restored patches are reassembled into full-resolution frames

https://doi.org/10.3390/electronics15010143

before YOLOv11 inference. A queue-based, asynchronous CPU–GPU execution structure enables the DnCNN and YOLOv11 engines to run in overlapping streams, allowing the system to achieve low-latency, real-time performance on the embedded platform.

Finally, Figure 1d outlines the visualization analysis framework, which is extensively discussed in Section 4. This panel serves as a conceptual preview of the qualitative evaluation, illustrating how the pipeline is analyzed in terms of intermediate feature preservation and detection robustness under diverse corruption scenarios. The specific visualization results corresponding to this framework are detailed later in Section 4.3

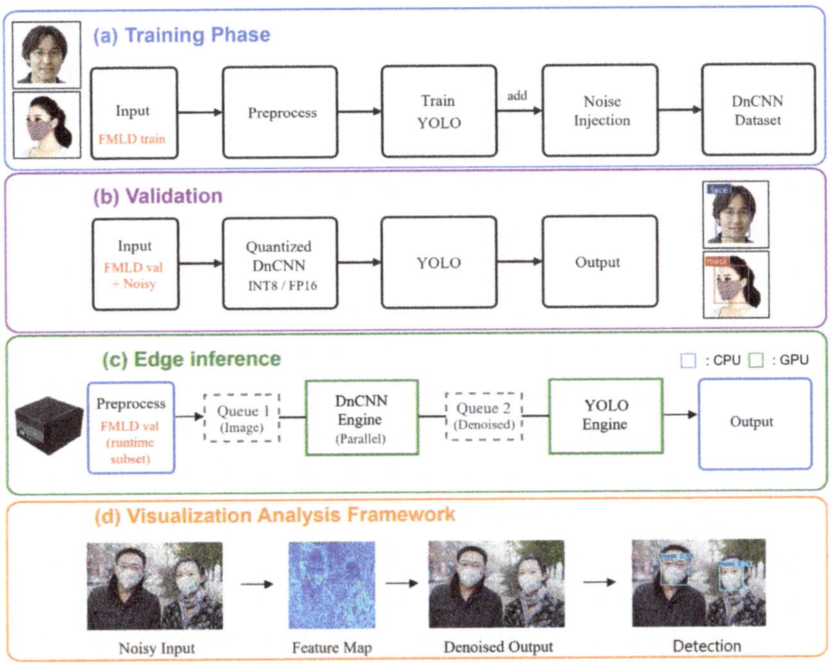


**Figure 1.** Overall architecture of the proposed three-stage noise-robust detection pipeline: (**a**) training phase with noise-injected data for YOLO learning, (**b**) validation step using quantized DnCNN and YOLO, (**c**) edge inference pipeline with parallel DnCNN–YOLO execution on embedded devices, (**d**) visualization analysis framework illustrating noisy inputs, intermediate feature maps, denoised outputs, and final detection results.

The following subsections describe the denoising strategy, noise construction process, quantization method, frame-reconstruction pipeline, and Jetson-based execution architecture in detail.

### 3.2. Denoising Strategy Using DnCNN

This subsection describes the denoising module used in the proposed pipeline. A pre-trained DnCNN model is employed as a fixed restoration backbone to suppress Gaussian noise before YOLOv11 detection. The denoising process operates on each RGB channel independently, and the channels are recombined to produce a restored full-resolution image. Channel-wise inference prevents parameter growth that would occur in a joint three-channel model and reduces GPU memory usage. This decomposition also improves CPU–GPU parallelization on Jetson devices, allowing independent patch streams to be scheduled concurrently without cross-channel synchronization overhead.

https://doi.org/10.3390/electronics15010143

### 3.2.1. Comparison with Other Denoising Models

To determine an appropriate denoising module for our masked-face detection pipeline, we compared three representative deep-learning–based denoisers: DnCNN, FFDNet, and SwinIR. Table 1 summarizes their quantitative performance under Gaussian noise with different $\sigma$ values. SwinIR achieves the highest PSNR and SSIM across most noise levels due to its Transformer-based architecture; however, its extremely low inference speed (0.17 FPS) renders it unsuitable for real-time or edge-device applications.

**Table 1.** Quantitative comparison of denoising models under Gaussian noise with different $\sigma$ values. Best performance per noise level is highlighted in bold.

| Algorithm | Noise Level | PSNR (dB) | SSIM |
|---|---|---|---|
| DnCNN [5] | $\sigma = 15$ | 36.72 | 0.945 |
| FFDNet [17] | $\sigma = 15$ | 35.62 | 0.936 |
| **SwinIR [16]** | $\sigma = 15$ | **37.69** | **0.955** |
| DnCNN [5] | $\sigma = 25$ | 34.70 | 0.920 |
| FFDNet [17] | $\sigma = 25$ | 34.69 | 0.925 |
| **SwinIR [16]** | $\sigma = 25$ | **35.45** | **0.935** |
| DnCNN [5] | $\sigma = 50$ | 31.14 | 0.868 |
| FFDNet [17] | $\sigma = 50$ | 31.55 | 0.880 |
| **SwinIR [16]** | $\sigma = 50$ | **32.41** | **0.897** |

FFDNet provides the fastest throughput (64.91 FPS), but its usability is fundamentally limited by its non-blind design. DnCNN, in contrast, offers a balanced trade-off between restoration quality and computational efficiency, making it a practical candidate for deployment-focused pipelines.

Although SwinIR demonstrates superior restoration accuracy, its computational cost makes it unsuitable for embedded use. Meanwhile, FFDNet exhibits impressive runtime performance but requires a noise-level map as an additional input, restricting its applicability in real-world environments where noise intensity cannot be estimated.

Table 2 reports the inference speed comparison. The denoising benchmarks reported in Tables 1 and 2 follow the standard evaluation pipeline provided by the KAIR image restoration toolbox [26], which is widely used for reproducible comparison of CNN-based denoising models.

**Table 2.** Runtime performance of denoising models at $\sigma = 15$.

| Algorithm | FPS |
|---|---|
| DnCNN [5] | 17.02 |
| FFDNet [17] | 64.91 |
| SwinIR [16] | 0.17 |

A decisive factor in selecting DnCNN is its structural suitability for uncontrolled real-world settings. The following properties highlight its advantages:

- **Structural Difference (DnCNN vs. FFDNet):** FFDNet is a non-blind denoiser that requires a noise level $\sigma$ as an additional input channel. This dependency is impractical in dynamic scenes where the noise level varies unpredictably and cannot be measured in advance.
- **Blind Denoising Capability:** DnCNN operates as a blind denoiser, removing noise without any external knowledge of $\sigma$. Its residual-learning structure allows it to

https://doi.org/10.3390/electronics15010143

handle diverse and unknown degradation patterns, ensuring stable preprocessing across a wide range of conditions.

Following the residual-learning formulation of DnCNN [5], the adopted denoising network consists of a sequence of convolutional layers with batch normalization and ReLU activation. In this work, the same principle is applied in a channel-wise manner to facilitate parallel execution on edge devices. Let $I_c \in \mathbb{R}^{H \times W}$ denote the noisy input of the $c$-th color channel, where $c \in \{R, G, B\}$. For the $l$-th layer ($1 \leq l < L$), the intermediate feature map is computed as

$$F_c^{(l)} = \sigma\Big(\text{BN}\Big(W^{(l)} * F_c^{(l-1)} + b^{(l)}\Big)\Big), \tag{1}$$

where $*$ denotes the convolution operator, $W^{(l)}$ and $b^{(l)}$ are the learnable kernels and biases, $\text{BN}(\cdot)$ denotes batch normalization, and $\sigma(\cdot)$ represents the ReLU activation function. The input feature map is given by $F_c^{(0)} = I_c$. The final layer predicts the noise residual without a nonlinear activation,

$$\hat{n}_c = W^{(L)} * F_c^{(L-1)} + b^{(L)}. \tag{2}$$

The denoised output is obtained by residual subtraction,

$$\hat{I}_c = I_c - \hat{n}_c. \tag{3}$$

This channel-wise formulation enables independent denoising of each color component, reducing model complexity and facilitating parallel execution on edge devices.

Given these considerations, DnCNN provides a rational trade-off between accuracy, computational cost, and practical deployability. Accordingly, our pipeline adopts a MATLAB-pretrained DnCNN model [27]. The model was obtained using MATLAB R2024b (MathWorks, Natick, MA, USA) with the Image Processing Toolbox, providing a stable and well-validated implementation without the need for additional training.

### 3.2.2. Noise Construction and Parameter Definition

Additive Gaussian noise is adopted in this work not as a comprehensive model of real-world degradation, but as a controlled baseline that enables explicit parameterization of noise strength and direct correspondence with widely used denoising benchmarks. To model realistic degradation, Gaussian noise is added to RGB images normalized to the $[0, 1]$ range. Let $I = (R, G, B)$ denote a clean pixel and let $n = (n_R, n_G, n_B)$ denote an independent noise vector. The noisy pixel is generated according to

$$I_{\text{noisy}} = I + n, \tag{4}$$

where each component of $n$ is sampled from $\mathcal{N}(0, \sigma_{\text{inj}}^2)$. The term $\sigma_{\text{inj}}^2$ represents the variance of the injected noise used in our system-level robustness evaluation.

In contrast, denoiser benchmarks such as DnCNN, FFDNet, and SwinIR typically express noise intensity using the standard deviation $\sigma$ on a $[0, 255]$ scale. To relate the injected variance to this benchmark notation, the equivalent standard deviation is given by

$$\sigma_{\text{eq}} = 255\sqrt{\sigma_{\text{inj}}^2}, \tag{5}$$

consistent with standard practice in denoising studies [5,28]. This conversion clarifies how our injected noise levels correspond to common benchmark settings (e.g., $\sigma = 25$ or 50).

The preprocessing pipeline used to generate noisy and restored images is shown in Figure 2. The procedure consists of (a) additive noise injection, (b) RGB channel splitting,

https://doi.org/10.3390/electronics15010143

(c) independent DnCNN inference per channel, and (d) channel merging to form a restored image. Each input image is first corrupted using a controlled noise model and then processed in a channel-wise manner. The RGB channels are separated and independently fed into the DnCNN model trained to predict the residual noise component. The DnCNN processes each channel independently to estimate and suppress the noise component, and the restored channels are subsequently merged to form a denoised image. This channel-wise residual learning strategy allows the denoiser to effectively suppress high-frequency noise while preserving structural image features that are critical for downstream detection. By operating independently on each channel, the pipeline avoids cross-channel interference and maintains color consistency under severe noise conditions.

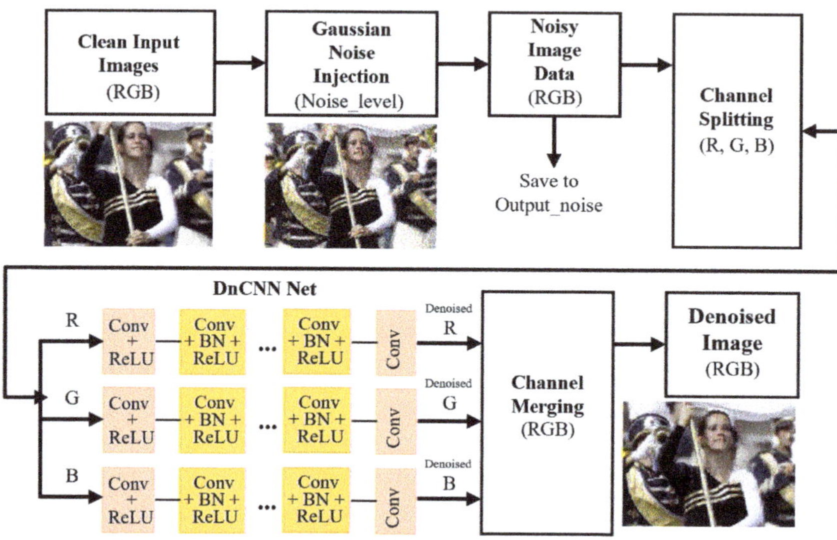


**Figure 2.** Architecture of the Channel-wise DnCNN Denoising Pipeline.

For evaluation, three injected noise variances are considered, $\sigma_{\text{inj}}^2 \in \{0.01, 0.05, 0.10\}$, corresponding to increasing levels of degradation. The largest setting corresponds to $\sigma_{\text{eq}} \approx 80$, capturing severe sensor noise and compression artifacts often encountered in surveillance imagery, and aligns with extended evaluation protocols such as FFDNet [17].

### 3.3. Quantized DnCNN

To enable efficient execution on edge devices, we convert the DnCNN denoiser into low-precision formats using post-training quantization (PTQ). Quantization reduces the precision of weights and activations, lowering memory usage and enabling fast INT8 inference while preserving robust denoising capability.

#### 3.3.1. Post-Training Quantization

Post-training quantization (PTQ) converts a pretrained floating-point model into an integer representation without additional training. Following the symmetric linear quantization scheme of Jacob et al. [7], a real-valued tensor $x$ is quantized using a scale factor $s$ as

$$x_q = \text{round}\left(\frac{x}{s}\right), \tag{6}$$

and the corresponding dequantized approximation is obtained by

$$x \approx s\, x_q. \tag{7}$$

The scale factor $s$ is typically computed from the dynamic range of $x$ using max-abs scaling for signed INT8, ensuring that the representable integer range covers the majority of the activation or weight distribution. This quantization scheme substantially reduces memory bandwidth and enables efficient INT8 inference on embedded devices such as the NVIDIA Jetson AGX Orin.

Although PTQ introduces quantization noise due to discrepancies between floating-point and integer arithmetic, DnCNN remains stable under INT8 conversion. Its residual-learning architecture inherently mitigates small perturbations in feature representations, allowing the quantized DnCNN to maintain effective denoising performance in our experiments.

#### 3.3.2. QDQ-Based Post-Training Quantization (TensorRT INT8)

For deployment on Jetson AGX Orin, we employ TensorRT's QDQ-based PTQ pipeline [29], which inserts Quantize (Q) and Dequantize (DQ) nodes around each operator to form a hardware-optimized INT8 computation graph compliant with the ONNX Quantization Specification [30]. Scale factors for weights and activations are obtained through PTQ calibration using representative samples, with no retraining or QAT involved. The resulting QDQ INT8 engine achieves significant latency reduction while maintaining consistent denoising performance. The quantized DnCNN outputs are directly fed into YOLOv11, forming a lightweight two-stage pipeline for robust masked-face detection on edge devices.

### 3.4. *YOLOv11-Based Masked Face Detection with Frame Reconstruction*

In the proposed framework, YOLOv11 serves as the downstream detector that consumes the restored output from the quantized DnCNN (Q-DnCNN) module. Unlike standard detection pipelines that process raw input frames directly, our system incorporates an intermediate reconstruction mechanism to bridge the patch-based denoiser and the full-frame detector.

**Frame Reconstruction and Input Processing:** Since the Q-DnCNN module processes the input stream in localized patches to maximize GPU parallelization efficiency (see Section 3.5), the denoised patches must be spatially reassembled before detection. As illustrated in Figure 3, the CPU-based reconstruction module stitches the asynchronous stream of denoised patches into a coherent full-resolution frame. Subsequently, this restored frame is resized to the standard input resolution of 640 × 640 pixels required by the YOLOv11 architecture. This decoupled design ensures that the detector operates on globally consistent spatial features, which is critical for recognizing masked faces across varying scales and aspect ratios.

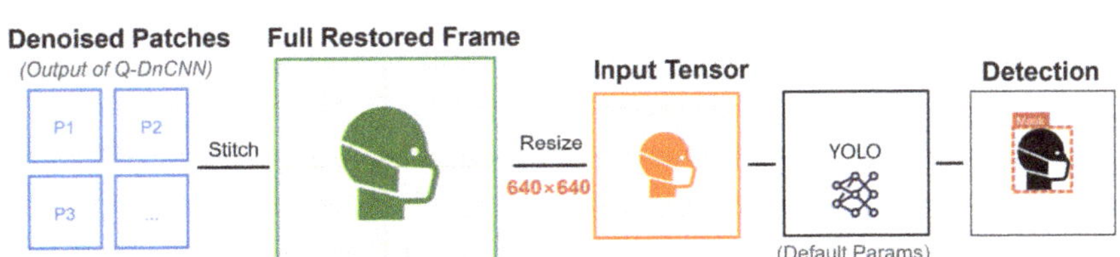


**Figure 3.** Frame Reconstruction and Detection Pipeline.

https://doi.org/10.3390/electronics15010143

**Training Configuration:** To isolate the performance gains attributed solely to the proposed denoising preprocessing, we trained the YOLOv11 model using the default hyperparameters provided by the official Ultralytics repository. The model was trained on the clean FMLD training set without any additional architectural modifications. Using default parameters (e.g., SGD optimizer, initial learning rate of 0.01, and momentum of 0.937) ensures that the reported improvements in robustness (Section 4) result directly from the superior quality of the Q-DnCNN-enhanced input, rather than from extensive hyperparameter tuning or detector-specific optimizations.

**Rationale for Choosing YOLOv11:** While various lightweight detectors exist, YOLOv11 was selected for its superior trade-off between detection accuracy and computational efficiency on edge hardware. Recent comparative studies on YOLO architectures indicate that newer iterations, such as YOLOv11, not only achieve higher mAP but also exhibit improved inherent robustness against input perturbations and adversarial distortions compared to predecessors and other lightweight models [25,31]. This characteristic is particularly critical for our framework, where the detector must operate reliably on denoised outputs that may still contain residual artifacts.

### *3.5. Edge Device Implementation on Jetson AGX Orin*

This subsection describes the edge-device implementation of the proposed framework on the NVIDIA Jetson AGX Orin platform. Since both DnCNN denoising and YOLOv11 detection are computationally intensive operations, achieving real-time performance requires a pipelined architecture that leverages multi-threaded CPU processing together with asynchronous GPU execution. Figure 4 illustrates the overall pipeline architecture adopted in this study.

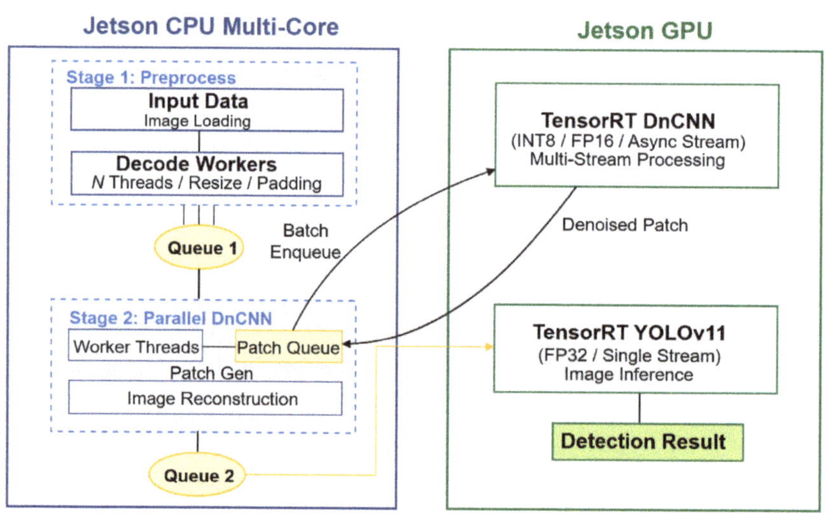


**Figure 4.** Pipeline Architecture: Multi-threaded CPU + Async GPU Processing on Jetson Orin AGX.

The overall design consists of two cooperating subsystems—a CPU-side preprocessing pipeline and a GPU-side inference pipeline—connected through decoupled FIFO queues. On the CPU side, incoming images are loaded and decoded by multiple worker threads, which perform resizing, normalization, and partitioning into patches. The preprocessed patches are then pushed into a patch queue that feeds the GPU-based denoising stage.

System-level parallelism is achieved by decoupling CPU-side preprocessing, result aggregation, and frame reconstruction from GPU-based inference. While the GPU exe-

https://doi.org/10.3390/electronics15010143

cutes denoising and detection kernels, the CPU concurrently handles input acquisition, basic preprocessing, and reconstruction of denoised patches, enabling pipeline overlap across successive frames. The use of FIFO queues decouples stage execution timing and avoids frame-level synchronization barriers, allowing each stage to progress independently and efficiently.

Memory usage is managed at the frame level, and intermediate feature maps are not persistently stored. Instead, denoised patches are immediately accumulated into frame-level buffers and discarded after reconstruction, which limits memory overhead and avoids unnecessary data transfers. As a result, CPU–GPU communication overhead is amortized across the asynchronous pipeline and does not dominate the overall end-to-end latency, making the implementation suitable for real-time edge deployment under constrained computational and memory resources.

On the GPU side, two TensorRT engines operate in a pipelined manner. The DnCNN engine executes denoising using FP16 or INT8 precision and supports asynchronous inference, allowing multiple patches to be processed efficiently. Once denoising is completed, the reconstructed frame is transferred back to the CPU and pushed to the next queue for detection. The YOLOv11 engine retrieves denoised frames from this queue and performs single-stream object detection.

This hybrid execution model enables overlapping data transfer, denoising, reconstruction, and detection on the embedded platform. For example, while the GPU performs YOLOv11 inference on frame $i$, it can concurrently apply DnCNN denoising to patches of frame $i + 1$, ensuring high hardware utilization and reduced latency. Low-level kernel scheduling and driver-specific optimizations are intentionally abstracted, as the focus of this work is on system-level execution behavior and deployability rather than hardware-specific micro-optimizations.

### 3.6. Overall System Operation

Figure 5 summarizes the end-to-end operational flow of the proposed denoising–detection pipeline during deployment. Incoming frames are sequentially processed through normalization, patch-wise denoising, frame reconstruction, and masked-face detection.

**Figure 5.** End-to-end operation flow of the proposed denoising–detection pipeline.

In addition to quantitative performance metrics, qualitative visualization analyses are employed to examine the effects of denoising and quantization on intermediate feature representations and detection outputs. These visual comparisons are presented later in Section 4.3 to provide intuitive insights into the behavior of the proposed pipeline under noisy conditions.

From a system-level perspective, the pipeline is designed to maintain continuous throughput by allowing preprocessing and inference stages to proceed without strict frame-level synchronization. While denoising and detection are executed on different stages of the pipeline, the overall system behavior is governed by the availability of restored frames rather than individual module latency. This execution flow enables stable and predictable performance under severe noise conditions, ensuring that detection accuracy is preserved without introducing excessive end-to-end delay. As a result, the proposed framework

https://doi.org/10.3390/electronics15010143

achieves a practical balance between robustness and real-time feasibility on embedded edge platforms.

## 4. Experiment Results

This section evaluates the proposed noise-resilient detection framework across two computational environments: a desktop workstation and the NVIDIA Jetson AGX Orin edge platform. Section 4.1 introduces the evaluation metrics used throughout the experiments. Section 4.2 describes the dataset preparation and baseline experimental settings. Section 4.3 analyzes noise robustness on the desktop platform under controlled Gaussian and real-world degradation conditions. Section 4.4 investigates quantization stability and detection accuracy on the Jetson AGX Orin under severe noise. Finally, Section 4.5 assesses real-time performance, throughput, and energy efficiency on the embedded platform.

### *4.1. Evaluation Metrics*

Detection performance is evaluated using standard object detection metrics, including Precision, Recall, mAP@0.5, and mAP@0.5:0.95, which are widely adopted in object detection benchmarks. Precision and Recall are defined as

$$\text{Precision} = \frac{TP}{TP+FP}, \quad \text{Recall} = \frac{TP}{TP+FN}, \tag{8}$$

where $TP$, $FP$, and $FN$ denote true positives, false positives, and false negatives, respectively. Mean Average Precision (mAP) is computed as the average of class-wise Average Precision (AP), where AP corresponds to the area under the precision–recall curve for each class. The mAP@0.5 metric evaluates detection performance at an Intersection-over-Union (IoU) threshold of 0.5, while mAP@0.5:0.95 further assesses robustness by averaging AP values across multiple IoU thresholds from 0.5 to 0.95 with a step size of 0.05.

### *4.2. Dataset Preparation and Settings*

This subsection describes the baseline configuration used to assess the fundamental detection capability of YOLOv11 before introducing noise or quantization effects. All experiments in Sections 4.2 and 4.3 were performed on a desktop workstation equipped with an NVIDIA RTX 3090 GPU and an AMD Ryzen 9 processor, using the full FMLD validation set (7148 images). These baseline results serve as a reference point for the subsequent robustness and edge-deployment analyses presented in Sections 4.4 and 4.5.

FMLD [24], which integrates the MAFA and Wider Face datasets [4], contains three annotation categories that reflect real mask-wearing conditions: masked face, incorrectly masked face, and unmasked face. FMLD was selected for this study because it provides a realistic and challenging benchmark for masked face detection under adverse conditions. By integrating the MAFA and WIDER Face datasets, FMLD captures diverse real-world variations in face scale, pose, occlusion, illumination, and mask placement, including correctly worn masks, incorrectly worn masks, and unmasked faces. These characteristics make the dataset particularly suitable for evaluating noise robustness and detection stability in practical surveillance scenarios.

Table 3 summarizes the number of images and annotated instances after applying an automated bounding box correction step. To ensure training stability and evaluation reliability, we applied an automated quality-control pipeline that filters out only corrupted images and structurally invalid annotations (e.g., coordinates exceeding normalized bounds or missing label files). This procedure follows standard practices for object detection dataset preparation [32] and is recommended in official YOLO documentation to prevent parsing errors. Importantly, this step is a technical quality-assurance measure that does not alter the semantic content or class distribution of the dataset. This refinement resulted in a minor reduction from 12,688 to 12,675 validation instances. Because these removed samples constitute a negligible proportion of the dataset, their impact on model evaluation is minimal, while the improved annotation consistency enhances the reliability of downstream detection.

**Table 3.** Instance Counts Before and After Bounding Box Filtering.

| Dataset | Images | Instances | Masked Face | Incorrectly Masked Face | Unmasked Face |
|---|---|---|---|---|---|
| FMLD (Updated) | 34,781 | 50,384 | 24,603 | 1204 | 24,576 |
| Validation (Updated) | 7148 | 12,675 | 7423 | 324 | 4928 |
| **Totals** | 41,934 | 63,059 | 32,026 | 1528 | 29,505 |

Figure 6 illustrates the training and validation box-loss curves. Both losses decrease rapidly in the initial epochs (0–20), indicating that the model quickly acquires the core localization features needed for face and mask detection. After approximately 50 epochs, the validation curve stabilizes, showing no oscillatory behavior that would signal poor generalization. The continuous decline of the training loss, contrasted with the near-flat validation loss, suggests a limited overfitting tendency; however, its magnitude is small and does not meaningfully affect the downstream experiments. These trends confirm that the YOLOv11 detector was trained stably and provides a reliable baseline for evaluating the effectiveness of the proposed denoising–detection pipeline. The training and validation losses exhibit similar convergence patterns, and no increasing gap is observed as training progresses, suggesting that overfitting is effectively controlled under the current training protocol.

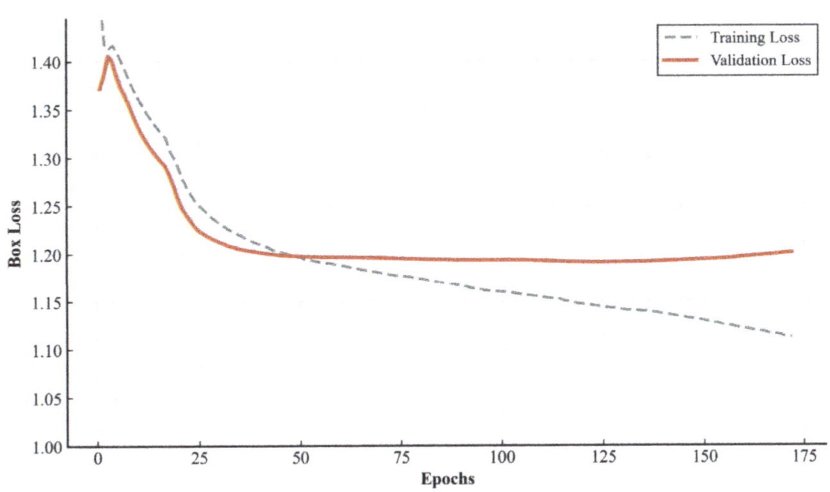


**Figure 6.** Training and Validation Box Loss Curves.

The normalized confusion matrix for the three-class prediction task is shown in Figure 7. The detector achieves strong classification performance for the *mask* (0.97) and *face* (0.83) categories, while performance for the *incorrectly masked face* category is notably lower (true positive rate of 0.65). Unlike a standard closed-set classifier, the columns of this detection-oriented confusion matrix do not sum to one because false negatives arising from missed detections (bounding box not generated) are accumulated outside the matrix. As a result, the matrix more accurately reflects the detector's localization behavior under partially occluded or irregular mask-placement conditions.

https://doi.org/10.3390/electronics15010143

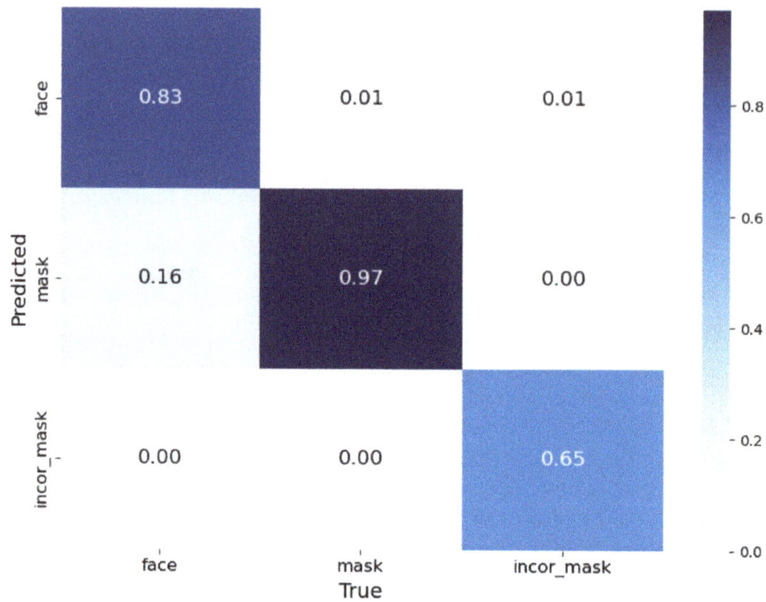


**Figure 7.** Normalized Confusion Matrix.

Performance per class is detailed in Table 4. The overall mAP@0.5 reaches 0.859 across the full validation set, demonstrating strong baseline capability. The *mask* class exhibits the highest performance (mAP@0.5 = 0.978, recall = 0.955), confirming that properly worn masks are consistently detected. Conversely, the *incorrectly masked face* class yields a lower mAP@0.5 of 0.720, reflecting the difficulty of detecting subtle variations in mask misuse. Because these statistics are computed over all 7,148 validation images, they carry sufficient statistical significance and constitute a robust reference point for evaluating noise robustness in later sections.

**Table 4.** Face Mask Detection Performance of YOLOv11 by Class.

| Class | Precision | Recall | mAP@0.5 | mAP@0.5:0.95 |
|---|---|---|---|---|
| Face | 0.817 | 0.824 | 0.880 | 0.623 |
| Mask | 0.940 | 0.955 | 0.978 | 0.654 |
| Incorrect Mask | 0.796 | 0.670 | 0.720 | 0.443 |
| **Average** | **0.851** | **0.816** | **0.859** | **0.573** |

### *4.3. Noise Robustness on Desktop*

This subsection evaluates how synthetic Gaussian noise affects the detection performance of YOLOv11 and examines the extent to which DnCNN preprocessing— in both full-precision and quantized forms—recovers accuracy. All experiments here were conducted exclusively on the desktop workstation described in Section 4.1, ensuring that the analysis isolates the intrinsic noise sensitivity of the detector without hardware-dependent effects.

Table 5 reports Precision, Recall, mAP@0.5, and mAP@0.5:0.95 under three noise levels ($\sigma^2_{inj} \in \{0.01, 0.05, 0.10\}$). Gaussian noise was injected using the Albumentations library, a widely adopted and reproducible data augmentation framework for computer vision experiments [33]. For the real-world distortion scenarios (Motion Blur, Low Illumination, and JPEG Compression) presented in Table 5, we adopted the severity levels

https://doi.org/10.3390/electronics15010143

L1, L3, and L5 following the corruption benchmark protocol established by Hendrycks and Dietterich [34] Across all metrics, noise substantially degrades performance. Under severe noise ($\sigma^2_{inj} = 0.10$), precision drops from 0.851 to 0.577, recall from 0.816 to 0.214, and mAP@0.5 from 0.859 to 0.262. These results confirm that YOLOv11 is highly vulnerable to high-frequency perturbations, leading to missed detections and unstable localization.

**Table 5.** Performance comparison of YOLOv11 with the proposed Q-DnCNN framework. The table compares the Baseline (Noise only), Full-Precision (FP32), and Quantized models (16-bit, 8-bit) to analyze the trade-off between precision and detection accuracy (Desktop).

| Distortion | Intensity | Method | Precision | Recall | mAP@0.5 | mAP@0.5:0.95 |
|---|---|---|---|---|---|---|
| **Baseline** | – | Original YOLOv11 | 0.851 | 0.816 | 0.859 | 0.573 |
| | | *Primary Target: Gaussian Noise* | | | | |
| Gaussian Noise | $\sigma^2 = 0.01$ | Noise only | 0.830 | 0.712 | 0.793 | 0.510 |
| | | DnCNN (FP32) | 0.842 | **0.800** | 0.844 | **0.619** |
| | | Q-DnCNN (FP16) | **0.849** | 0.793 | **0.846** | 0.561 |
| | | **Q-DnCNN (INT8)** | 0.841 | 0.780 | 0.760 | 0.554 |
| | $\sigma^2 = 0.05$ | Noise only | 0.742 | 0.416 | 0.489 | 0.295 |
| | | DnCNN (FP32) | **0.831** | **0.733** | **0.812** | **0.527** |
| | | Q-DnCNN (FP16) | 0.819 | 0.722 | 0.801 | 0.517 |
| | | **Q-DnCNN (INT8)** | 0.761 | 0.700 | 0.768 | 0.492 |
| | $\sigma^2 = 0.10$ | Noise only | 0.577 | 0.214 | 0.262 | 0.151 |
| | | DnCNN (FP32) | **0.751** | **0.655** | **0.723** | **0.456** |
| | | Q-DnCNN (FP16) | 0.732 | 0.637 | 0.704 | 0.441 |
| | | **Q-DnCNN (INT8)** | 0.708 | 0.598 | 0.659 | 0.414 |
| | | *Verification: Real-world Distortions* | | | | |
| Motion Blur | L1 | Noise only | 0.806 | 0.594 | 0.676 | 0.426 |
| | L3 | Noise only | 0.677 | 0.348 | 0.406 | 0.235 |
| | L5 | Noise only | 0.578 | 0.208 | 0.241 | 0.130 |
| Low Illumination | L1 | Noise only | 0.850 | 0.815 | 0.857 | 0.572 |
| | L3 | Noise only | 0.831 | 0.797 | 0.838 | 0.545 |
| | L5 | Noise only | 0.802 | 0.710 | 0.761 | 0.470 |
| JPEG Compression | L1 | Noise only | 0.846 | 0.815 | 0.855 | 0.572 |
| | L3 | Noise only | 0.843 | 0.811 | 0.854 | 0.570 |
| | L5 | Noise only | 0.843 | 0.807 | 0.850 | 0.567 |

Applying DnCNN effectively restores performance across all noise levels. For $\sigma^2_{inj} = 0.10$, the denoiser increases precision from 0.577 to 0.751, recall from 0.214 to 0.655, and mAP@0.5 from 0.262 to 0.723—recovering more than 60% of the performance lost due to noise. This substantial improvement indicates that DnCNN successfully suppresses noise-induced distortions and restores the structural cues required for stable detection.

An additional observation arises under mild noise ($\sigma^2_{inj} = 0.01$): the quantized 16-bit and 8-bit DnCNN variants achieve precision values (0.849 and 0.841) comparable to or slightly higher than the full-precision model (0.842). A similar trend is observed for mAP@0.5 (0.846 and 0.843 vs. 0.844). This counterintuitive behavior suggests that reduced bit precision may act as an implicit regularizer. By constraining the representational dynamic range, quantization suppresses minor fluctuations in the activation space and stabilizes inference under weak perturbations, consistent with prior studies on quantization regularization [8]. Recent work further shows that quantization reduces overfitting in noisy environments [9] and enhances consistency in low-precision networks [10], which aligns with the observed trend that Q-DnCNN matches or slightly exceeds floating-point performance at low noise levels.

https://doi.org/10.3390/electronics15010143

As noise severity increases, quantized models exhibit a gradual performance drop relative to full-precision DnCNN, as expected from the reduced numerical resolution. However, even at $\sigma_{inj}^2 = 0.10$, the 16-bit and 8-bit variants preserve a meaningful portion of the denoising benefit (mAP@0.5 = 0.704 and 0.659), demonstrating that quantization does not undermine the fundamental noise-removal capability of DnCNN.

To complement the quantitative results in Table 5, Figure 8 presents qualitative visualizations illustrating how denoising preprocessing stabilizes feature representations and detection outputs under severe noise. In particular, backbone feature maps are visualized to provide insight into how high-frequency noise affects intermediate representations and how denoising preprocessing modulates these responses prior to detection. The detection results in Figure 8c reflect the differences observed in the preceding restoration and feature map visualizations, illustrating how changes in intermediate representations are manifested at the final detection stage. This qualitative comparison provides visual context for the quantitative performance trends reported in Table 5, without replacing the metric-based evaluation.

(**a**) Visual comparison of image restoration results, including the noisy input, the FP16 DnCNN output, and the INT8 DnCNN output.

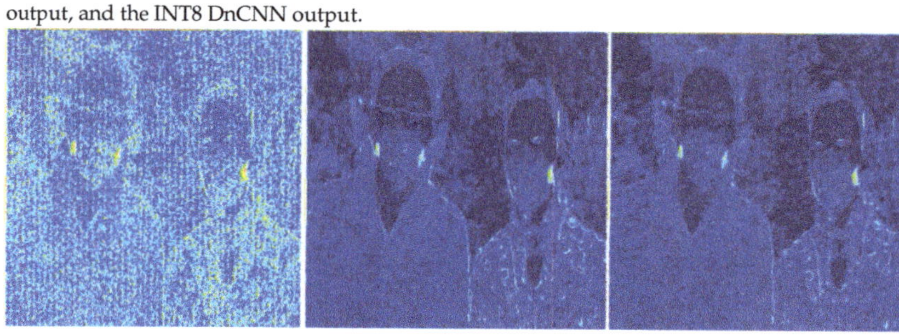

(**b**) Visualization of YOLOv11 backbone feature maps corresponding to the noisy input, FP16 DnCNN preprocessing, and INT8 DnCNN preprocessing.

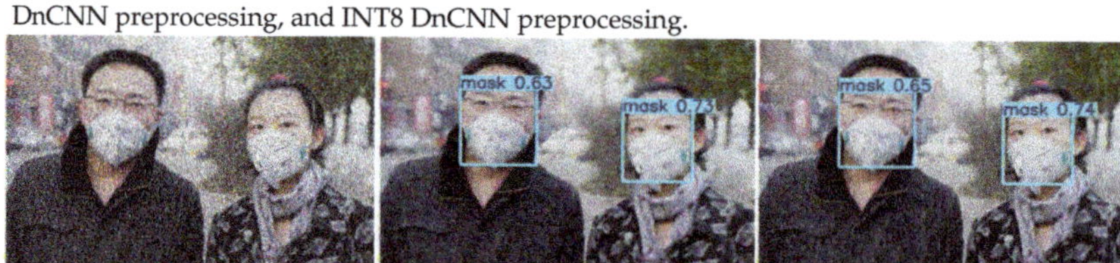


(**c**) Final masked-face detection results produced by YOLOv11 for each input condition.

**Figure 8.** Qualitative comparison of the proposed denoising–detection pipeline under severe Gaussian noise ($\sigma^2 = 0.10$).

To further validate the practical applicability of the proposed framework, we extended the qualitative analysis to real-world degradation scenarios beyond Gaussian noise. Figure 9 presents representative denoising and detection results under severe motion blur, JPEG compression, and low illumination conditions. While the visual restoration of motion-blurred images (Figure 9a) remains inherently challenging due to the design of DnCNN for

https://doi.org/10.3390/electronics15010143

additive noise removal, the proposed pipeline consistently preserves essential structural cues required for detection.

(a) Robustness against severe motion blur (Level 5).

(b) Robustness against JPEG compression artifacts (Level 5).

(c) Robustness against low-illumination conditions (Level 5).

**Figure 9.** Qualitative robustness evaluation under severe real-world degradations (Severity Level 5) using CLAHE-enhanced ROI heatmaps. From left to right: degraded input, INT8-quantized DnCNN output, and YOLO detection result. Enlarged insets show magnified mask regions.

To support a clearer interpretation of this structural preservation, enhanced ROI heatmaps are provided in Figure 9. Specifically, contrast-limited adaptive histogram equalization (CLAHE) is applied to cropped mask regions to amplify local contrast, thereby revealing noise distribution patterns and fine structural details that are less discernible in raw RGB images. These visualizations indicate that the INT8-quantized denoising retains critical ROI structures across all degradation types, enabling stable bounding box localization. Consequently, the detector successfully localizes masked faces under all tested scenarios, reinforcing the robustness of the proposed quantized inference pipeline against diverse real-world environmental distortions.

Overall, these desktop observation results provide a hardware-neutral assessment of noise robustness and establish a controlled baseline for interpreting the quantized inference behavior on the Jetson AGX Orin in Section 4.4.

### 4.4. Quantization Stability on Jetson AGX Orin

This subsection investigates how reduced numerical precision affects denoising robustness and downstream detection accuracy when deploying the proposed pipeline on the NVIDIA Jetson AGX Orin. In contrast to the desktop evaluation in Section 4.2, which analyzes noise robustness under controlled conditions, this section focuses on the stability of detection accuracy across FP16 and INT8 DnCNN variants on an embedded platform.

Unless otherwise specified, all detection accuracy metrics (Precision, Recall, mAP@0.5, and mAP@0.5:0.95) reported in this subsection are computed over the full FMLD validation set (7148 images). However, to enable controlled and repeatable runtime profiling on the

https://doi.org/10.3390/electronics15010143

embedded platform, runtime-related measurements (FPS, power consumption, energy efficiency) are evaluated using a fixed, class-balanced subset of 100 validation images.

Table 6 reports detection performance under severe Gaussian noise ($\sigma^2_{inj} = 0.10$), together with the corresponding throughput for reference. YOLO-only inference exhibits a severe degradation in robustness: although precision remains high (0.8921), recall collapses to 0.1427 due to missed detections, resulting in a substantial drop in localization accuracy (mAP@0.5 = 0.5223). This phenomenon is consistent with the noise sensitivity trends observed in Section 4.2 and highlights the necessity of denoising for stable detection on edge hardware.

**Table 6.** Combined quantitative comparison of detection performance and runtime efficiency on Jetson AGX Orin under severe noise ($\sigma^2_{inj} = 0.10$). The proposed INT8 Parallel pipeline achieves a favorable trade-off between accuracy and speed.

| Model/Setting | Precision | Recall | mAP@0.5 | mAP@0.5:0.95 | FPS |
|---|---|---|---|---|---|
| YOLO (Clean) | 0.8649 | 0.8031 | 0.8426 | 0.5893 | 14.58 |
| YOLO (Noise) | 0.8921 | 0.1427 | 0.5223 | 0.3238 | 26.09 |
| DnCNN FP16 (Serial) | 0.8387 | 0.4269 | 0.6427 | 0.4369 | 4.42 |
| DnCNN FP16 (Parallel) | 0.8465 | **0.4274** | **0.6464** | 0.4397 | 5.82 |
| DnCNN INT8 (Serial) | 0.8384 | 0.4172 | 0.6367 | 0.4364 | 6.24 |
| **DnCNN INT8 (Parallel) (Ours)** | **0.8471** | 0.4154 | 0.6402 | **0.4407** | **7.66** |

When DnCNN preprocessing is applied, detection performance is substantially restored. The FP16 variant achieves an mAP@0.5 of 0.6464, effectively mitigating the noise impact. Notably, the INT8 model maintains competitive accuracy (mAP@0.5 = 0.6402), with less than 1% degradation relative to FP16, demonstrating that aggressive quantization does not compromise denoising robustness on the embedded platform.

This behavior is consistent with prior observations on quantization-induced regularization effects. By constraining the dynamic range of activations, quantization can suppress minor perturbations and promote more stable feature representations [8]. Related studies further report that quantization reduces overfitting in noisy or perturbed environments [9] and improves in-distribution consistency in low-precision networks [10]. In addition, integer-arithmetic inference has been shown to preserve semantic fidelity with minimal degradation in detection backbones [7]. While this effect is not claimed as a novel theoretical contribution, the empirical stability observed here aligns well with these prior findings.

Overall, the results demonstrate that INT8 quantization preserves the robustness of DnCNN-based denoising while maintaining detection accuracy comparable to higher-precision models.

### 4.5. Real-Time Edge Efficiency on Jetson AGX Orin

This subsection evaluates whether the proposed denoising–detection pipeline can operate effectively in real time on the NVIDIA Jetson AGX Orin. While Section 4.3 analyzed detection accuracy stability under different quantization levels, the present analysis focuses on throughput, power consumption, and energy efficiency, which are critical metrics for power- and resource-constrained embedded systems.

Table 7 summarizes the throughput, power usage, and energy efficiency (FPS/W) for each pipeline configuration. A subset of 100 validation images was used to measure stable power metrics. Notably, the baseline detector under noise achieves 26.09 FPS, effectively satisfying standard high-speed real-time requirements ($\geq$20 FPS). However, as discussed in Section 4.3, this speed gain comes at the cost of a severe collapse in detection performance, making the noise-only condition impractical.

https://doi.org/10.3390/electronics15010143

**Table 7.** Performance comparison of runtime throughput, power consumption, and energy efficiency on Jetson AGX Orin. Energy metrics are measured over the validation subset (100 frames). The proposed INT8 Parallel pipeline demonstrates the best balance, achieving 1.222 FPS/W.

| Pipeline | FPS | Avg Power (W) | Max Power (W) | Energy (Wh) | FPS/W |
|---|---|---|---|---|---|
| YOLO-only (Clean) | 14.58 | 5.59 | 6.99 | 0.010 | 2.671 |
| YOLO-only (Noise) | 26.09 | 6.77 | 7.19 | 0.007 | 4.000 |
| DnCNN FP16 (Parallel) | 5.82 | 5.79 | 6.08 | 0.028 | 0.982 |
| **DnCNN INT8 (Parallel)** | **7.66** | **5.93** | **6.18** | **0.023** | **1.222** |

To restore accuracy within a reasonable computational budget, our pipeline leverages parallel CPU–GPU execution and INT8 quantization. As shown in Table 7, introducing DnCNN restores robustness but incurs computational overhead. However, the proposed **INT8 quantization significantly mitigates this burden**. The **INT8 Parallel pipeline achieves 7.66 FPS**, representing a **31.6% throughput improvement** over the FP16 Parallel baseline (5.82 FPS). This confirms that integer-arithmetic inference effectively accelerates the denoising workload on the Jetson edge platform.

Furthermore, the energy efficiency analysis highlights the benefits of quantization. While the YOLO-only baseline exhibits high throughput-to-power efficiency (4.00 FPS/W), it fails to detect targets under noise. Among the denoising pipelines, the proposed INT8 parallel model achieves an efficiency of **1.222 FPS/W**, representing a **24.4% improvement** over the FP16 implementation (0.982 FPS/W). This indicates that INT8 quantization not only accelerates inference speed but also effectively reduces the energy cost per frame, enhancing the sustainability of edge surveillance systems.

It should be noted that real-time object detection does not universally require 30 FPS operation; depending on the application, frame processing rates of approximately 3–10 FPS can be sufficient when end-to-end latency remains bounded, as reported in prior studies [35]. By balancing throughput ( 7.7 FPS), accuracy (mAP retention), and energy efficiency (1.222 FPS/W), the proposed INT8+Parallel framework offers the most favorable configuration for robust real-time deployment on the Jetson AGX Orin.

## 5. Discussion

This section discusses the empirical observations, limitations, and system-level implications of the proposed noise-resilient masked-face detection framework.

### 5.1. Quantization Effects and Interpretation

An important empirical observation from our experiments is that low-bit quantized DnCNN models occasionally exhibit performance comparable to, or slightly exceeding, their full-precision counterparts under mild noise conditions. Similar behaviors have been reported in prior studies on quantized inference, where reduced numerical precision constrains activation dynamics and limits sensitivity to small perturbations. It is emphasized that this phenomenon is reported here as an empirical observation at the system level, rather than as a claimed noise suppression mechanism or theoretical contribution. The primary contribution of this work lies in the system-level integration and validation of quantized denoising for robust detection, rather than in proposing a new regularization principle.

It should be noted that the observed robustness gain under quantization should not be interpreted as a definitive noise suppression mechanism. Rather, quantization constrains the numerical dynamic range of activations, which may indirectly stabilize inference under mild noise conditions by reducing sensitivity to small perturbations. This explanation is provided as a retrospective and empirical interpretation rather than a claimed theoretical contribution, and alternative interpretations—such as effective model capacity reduction—cannot be excluded. Accordingly, the reported behavior should be interpreted within this bounded empirical context, rather than as evidence of a causal regularization effect.

Beyond the empirical observations, a plausible interpretation of the improved performance of quantized models under low-noise conditions can be discussed from the perspective of numerical stability and activation distribution compression. Low-bit quantization effectively limits the dynamic range of intermediate activations, which suppresses minor fluctuations caused by residual noise and prevents excessive amplification of such variations through successive layers. When the input noise level is moderate, this implicit constraint can stabilize feature propagation and lead to more consistent inference behavior. As noise becomes more severe, however, such compression may also attenuate semantically meaningful features, diminishing its beneficial effect. This suggests that the apparent robustness gain of quantized inference is most pronounced within a practical noise regime and may reflect a form of survivorship bias in the observed operating range, rather than a universal robustness property under extreme corruption conditions.

### *5.2. Noise Modeling and Robustness Scope*

In this study, additive Gaussian noise was adopted as a controlled baseline to enable reproducible robustness analysis and direct comparison with standard denoising benchmarks. Gaussian corruption provides a well-established proxy for high-frequency sensor noise and compression artifacts, allowing systematic evaluation of noise-induced performance degradation.

To reflect realistic operating conditions, noise variance was incrementally increased to analyze robustness across distinct degradation regimes. Qualitative and quantitative results indicate that up to $\sigma^2_{\text{inj}} = 0.10$, the proposed pipeline maintains structurally consistent facial representations sufficient for reliable detection, even under visually severe corruption. This range therefore represents the upper bound of stable operation for edge-based vision sensors, where perceptual recognition remains possible despite significant noise contamination.

Although real-world degradations often involve mixed effects such as motion blur, low illumination, and compression artifacts, the controlled Gaussian setting allows isolation of noise-related failure mechanisms. Complementary qualitative evaluations under such non-Gaussian conditions further suggest that the proposed denoising–detection pipeline preserves essential structural cues beyond the strict Gaussian assumption, supporting its practical applicability.

### *5.3. Performance Boundaries and Failure Modes*

Figure 10 illustrates the progressive degradation of detection performance as noise severity increases beyond the stable operating range, using an 8-bit quantized DnCNN followed by YOLO-based detection.

At $\sigma^2_{\text{inj}} = 0.10$ (Figure 10a), detection remains stable and confident for both masked faces. Although the input exhibits heavy grain noise, core facial structures such as contours and mask boundaries are sufficiently preserved by the denoising stage, allowing the detector to operate within a practical "safe zone." This noise level therefore defines the effective operational limit of the proposed pipeline.

As noise increases to $\sigma^2_{\text{inj}} = 0.15$ (Figure 10b), the system enters a transition regime where denoising begins to introduce over-smoothing effects. While detections are still produced, confidence scores become unstable, particularly for faces with weaker contrast or partial occlusion. For example, the confidence of the left masked face decreases from 0.63 to 0.37, indicating the onset of structural attenuation that directly impacts detection reliability.

https://doi.org/10.3390/electronics15010143

(**a**) Limit ($\sigma^2_{\text{inj}} = 0.10$): Safe Zone. The system successfully detects both masked faces with high confidence, representing the effective operational limit.

(**b**) Failure Start ($\sigma^2_{\text{inj}} = 0.15$): Over-smoothing. As noise increases, the denoised output exhibits excessive smoothing, causing a significant drop in detection confidence (e.g., left face: $0.63 \rightarrow 0.37$), indicating the onset of instability.

(**c**) Total Failure ($\sigma^2_{\text{inj}} = 0.20$): Feature Collapse. Under extreme corruption, the structural features of the left face are lost (Feature Collapse), resulting in a missed detection.

**Figure 10.** Qualitative visualization of system failure boundaries and performance degradation under extreme noise conditions.

Under extreme corruption at $\sigma^2_{\text{inj}} = 0.20$ (Figure 10c), denoising is no longer able to recover semantically meaningful facial features. Patch-wise residual estimation collapses fine-scale structures, resulting in feature collapse and eventual missed detections. This failure mode is characterized not by erroneous classifications, but by the absence of detectable bounding boxes, reflecting a fundamental loss of discriminative information.

These observations indicate that performance degradation beyond $\sigma^2_{\text{inj}} = 0.10$ arises from intrinsic limitations of image restoration under extreme noise, rather than from deficiencies in the proposed framework. The transition from noise-robust operation to feature-collapse-driven failure defines a practical system boundary, beyond which preprocessing and detection are no longer effective. Systematic extension to adaptive noise modeling or cross-patch contextual restoration is therefore identified as an important direction for future work.

### *5.4. System-Level Implications for Edge Deployment*

From a system perspective, the proposed framework is directly applicable to a range of edge-based vision systems, including intelligent surveillance cameras, access-control terminals, healthcare monitoring platforms, and perception modules for human–robot interaction. In such systems, robustness to image degradation, low-latency inference, and limited computational resources are critical constraints. The proposed noise-aware and quantization-friendly design explicitly addresses these constraints through lightweight preprocessing, low-bit inference, and parallel CPU–GPU execution.

https://doi.org/10.3390/electronics15010143

The current evaluation focuses on a single-stream, fixed-resolution scenario, which reflects a common operational mode for embedded vision sensors. Specifically, the patch size was determined through preliminary profiling to identify the optimal operating point that balances GPU compute density with memory transfer latency. We observed that the selected patch dimension maximizes the throughput of the asynchronous CPU–GPU pipeline on the Jetson AGX Orin. Deviating from this optimal size (e.g., larger patches) resulted in memory bandwidth saturation and increased single-inference latency, which disrupted the continuous flow of the asynchronous pipeline. Therefore, the patch size was treated as a fixed hardware-aware design parameter to ensure stable real-time performance, rather than a tunable hyperparameter. Extensions to dynamic sizing or multi-stream scheduling are considered valuable directions for future investigation.

Power consumption was evaluated using the NVIDIA Jetson AGX Orin's built-in monitoring interfaces during runtime execution, rather than external power measurement instrumentation. The reported average and peak power values in Table 7 therefore reflect system-level readings collected under fixed power mode and workload conditions, and are intended to provide a relative comparison of energy efficiency across pipeline configurations rather than absolute power characterization. While such measurements may be affected by platform-specific variability, they are sufficient for comparing the relative efficiency of FP16 and INT8 pipelines under identical experimental settings.

A direct speed–accuracy comparison with other lightweight denoising models on the same edge platform was not conducted in this study. While such an evaluation would further strengthen the real-time performance analysis, the selection of DnCNN was motivated by its well-established balance between restoration quality, architectural simplicity, and blind denoising capability, as demonstrated in the desktop benchmarks. In contrast, alternative models such as FFDNet require explicit noise-level estimation, and transformer-based models incur substantial computational overhead that limits their suitability for embedded deployment. Comprehensive edge-level comparisons across denoising architectures are therefore identified as an important direction for future work.

## 6. Conclusions

This study proposed a noise-resilient masked-face detection framework that integrates DnCNN-based image denoising with the YOLOv11 detector, together with low-bit quantization and an optimized edge-device execution pipeline. Experimental results demonstrated that high-frequency noise severely degrades masked-face detection performance, and that lightweight residual denoising prior to detection substantially improves robustness under moderate to severe degradation.

Comprehensive evaluations showed that 16-bit and 8-bit quantized denoisers preserve most of the denoising benefit while significantly reducing computational cost. Edge deployment experiments on the NVIDIA Jetson AGX Orin further confirmed that quantization and parallel CPU–GPU execution enable near–real-time operation under noisy conditions, providing a practical foundation for deployable edge-AI systems.

Future work will focus on extending the proposed framework to continuous video pipelines, multi-stream scenarios, and broader real-world degradation models. Furthermore, we plan to integrate the framework into concrete edge applications such as intelligent surveillance cameras, access-control terminals, and healthcare monitoring platforms. Exploring its applicability to multi-task facial analysis—including facial landmark detection, identity recognition, and physiological signal estimation—represents another promising direction for future research.

https://doi.org/10.3390/electronics15010143

**Author Contributions:** Conceptualization, R.C. and M.Y.K.; Methodology, R.C., S.K. and M.Y.K.; Software, R.C. and S.K.; Validation, R.C., B.-s.K. and H.L.; Formal analysis, R.C. and B.-s.K.; Investigation, R.C. and B.-s.K.; Resources, M.Y.K. and H.L.; Technical support, H.L.; Data curation, R.C.; Writing—original draft preparation, R.C.; Writing—review and editing, M.Y.K., B.-s.K., S.K. and H.L.; Visualization, R.C.; Supervision, M.Y.K.; Project administration, M.Y.K.; Funding acquisition, M.Y.K. All authors have read and agreed to the published version of the manuscript.

**Funding:** This work was supported by the DGIST R&D Program of the Ministry of Science and ICT (25-IT-02). This research was supported by the Regional Innovation System & Education (RISE) Glocal 30 program through the Daegu RISE Center, funded by the Ministry of Education (MOE) and the Daegu, Republic of Korea (2025-RISE-03-001).

**Data Availability Statement:** The Face Mask Label Dataset (FMLD) used in this study is publicly available at https://github.com/borutb-fri/FMLD. The pretrained DnCNN model is provided by MathWorks (https://www.mathworks.com/help/images/ref/denoisingnetwork.html). Noise injection and denoising benchmarks were implemented using publicly available toolboxes, including the KAIR image restoration framework (https://github.com/cszn/KAIR) and the Albumentations library (https://github.com/albumentations-team/albumentations, all accessed on 4 December 2025). The source code for the proposed edge-deployment pipeline is available from the corresponding author upon reasonable request due to hardware-specific dependencies on NVIDIA Jetson platforms.

**Acknowledgments:** The authors would like to thank the anonymous reviewers for their constructive and insightful comments, which greatly improved the quality of this manuscript. We also express our gratitude to the Intelligent Robotics Research Division at DGIST for providing technical support and experimental resources. Finally, the first author would like to acknowledge Mercury and Depence for their continuous encouragement and support during the preparation of this study.

**Conflicts of Interest:** The authors declare no conflicts of interest.

## References

1. Chen, L.; Wang, H.; Wang, X.; Gao, J.; Deng, W. The Devil of Face Recognition Is in the Noise. In Proceedings of the European Conference on Computer Vision (ECCV), Munich, Germany, 8–14 September 2018; pp. 765–782.
2. Esmaeilzehi, A.; Ahmad, M.O.; Swamy, M.N.S. SRNHARB: A deep light-weight image super resolution network using hybrid activation residual blocks. *Signal Processing: Image Commun.* **2021**, *99*, 116509. [CrossRef]
3. Guo, Y.; Zhang, L.; Hu, Y.; He, X.; Gao, J. A Dataset and Benchmark for Large-Scale Face Recognition. In Proceedings of the IEEE Conference on Computer Vision and Pattern Recognition (CVPR), Las Vegas, NV, USA, 27–30 June 2016; pp. 4873–4882.
4. Batagelj, B.; Peer, P.; Struc, V.; Dobrisek, S. How to Correctly Detect Face-Masks for COVID-19 from Visual Information? *Appl. Sci.* **2021**, *11*, 2070. [CrossRef]
5. Zhang, K.; Zuo, W.; Chen, Y.; Meng, D.; Zhang, L. Beyond a Gaussian Denoiser: Residual Learning of Deep CNN for Image Denoising. *IEEE Trans. Image Process.* **2017**, *26*, 3142–3155. [CrossRef] [PubMed]
6. He, L.; Zhou, Y.; Liu, L.; Ma, J. Research and Application of YOLOv11-Based Object Segmentation in Intelligent Construction-Site Recognition. *Buildings* **2024**, *14*, 3777. [CrossRef]
7. Jacob, B.; Kligys, S.; Chen, B.; Zhu, M.; Tang, M.; Howard, A.; Adam, H. Quantization and Training of Neural Networks for Efficient Integer-Arithmetic-Only Inference. In Proceedings of the IEEE Conference on Computer Vision and Pattern Recognition (CVPR), Salt Lake City, UT, USA, 18–23 June 2018; pp. 2704–2713.
8. Nagel, S.; Shao, R.; Gouk, H.; Hospedales, T.M. QReg: On Regularization Effects of Quantization. *arXiv* **2022**, arXiv:2206.12372. [CrossRef]
9. Xu, Y.; Wang, Z.; Li, Z.; Xu, Y.; Tao, D. Fighting Overfitting with Quantization for Deep Neural Networks on Noisy Labels. *arXiv* **2023**, arXiv:2303.11803.
10. Wang, R.; Tang, Y.; Gong, C.; Liu, Y. In-Distribution Consistency Regularization for QAT Generalization. *arXiv* **2024**, arXiv:2402.13497.
11. Dabov, K.; Foi, A.; Katkovnik, V.; Egiazarian, K. Image Denoising by Sparse 3D Transform-Domain Collaborative Filtering. *IEEE Trans. Image Process.* **2007**, *16*, 2080–2095. [CrossRef] [PubMed]
12. Pande-Chhetri, R.; Abd-Elrahman, A. De-Striping Hyperspectral Imagery Using Wavelet Transform and Adaptive Frequency Domain Filtering. *ISPRS J. Photogramm. Remote Sens.* **2011**, *66*, 620–636. [CrossRef]

https://doi.org/10.3390/electronics15010143

13. Cui, H.; Jia, P.; Zhang, G.; Jiang, Y.-H.; Li, L.-T.; Wang, J.-Y.; Hao, X.-Y. Multiscale Intensity Propagation to Remove Multiplicative Stripe Noise From Remote Sensing Images. *IEEE Trans. Geosci. Remote Sens.* **2020**, *58*, 2308–2323. [CrossRef]
14. Chang, Y.; Yan, L.; Liu, L.; Fang, H.; Zhong, S. Infrared Aerothermal Nonuniform Correction via Deep Multiscale Residual Network. *IEEE Geosci. Remote Sens. Lett.* **2019**, *16*, 1120–1124. [CrossRef]
15. Sun, W.; Ren, K.; Meng, X.; Yang, G.; Xiao, C.; Peng, J.; Huang, J. MLR-DBPFN: A Multi-scale Low Rank Deep Back Projection Fusion Network for Anti-noise Hyperspectral and Multispectral Image Fusion. *IEEE Trans. Geosci. Remote Sens.* **2022**, *60*, 5522914. [CrossRef]
16. Liang, J.; Cao, J.; Sun, G.; Zhang, K.; Van Gool, L.; Timofte, R. SwinIR: Image Restoration Using Swin Transformer. In Proceedings of the IEEE/CVF International Conference on Computer Vision (ICCV), Montreal, QC, Canada, 10–17 October 2021; pp. 1833–1844.
17. Zhang, K.; Zuo, W.; Zhang, L. FFDNet: Toward a Fast and Flexible CNN-Based Image Denoiser. *IEEE Trans. Image Process.* **2018**, *27*, 4608–4622. [CrossRef] [PubMed]
18. Guo, S.; Li, Q.; Zuo, W. Toward Convolutional Blind Denoising of Real Photographs. In Proceedings of the IEEE/CVF Conference on Computer Vision and Pattern Recognition (CVPR), Long Beach, CA, USA, 16–20 June 2019; pp. 1712–1722.
19. Li, L.; Jiang, L.; Zhang, J.; Wang, S.; Chen, F. A Complete YOLO-Based Ship Detection Method for Thermal Infrared Remote Sensing Images under Complex Backgrounds. *Remote Sensing* **2022**, *14*, 1534. [CrossRef]
20. Rodríguez-Rodríguez, J.A.; López-Rubio, E.; Ángel-Ruiz, J.A.; Molina-Cabello, M.A. The Impact of Noise and Brightness on Object Detection Methods. *Sensors* **2024**, *24*, 821. [CrossRef] [PubMed]
21. Li, J.; Zhang, S.; Zhang, X.; Wang, A. DiffuYOLO: A Novel Method for Small Vehicle Detection in Remote Sensing Based on Diffusion Models. *Alex. Eng. J.* **2025**, *114*, 485–496. [CrossRef]
22. Liu, Y.; Li, S.; Zhou, L.; Liu, H.; Li, Z. Dark-YOLO: A Low-Light Object Detection Algorithm Integrating Multiple Attention Mechanisms. *Appl. Sci.* **2025**, *15*, 5170. [CrossRef]
23. Ge, S.; Li, J.; Ye, Q.; Luo, Z. Detecting Masked Faces with LLE-CNNs. In Proceedings of the IEEE Conference on Computer Vision and Pattern Recognition (CVPR), Honolulu, HI, USA, 21–26 July 2017; pp. 2682–2690.
24. Batagelj, B. Face Mask Label Dataset (FMLD). GitHub Repository. 2024. Available online: https://github.com/borutb-fri/FMLD (accessed on 3 September 2025).
25. Wang, A.; Chen, H.; Liu, L.; Chen, K.; Lin, Z.; Han, J.; Ding, G. YOLOv10: Real-Time End-to-End Object Detection. In Advances in Neural Information Processing Systems (NeurIPS), Vancouver, BC, Canada, 10–16 December 2024; Curran Associates, Inc.: Red Hook, NY, USA, 2024; Volume 37.
26. Zhang, K.; Zuo, W.; Zhang, L. KAIR: Image Restoration Toolbox for Reproducible Research. GitHub Repository. 2021. Available online: https://github.com/cszn/KAIR (accessed on 3 September 2025).
27. MathWorks. Denoising Network (MATLAB R2024b, Image Processing Toolbox). Available online: https://www.mathworks.com/help/images/ref/denoisingnetwork.html (accessed on 12 February 2025).
28. Ke, R. Deep Variation Prior: Joint Image Denoising and Noise Variance Estimation Without Clean Data. *IEEE Trans. Image Process.* **2024**, *33*, 2908–2923. [CrossRef] [PubMed]
29. NVIDIA Corporation. *TensorRT Developer Guide: Quantization and Calibration*; NVIDIA: Santa Clara, CA, USA, 2023.
30. ONNX Working Group. ONNX Quantization Specification (Q/DQ Format). 2022. Available online: https://github.com/onnx/onnx/blob/main/docs/Operators.md (accessed on 17 December 2025).
31. Apostolidis, K.D.; Papakostas, G.A. Delving into YOLO Object Detection Models: Insights into Adversarial Robustness. *Electronics* **2025**, *14*, 1624. [CrossRef]
32. Ultralytics. Detection Datasets. Available online: https://docs.ultralytics.com/datasets/detect/ (accessed on 17 December 2025).
33. Buslaev, A.; Iglovikov, V.I.; Khvedchenya, E.; Parinov, A.; Druzhinin, M.; Kalinin, A.A. Albumentations: Fast and Flexible Image Augmentations. GitHub Repository. 2020. Available online: https://github.com/albumentations-team/albumentations (accessed on 3 September 2025).
34. Hendrycks, D.; Dietterich, T. Benchmarking Neural Network Robustness to Common Corruptions and Perturbations. In Proceedings of the International Conference on Learning Representations (ICLR), New Orleans, LA, USA, 6–9 May 2019. Available online: https://openreview.net/forum?id=HJz6tiCqYm (accessed on 3 September 2025).
35. Lee, J.; Hwang, K.-I. YOLO with Adaptive Frame Control for Real-Time Object Detection Applications. *Multimed. Tools Appl.* **2022**, *81*, 36375–36396. [CrossRef]




https://doi.org/10.3390/electronics15010143

electronics

MDPI

Article

# Visualizing Urban Dynamics: Insights from Electric Scooter Mobility Data

**Robert Bembenik *, Alicja Dąbrowska and Jarosław Chudziak**

Institute of Computer Science, Warsaw University of Technology, Nowowiejska 15/19, 00-665 Warsaw, Poland
* Correspondence: robert.bembenik@pw.edu.pl

**Abstract**

This paper showcases how electric scooter data can be used to visually explore and interpret urban dynamics, offering a perspective on city structure and mobility patterns. The goal of the study is to investigate how visual analysis of micromobility data can reveal spatial and temporal patterns that support urban planning and operational decision-making. Through a series of visual analyses, the article identifies high-demand areas and popular travel routes, with areas of particularly strong traffic—insights valuable for infrastructure planning and operational optimization. Temporal visualizations reveal distinct peaks in e-scooter activity during lunch hours and late evenings, highlighting behavior patterns that may inform service adjustments. Clustering techniques are used to delineate functional zones within the city, which are then visualized to reflect how users interact with urban space. These visuals help uncover mobility-based boundaries and support a deeper understanding of the city's layout. Additionally, the approach highlights key locations that may be attractive for business development, such as new commercial spots, based on user behavior. By focusing on visual storytelling rather than predictive modeling, this work proposes analyses suitable for urban planners, mobility providers, and other stakeholders with actionable insights into urban movement and structure.

**Keywords:** spatial analyses; city structure; electric scooters; E-scooters; open data; GBFS; shared micromobility

## 1. Introduction

Cities can be compared to living organisms—constantly changing and consisting of thousands of elements through which millions of particles move [1]. Understanding such a complex structure has been studied by urbanists for hundreds of years. As a result of technological progress, cities are constantly changing, and therefore, their research must also evolve [2]. Knowledge of the city's structure is necessary for spatial planning, infrastructure management, and the development of new technologies that transform an ordinary city into a "smart city" [2]. At the same time, fine-grained mobility traces raise privacy and security concerns, as repeated location observations may reveal sensitive movement patterns if handled or shared improperly. In this study, we mitigate these risks by working with publicly accessible GBFS snapshots and reporting results only in aggregated forms (e.g., grid-based intensities and corridor summaries), rather than analyzing individual users or personal identifiers. Recent advancements in data availability have enabled new ways of observing urban mobility. Tools such as mobile phone logs, GPS traces from car navigation systems, and people-flow monitoring, collectively referred to as urban computing, have all been used to model movement and spatial relationships in cities [3]. Another very good source of data on people's movement around the city was completely unknown until recently: electric scooters (also referred to as e-scooters; we will use both of these terms in the paper). Electric scooters are becoming an increasingly popular means of transportation in the city. They provide a sustainable and cheap alternative to reducing the number of private vehicle trips [3], and thus pollution, traffic congestion [4], and land-use [5]. Electric scooters are one of the fastest-growing electric micro-mobility vehicles [6]. Since 2017, several e-scooter companies have started their services in many cities in North America and Europe. The number of companies offering e-scooters for rent and the cities where the service is available are constantly growing.

E-scooters interact with existing mobility systems by simultaneously complementing and substituting traditional transport modes. They typically fill gaps in transit networks, solving first-mile/last-mile connectivity issues, especially evident during disruptions like COVID-19, where e-scooters became a preferred transport mode due to health and safety concerns [7,8]. Rider behaviors and safety perceptions significantly depend on infrastructure quality. Dedicated lanes improve rider comfort and safety, whereas mixed traffic conditions elevate perceived risks, influencing rider choices and interactions [9]. Infrastructure safety, cost, and accessibility are factors affecting commuters' willingness to shift from cars to electric micromobility options such as e-scooters [10]. User experiences, perceptions, and adoption are influenced by demographic and psychological factors, including attitudes towards sustainability, cost sensitivity, service convenience, and satisfaction with service reliability. Adoption studies revealed that positive user experiences (ease of use, enjoyment) significantly boost e-scooter adoption, whereas technical malfunctions, pricing, limited service areas, and poor infrastructure deter potential users [11–13]. Barriers to micromobility implementation primarily encompass infrastructural deficiencies (e.g., poorly maintained paths, inadequate signage), operational issues (high cost, battery limitations, complicated app usage), and personal barriers like safety concerns, weather sensitivity, and perceived health risks. Effective integration into smart city frameworks necessitates addressing these barriers through infrastructure enhancement, operational simplification, policy adjustments, and robust maintenance practices [14].

Electric scooter users can be grouped into distinct types based on factors such as access to infrastructure, cost sensitivity, and personal background. These groups have different mobility needs, highlighting the importance of tailored policies and infrastructure improvements. Common patterns in e-scooter use include specific times of day and popular locations, and users can generally be categorized as one-time, casual, regular, or non-users. These patterns support the development of more targeted and effective urban mobility strategies [15,16].

Despite the growing popularity of e-scooters, their potential to reveal structural characteristics of cities remains underexplored. This study seeks to investigate whether shared e-scooter data can be used to analyze the spatial structure of a city. Given the high volume of movement data they generate, these devices may offer a new perspective on how urban areas function and interact [17–20]. While many previous studies rely on long-term, large-scale datasets to produce detailed and comprehensive analyses of micromobility systems, such as multi-month examinations of e-scooter dynamics in Chicago [21] or extensive spatiotemporal segmentations of shared e-scooter usage patterns across Berlin [22], our work adopts a different perspective. The aim of this study is not to perform a longitudinal assessment of an entire urban area over extended periods, but rather to demonstrate how much can be learned from visual analysis of a relatively short temporal window of shared e-scooter data.

The goal of the work is thus to investigate the structure of a selected city using various spatial analyses with the use of data from electric scooters and presenting the results


https://doi.org/10.3390/electronics15010187

visually. Rome has been chosen for the study due to the availability of data from this city and its characteristics: it is a city with a very high tourist potential, also being the European capital composed of typically administrative, residential, and office districts. The aim of the work is also to find a way to obtain data on actual journeys.

We argue that even a limited dataset, when examined through carefully designed visual analytics, can yield meaningful and actionable insights into urban structure, travel behavior, and potential interventions. This emphasis on visual reasoning sets our approach apart from prior research focused primarily on predictive modeling [23], behavioral determinants [10], or multi-quarter demand and usage analyses [15,16]. Instead, our perspective is pragmatic: we evaluate the practical utility of visually inspecting a compact sample of micromobility data to reveal spatial patterns, functional zones, and mobility flows that are directly interpretable by planners, operators, and other stakeholders.

We position this work within urban computing and mobility visual analytics, where heterogeneous urban sensing data are transformed into representations that support human-centered reasoning and operational decisions. In this framing, our contribution is a descriptive visual-analytics workflow that converts publicly available GBFS snapshots into reconstructed trips and grid-based indicators, which are then communicated through hotspot, corridor, and zoning views. The pipeline emphasizes transparency of assumptions and reproducibility under minimal data access, and is intended for exploratory decision support rather than predictive modeling or causal inference.

Our goal is not to propose a new visualization technique per se, but to present a reproducible visual-analytics workflow for extracting interpretable urban mobility cues from high-frequency GBFS snapshots, which are often the only publicly accessible source of micromobility data. In particular, we demonstrate how a compact observation window (one operator, one week) can still support consistent descriptive analyses of demand, mobility corridors, temporal peaks, and mobility-based functional zoning when the data are reconstructed and summarized transparently.

The main contributions of this paper are as follows:

- GBFS-to-trips reconstruction pipeline: we describe how real-time GBFS snapshots sampled every 5 s are transformed into historical rentals and idle episodes using simple continuity rules ($\leq$15 s temporal continuity for rentals; 50 m spatial threshold for idle segmentation), without interpolating missing positions.
- A consistent set of map-centered visual products for urban interpretation, including (i) spatial demand/idle-time patterns, (ii) frequently used route structure, and (iii) complementary views of short vs. long trips to separate local mobility from longer cross-city movements.
- Mobility-based zoning from reconstructed trips: we show how a 200 m grid and k-means clustering over interpretable descriptors (arrivals, spatial dispersion of starts, average trip distance) yields functional zones that support qualitative reading of city structure.
- Transparent, criterion-based location scoring (descriptive, not causal): we provide top-location visualizations under simple criteria (trip-start frequency, average trip distance, dominant time-of-day), explicitly avoiding composite "optimal location" claims.
- Decision-support framing for stakeholders: we illustrate how the same descriptive outputs can be mapped to operator and city questions (rebalancing, parking/drop-off zones, and location salience), while explicitly stating the limits of single-operator, single-week generalization.

The rest of the paper is structured as follows. In Section 2 we discuss related work. In Section 3 we focus on the data acquisition process. We then conduct initial analyses of electric scooter travel patterns in Rome, categorizing journeys into long and short routes.

 https://doi.org/10.3390/electronics15010187

This section also includes a zoning analysis of the city, identifying distinct areas based on e-scooter usage patterns. A detailed ranking of city locations based on various criteria provides insights into popular spots and potential areas for infrastructure development. In Section 4, we synthesize our findings to demonstrate their practical applications. In Section 5, we discuss the scope, limitations, robustness, and transferability of the proposed GBFS-based workflow and interpret the results in light of the data constraints. We conclude the paper in Section 6.

## 2. Related Work

Recent work on spatio-temporal data visualization is often framed within the broader paradigm of visual analytics, where interactive visual representations are combined with analytical reasoning to support insight and decision-making [24,25]. Foundational work by Andrienko and Andrienko systematizes exploratory analysis for spatial and temporal data and extends these principles to movement data, emphasizing trajectory transformation and multi-scale visual reasoning [26,27], (Andrienko & Andrienko, 2006; Andrienko et al., 2013). Building on these principles, we review prior work on visual analysis of micromobility and urban mobility traces, and then position our GBFS-snapshot-driven workflow with respect to these studies.

City structure analysis is a research goal which has been pursued by researchers for quite some time. Depending on available data different analyses can be realized. With the advent of mass data generation and processing (e.g., smartphones, cars, e-scooters, city bikes, etc.) these data become easier and easier to get hold of and be utilized for particular needs. The purpose of such analyses can be, e.g., predicting success of city businesses, ranking business locations, location recommendations, analysis of micro-mobility usage patterns, modeling the demand for POIs or visual analyses of urban data.

Predicting success of city businesses like restaurants or shops, based on various factors using different methods and features are studied in, e.g., [28–30]. The authors of these papers use a variety of data sources, including user reviews, check-in data, demographic data, and other online data. The features used in these models include geographical location, human mobility patterns, rating scores, and textual reviews. The models are trained using machine learning techniques, such as logistic regression, gradient boosted decision trees, and support vector machines. The goal is to provide insights that can help businesses improve their performance and survival chances.

Some researchers propose methods for selecting or ranking business locations based on demand or popularity (e.g., [31–33]). They aim to identify the most promising locations for businesses (such as stores or outlets) based on factors like demand, popularity, and competition. They use data from map queries, WiFi connections, and social media to identify demand centers and rank potential locations. The methods utilized to achieve the assumed goals include learning-to-rank, regression, and ensemble methods. Ref. [34] proposes a method for recommending shop types to users based on their preferences and the popularity of shop types. The offered model considers both the popularity of shop types and the preferences of individual users. The method involves collecting data from social media and LBSNs (Location-Based Social Networks), extracting relevant features, training a model (in this case, a matrix factorization approach), and evaluating the model's performance. The goal is to help users discover new shops and help shop owners attract more customers. Ref. [35] focuses on modeling the demand for Points of Interest (POIs) in urban regions. It proposes a framework for modelling the demand for POIs across various urban regions. The framework leverages large-scale human mobility data, specifically taxi GPS traces, to analyze and predict the need for services in different neighborhoods. Ref. [36] develops an approach for real estate appraisal by integrating human mobility patterns with

 https://doi.org/10.3390/electronics15010187

the functional diversity of communities. This approach leverages a geographic functional learning model that captures correlations among estate neighborhoods, urban functions, temporal effects, and user mobility patterns. The study makes use of extensive real-world data, including taxi GPS traces and Point of Interest (POI) data, to model the demand dynamics around properties.

These studies rely heavily on predictive modeling and structured features, whereas our work does not attempt to forecast demand or optimize business performance. Instead, we employ visual exploration of micromobility data to reveal mobility structures and identify potentially interesting locations, without building predictive models or inferring causality.

Analysis of micro-mobility usage patterns is the focus of these papers [21,37–44]. The studies seek to derive insights into user behavior and service usage. Whether through direct data analysis or through surveys, they try to understand the underlying reasons behind micro-mobility choices and how these choices impact urban mobility. The data used in these studies comes either from specific APIs (Application Programming Interfaces) provided by micro-mobility service operators or through comprehensive surveys. The studies employ spatial analysis techniques to overlay trip data onto maps or use statistical methods to explore temporal patterns.

In particular, the authors of [37] collected real-time data from a vendor's API, focusing on e-scooter trip origins, destinations, and trajectories. This data was analyzed at 30 s intervals to explore trip dynamics through descriptive statistics, spatial analysis on street maps, and cross-tabulations with street classifications and traffic volumes. The findings revealed spatial and temporal usage patterns, highlighting areas with high traffic and potential risks, which can guide urban planners and policymakers in enhancing urban mobility frameworks, targeting safety measures, and refining regulatory approaches. In [38] user behaviors and demographic characteristics between e-scooter and bike-sharing systems in the Tricity area of Poland is compared. By utilizing survey data, the study explores how different demographics interact with these micro-mobility services and the implications for urban transport planning, especially in understanding modal complementarity and substitution. Ref. [39] provides a comparative analysis of usage patterns for e-scooter-share and bike-share systems in Washington, D.C. It uses large datasets to examine how these services are utilized across different times and locations within the city, aiming to determine their functional roles and integration within the urban mobility landscape. Ref. [40] focuses on Turin, Italy. It analyzes and compares the spatiotemporal usage patterns of dockless bike sharing and e-scooter services. Through data gathered from service operators, the paper identifies key usage trends and geographical hotspots, providing insights into how these services are adopted in different urban contexts and their impact on urban mobility. Ref. [43] explores how shared micromobility interacts with public transport systems through an in-depth spatiotemporal analysis. Using trip data from Calgary's shared micromobility program, they identified temporal and spatial hotspots of micromobility use that serve as connectors to bus and rail stations. Their findings revealed that e-scooters and bikes are disproportionately used to bridge transit gaps during peak commuting periods, emphasizing their value in improving multimodal network efficiency. Ref. [21] conducts a large-scale analysis of shared e-scooter usage in Chicago, integrating trip data with sociodemographic, land-use, and transport-system characteristics. Their findings revealed that e-scooter usage is strongly associated with urban density, transit accessibility, and income levels, with significant differences between neighborhoods. The study concluded that shared e-scooters act as a supplementary mode to transit rather than a direct substitute, especially for short local trips. These results highlight wider socio-spatial inequalities in access and identify policy levers for promoting more equitable micromobility deployment. Ref. [44] is a survey-based study from Braga, Portugal. The authors identified


https://doi.org/10.3390/electronics15010187

key social, environmental, and psychological factors influencing e-scooter adoption. They found that perceived convenience, time savings, and environmental concern positively correlated with usage, while safety fears, inadequate infrastructure, and poor road conditions acted as major deterrents. Their analysis emphasized the need for improved cycling infrastructure and targeted regulations to encourage sustainable micromobility use. This work complements broader behavioral research by highlighting how local infrastructure quality and risk perception shape adoption patterns.

These works aim to explain or predict usage behavior, often using statistical inference or econometric modeling. Our study does not model determinants of e-scooter use; instead, it focuses on visualizing the spatial and temporal structure revealed by e-scooter traces. Where behavioral studies seek drivers of mobility, our goal is to reveal patterns and urban structure through visual interpretation.

Other studies go further in examining trip intent and infrastructure design. Ref. [41] utilizes topic modeling techniques to infer the purposes behind e-scooter trips in urban environments, specifically looking at data from Washington, D.C. By integrating e-scooter trip data with points of interest, the study offers novel insights into the motivations driving e-scooter usage and its implications for urban planning and policy-making. Ref. [42] analyzes the practical challenges of integrating e-scooters into urban transportation systems, focusing on Dallas, Texas. The study employs unsupervised learning techniques like DBSCAN to identify and manage e-scooter parking areas and employs methods such as shortest path analyses to pinpoint high-use corridors, aiming to enhance infrastructure and reduce vehicle clutter. The findings have the potential to improve parking management and tailor infrastructure to match actual usage patterns, leading to recommendations for policy changes to support the efficient integration of e-scooters in cityscapes. Ref. [23] uses deep learning and spatio-temporal graph neural networks (STGCapNet) to predict urban e-scooter flows. The proposed GCScoot model utilized real-world data, including GPS trajectories, points-of-interest, street networks, and weather conditions to forecast e-scooter distributions during dynamic reconfiguration scenarios (such as area expansions or reductions). The predictive capability offers valuable guidance for city planners and operators to optimize fleet management, operational decisions, and ultimately enhance micromobility efficiency. These studies analyze mode relationships, substitution effects, and integration with transit. Our study does not evaluate multimodal substitution nor first/last-mile connectivity; instead, it uses e-scooters as a lens to reveal urban form, focusing on routes, hotspots, and functional zones rather than modal interactions.

Another line of research focuses on visual analysis of urban mobility, where spatial data is not only analyzed but also presented in visual form to enhance interpretation. For example, Ref. [45] uses data from Austin, Texas to analyze electric scooter trips. The data includes rental times, trip durations, distances traveled, and starting and ending locations. The study finds that e-scooter usage varies based on the time of day and day of the week. The study also categorizes routes based on the pickup and drop-off points, revealing a division of the city into two parts. Similarly, in [46] data from Minneapolis and Louisville is used to determine the optimal number of e-scooters to meet user demand. The study presents charts depicting the popularity of different times of the day and week, and heat maps of e-scooter demand in the city. Ref. [33] uses data from Foursquare to determine the most popular locations in a city within a specific category. The study uses four methods to determine the level of popularity for a specific area: passenger volume, linear regression, collaborative filtering, and association rules. Each method highlights different characteristics. In [20] mobile phone data is used to determine the routes of Riyadh residents. The authors conduct an analysis of how the city can be divided based on the characteristics of the trips made to and from each region. The study divides the city

 https://doi.org/10.3390/electronics15010187

based on how users move between different zones and characterizes the features of the city's regions based on the spatial dispersion of starting locations. The study notes that the choice of analysis type should suit the characteristics of the city under investigation. The authors of [22] performed an extensive spatiotemporal study of e-scooter trips in Berlin, analyzing millions of rides over several months. The authors classified trip patterns into functional categories such as leisure rides, commuting flows, and multimodal transfers, revealing strong temporal regularities and spatial dependencies across districts. Their visual and statistical analysis underscored the heterogeneity of micromobility demand and its sensitivity to land-use structures. This study serves as an example of long-term, fine-grained mobility characterization based on large datasets. Closest in spirit to our visualization-focused objective are studies that visualize and summarize e-scooter usage for planning or system design. The authors of [45] estimate e-scooter traffic flow to support micromobility planning, whereas [46] leverages open data primarily from a system-design perspective.

In summary, existing visual approaches often complement model-driven frameworks or target operational optimization of micromobility systems. In contrast, we center our contribution on visual analytics as the primary analytical instrument, demonstrating that visual reasoning alone can reveal interpretable urban structure, such as mobility corridors, temporal peaks, functional zones, and candidate locations relevant to commercial or operational decisions, without relying on predictive modeling or demand estimation. By prioritizing intuitive, map-based representations, our approach aims to translate micromobility traces into actionable insights that are immediately usable by planners, policymakers, and operators. From a stakeholder perspective, visual analytics is often preferred when decisions must be auditable and quickly communicated (e.g., to justify parking zones, rebalancing priorities, or infrastructure changes). In practice, planners and operators frequently need transparent evidence of where and when demand concentrates, and how patterns change across time, rather than a black-box forecast. Visual summaries also remain useful when ground-truth labels or long historical series are limited, providing a robust descriptive baseline that can later be complemented by predictive models.

## 3. E-Scooter Data Acquisition and Route Classification

In this section, the process of obtaining data for the needs of this study is described. We discuss data availability, the way of transforming real-time data into historical data, as well as the presentation of the obtained data for the test period. Preliminary visualizations allowed for many conclusions to be drawn. The visualizations were not yet spatial analyses, but rather advanced data presentations. This section presents our analyses that allow for an understanding of the structure and construction of the city.

### 3.1. Data Acquisition

Despite the INSPIRE Directive (Infrastructure for Spatial Information in Europe) [47] mandating EU member states to make spatial data widely accessible, many datasets remain inaccessible or are fee-based [48,49]. E-scooter data faces similar challenges. Most e-scooters are owned by private companies, which are not obligated to share data unless specific agreements with local governments are established, as seen in Warsaw where five operators agreed to provide anonymized data for research purposes [19,50].

Typically, researchers obtain e-scooter data through local government sources. However, in Poland, no open datasets were found, likely due to the relatively recent adoption of this transport mode. Privacy concerns also restrict broader data sharing, especially regarding historical ride data.

 https://doi.org/10.3390/electronics15010187

While historical data is rarely shared, operators often publish real-time information to attract users, usually through public APIs based on the GBFS (General Bikeshare Feed Specification) standard [51]. GBFS enables standardized sharing of data on available vehicles, system status, docking stations (if any), and attributes such as availability (is_reserved, is_disabled) and last known location with timestamp, without compromising user privacy.

Due to these limitations, data for this study was collected from the Helbiz operator for the city of Rome, which had an open, test API. Data frames were downloaded every 5 s over a period of 7 days, from 15 to 22 November 2021. This resulted in over 80,000 files, capturing real-time snapshots of the system. While these snapshots allowed identification of general trends in e-scooter availability, further data processing was required to reconstruct actual ride trajectories. The data was cleaned and transformed into historical trip records, forming the basis for analyzing the spatial structure of the city.

Each GBFS snapshot provides time-stamped records per e-scooter ID. We reconstructed trips by first grouping records for each e-scooter chronologically, then segmenting the time series into (i) idle periods and (ii) rental (moving) periods. Consecutive records were treated as belonging to the same rental if the time gap between them did not exceed a temporal continuity threshold (set to 3× the sampling interval, i.e., $\leq$15 s for 5 s sampling); otherwise, a new segment was started. For idle periods, consecutive records were merged as long as the e-scooter location did not change materially (a spatial threshold of 50 m was used to separate distinct waiting episodes). Each rental segment was converted into a trajectory by connecting successive positions into a polyline, with start/end times taken from the first/last record in the segment; idle segments were stored as a point geometry with the corresponding start/end waiting times. We removed obviously invalid segments produced by missing snapshots (gaps > 15 s) by starting a new segment rather than interpolating positions.

The dataset covers one operator (Helbiz) and a single week, so the results should be interpreted as operator- and period-specific rather than a complete characterization of micromobility in Rome. Patterns may be biased by Helbiz's fleet size, service-area boundaries, pricing and promotions, vehicle availability/charging practices, and user base, as well as by short-term factors (weather, events, and seasonal tourism). Nevertheless, this scope is appropriate for our study objective: to demonstrate that visual analytics applied to high-frequency GBFS snapshots can yield actionable, stakeholder-oriented insights (e.g., hotspots, corridors, zoning cues) even without long-term, multi-operator coverage. Extending the analysis to multiple operators and longer periods, and cross-validating against external mobility indicators, is left for future work.

### 3.2. Collected Data Overview

We firstly present the collected data along with basic statistics that serve as an introduction to spatial analysis explaining the structure of the city.

The first statistic is the overall number of rides on specific days of the week (Figure 1). The days of the week are shown on the bottom axis, and the rides that started at midnight and noon are additionally marked with colors. Importantly, the smallest number of rides during a day occurs around 3:00 a.m. Therefore we do not divide the days equally at midnight, as it would result in losing some valuable information.

On workdays, the first peak occurs around 8–9 a.m., which can be explained by commuting to work and school (there are no such increases in these hours on Saturdays and Sundays). Then, another peak is observed around 1 p.m. In Italy, many people have lunch at this time, so there is greater mobility of residents. Additionally, from 2 p.m., the siesta begins, and some workers (including office workers) return home for a longer break. Further increases are visible in the afternoon, with the maximum during the day almost

 https://doi.org/10.3390/electronics15010187

always reached at 8 p.m. Interestingly, the later the day of the week, the lower the number of rentals at 8 p.m.

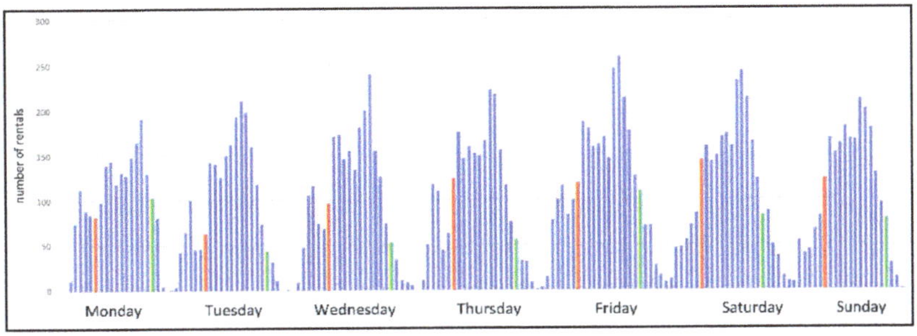


**Figure 1.** Histogram of hourly rentals in Rome during the period from 15 to 22 November 2021 (blue color), divided by days of the week. The red color indicates rentals around noon, and the green color indicates rentals around midnight.

In the case of non-working days, the characteristic is slightly different—there is no noticeable morning peak, and slightly more rentals take place during the siesta time, and the number of rentals after midnight is higher than on working days. An interesting day is Friday, which has features of both a working and a non-working day (which is obvious because on Friday evening, many people meet and treat this part of the day as a day off).

As a second characteristic, we analyzed distances travelled with electric scooters and cumulative number of rentals (Figure 2). The distances covered by e-scooters are very typical and practically always less than 4 km. Of course, longer rides are also visible (even above 7 km), but the most popular distance was less than a kilometer. Here are some statistical values giving more insight into the distances covered by e-scooters in the considered timeframe: avg = 1155 m, std = 1486 m, median = 1649 m, mode = 850 m. As for the ranges covered, here is a summary: 21% of all trips were shorter than 800 m, 68% of the trips were in the range 800 m–4 km, 10% were in the range 4 km–7 km, and 1% were trips longer than 7 km.

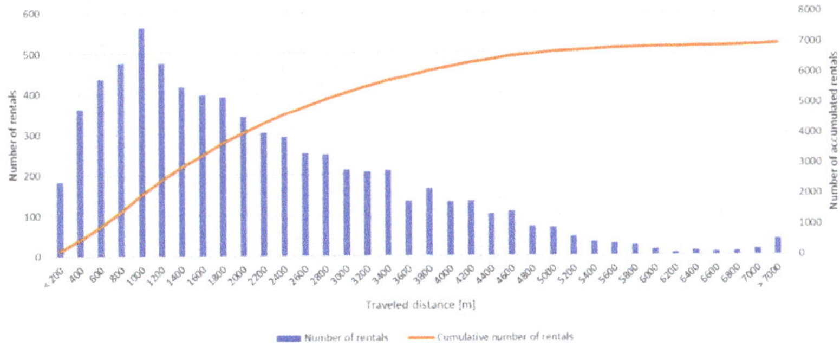


**Figure 2.** Distribution and cumulative frequency of e-scooter rentals in Rome from 15 to 22 November 2021.

The statistics presented above do not have a spatial character. With the use of a heat map, it is possible to show how the previously designated locations of rented e-scooters look (Figure 3). A logarithmic scale is used: points that existed for only an hour were better distinguishable than those that existed for many hours. From the analysis, it can be inferred that the "hottest" spot in the city is primarily the area around the main railway


https://doi.org/10.3390/electronics15010187

station (the largest red dot in the eastern part of the city). Additionally, e-scooters waited very shortly for re-rental in the very center of the city, around the Vatican (northwest part of the city), and at larger intersections in the southern part of the city. The visualization also shows areas where e-scooters cannot be ridden—for example, the closed for visitors part of Vatican, surrounded from west by a wall (area with red border and "1"), the area of the Palatino museum complex (area with blue border and "2"), and the historic Villa Doria Pamphili park (area with violet border and "3"). In this way, areas inaccessible to e-scooters were identified (whether due to an entry ban or a physical inability to pass).

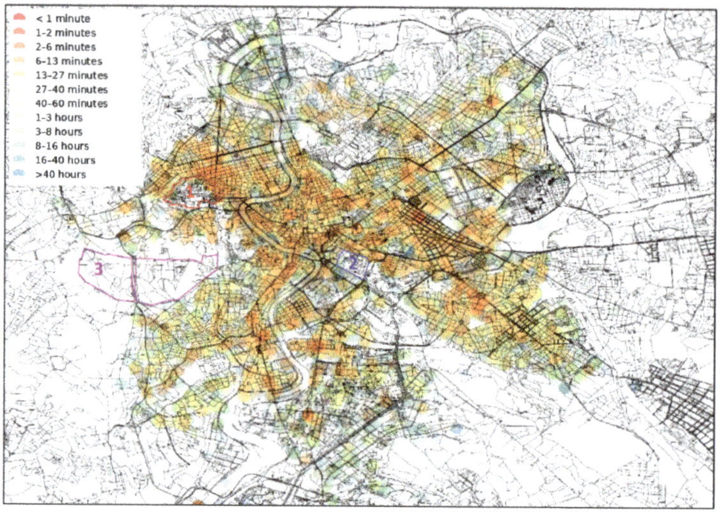


**Figure 3.** The heat map shows the time between successive rentals of the same e-scooter. The e-scooters that were rented again in less than a few minutes are marked in red, those that were rented in less than an hour are marked in green, and those that waited for a few hours are marked in blue. Numbers represent areas where e-scooters are banned (1—The Vatican, 2—The Palatino museum complex, 3—Villa Doria Pamphili park). All visualizations are oriented with north at the top. The figures are presented as visualizations rather than formal maps.

The next visualization shows the actual routes taken by users (Figure 4). The fading effect is not accidental—in the visualization, each route was drawn using an almost transparent line. The more visible the line, the more routes were taken on that street. Additionally, the thicker the line, the wider the street is in reality—users sometimes ride on one side of the street, sometimes on the other, naturally mapping its width. Thanks to this type of visualization, it is easy to check which streets are most frequently used by residents (which, in the case of other cities, could be used to, e.g., determine the order of snow removal on streets, but in Rome snow falls very rarely).

### 3.3. Long and Short Routes

All rides were divided into short and long rides. Based on the histogram showing the overall ride length (Figure 2), it was decided that the distance separating short rides from long rides would be 800 m (the distance close to the peak on the histogram). Short rides were further interpreted as points (according to their starting location), while long rides were represented as lines composed only of two points—the start and end.

Long rides are shown in Figure 5. Each ride is drawn with a transparent line, in order to better illustrate which areas of the city were most frequently connected in pairs. If users traveled long distances, they were most likely moving along the east–west axis. Despite

 https://doi.org/10.3390/electronics15010187

the fact that the visualization does not show the exact ride routes, only the lines connecting the start and end points, some of them overlap with the street grid. This may suggest that a large number of long rides are made almost in a straight line along one main street. If users were moving at the same rate between all areas of the city, the visualization would show a uniform structure resembling a complete graph. However, this is not the case, which proves that, for example, there are not many trips from the south to the east. It can also be seen that rides between adjacent districts are relatively rare, unless they are rides that pass through the city center or between districts on opposite ends of the city to the east and west.

**Figure 4.** Visualization of popular e-scooter routes in Rome from 15 to 22 November 2021.

**Figure 5.** Visualization of long rides (purple color) as pairs of start-end based on data from Rome recorded from 15 to 22 November 2021.



https://doi.org/10.3390/electronics15010187

Short rides are shown in Figure 6. The darker areas on the visualization show that more short trips (less than 800 m) took place in that area. Each square on the visualization has a width of 800 m, so it also shows how such a distance looks compared to the rest of the city. Most trips did not take place in the vicinity of the station or the Vatican, which were previously indicated as generally the most popular regions. Most trips took place in the center of Rome, in the historic part of the city. This may suggest that tourists mainly cover short distances when they want to quickly move between tourist attractions.

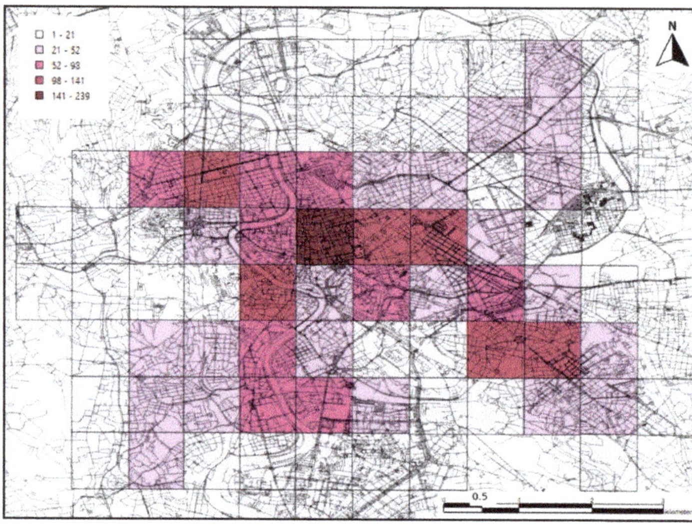


**Figure 6.** Visualization of short trips based on data recorded in Rome from 15 to 22 November 2021. The darker the area, the more trips were taken within its range.

## 4. Zoning and Location Popularity in E-Scooter Analytics

Building upon the foundational data and route classifications discussed in the previous section, we now turn our focus to the more advanced aspects of our spatial analysis: the division of the city into distinct zones based on e-scooter usage and the ranking of locations within these zones. This section presents a view of urban dynamics, exploring how e-scooter data can be utilized to demarcate different urban zones, each characterized by unique usage patterns. We also delve into the methodological approach for ranking locations within the city, providing insights into the most popular and frequented areas as revealed by e-scooter data. Furthermore, we discuss the potential beneficiaries of these analysis results, highlighting the practical implications and applications of our findings in urban planning and mobility management.

### *4.1. Division into Zones*

In [20] the authors divided the city into three types of zones based on mobile phone data. We create zones in our analysis as well. The clustering is applied to square areas with a side length of 200 m. This size was selected as its l (i) is comparable to a short walking distance and aligns with how users reach nearby devices, and (ii) reduces the likelihood that the start and end of the same trip fall into the same cell. To further support this assumption, trips shorter than 200 m were removed from the dataset. Each area is characterized by a different number of trips that end there. In addition, each trip has its unique features. To cluster the areas, it was decided to use three parameters for each area: (i) the number of rentals that end in the area, (ii) spatial dispersion of the starting locations,

 https://doi.org/10.3390/electronics15010187

(iii) average distance traveled. The decision on the number of clusters (the value of k) was made based on a comparison of results for k ranging from 2 to 4. We achieved the best results for k = 4 (based on the values of the centroids of each group) and the results for this value are presented in the paper. Smaller k values produced very coarse partitions that merged functionally distinct areas, while larger k values fragmented the city into smaller clusters that were harder to interpret in a visual-analytics context.

The values of the centroids for each cluster are presented in Figure 7. Clusters labeled 0 and 1 are similar to each other, with the rides in cluster 0 taking place at longer distances, being more spatially dispersed, and slightly more numerous. Cluster 3 stands out in terms of the number of rentals, having by far the highest number (over 60 compared to just under 10 for cluster 0). However, the rides in this cluster were neither very long nor spatially dispersed. The points in cluster 2 had the highest values in these two categories. For these points, spatial dispersion was twice as high as in cluster 0 and almost four times higher than in cluster 1.

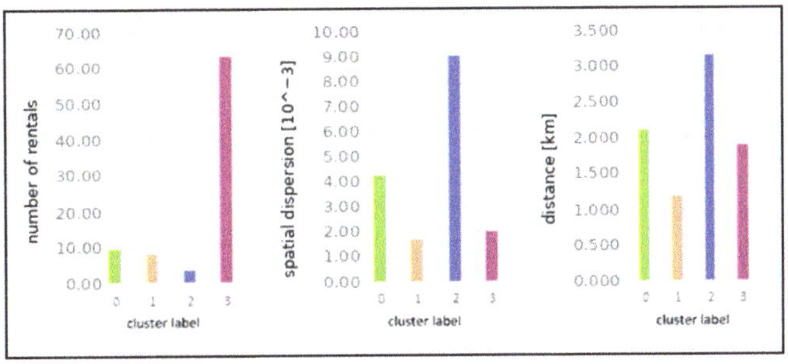


**Figure 7.** The charts present the values of cluster centroids. Green color represents cluster 0, light orange—cluster 1, blue—cluster 2, purple—cluster 3.

Figure 8 shows the visualization of how locations are distributed in specific clusters within the city. The charts in Figure 7 show that clusters 0 and 1 are similar to each other and this is also well visible on the cartographic visualization—both clusters cover most of the area and are adjacent to each other. The biggest difference between these two clusters is spatial dispersion of localizations in which users end their rentals. For cluster 1, the spatial dispersion is slightly lower. Taking into account the location of larger clusters of points from this cluster, one can conclude that these are areas where there are quite a few local trips. This is best seen in the example of the EUR district (in the south of the city, somewhat separated from the rest of the city)—the vast majority of it is covered by points from cluster 1. If users mainly traveled to the city center from there, the points would most likely be in cluster 0.

Locations of points from cluster 2 are of interest. They occur rather individually on the map, are less often grouped. Considering that these points are characterized by the smallest number of rentals and the highest dispersion, they can be interpreted as low-activity peripheral destinations. It is worth noting the location of points from this cluster in the city: they are mostly located on the outskirts of the city, and are rarely found in the center. Consistent with the overall temporal pattern of increased activity in the evening (Figure 1), one plausible interpretation is that a subset of these trips reflects return movements (e.g., toward residential areas).

The last cluster is characterized by the largest number of trips. It is therefore not surprising that the areas previously identified as popular are found in this cluster. Here, too, the vast majority of points belonging to this cluster are located close to each other, and


https://doi.org/10.3390/electronics15010187

almost all of them are in the city center. Single points occur in other districts. Most likely, these are local activity centers of users related to the proximity of a metro or railway station.

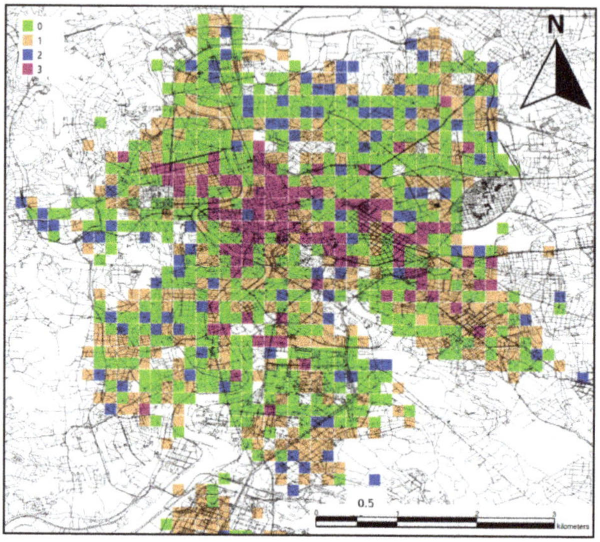


**Figure 8.** The cartographic visualization presents the division of locations into clusters using the k-means algorithm (for k = 4). On the left side, the legend explains the assignment of points on the map to the clusters.

Because ground-truth functional zoning is not uniquely defined, we validate zoning and ranking results via external consistency checks against independent urban structure proxies. First, we compare high-activity clusters and top-ranked cells to transport nodes (e.g., major rail/metro stations) and observe that the highest-demand areas align with known interchange and activity hubs. Second, we compare ranked locations to commercial/POI intensity (e.g., density of amenities and attractions) and find that many top-ranked cells coincide with areas of high POI concentration, consistent with the interpretation that e-scooter demand increases near activity centers.

While the paper focuses on an interpretable, map-centered visual pipeline, we note that the spatial patterns shown in hotspot and corridor maps can also be quantified using standard spatial statistics (e.g., global/local autocorrelation such as Moran's I on the 200 m grid, or network-based centrality measures after projecting flows onto the street graph). We deliberately prioritize a lightweight workflow that can be reproduced from GBFS snapshots without additional external datasets and without introducing further modeling choices; therefore, we present the link to urban morphology as an interpretive, exploratory perspective, not as a formal validation of land-use patterns.

### 4.2. Exploratory City Location Scoring

Another analysis that can be carried out based on electric scooters data was exploratory city location scoring. It can be used to identify which places in the city are distinctive and have an advantage over other locations. To conduct such an analysis, one needs to choose the criterion for classifying the locations (what makes one location better than another). For the purposes of this study, three classifications were carried out, each taking into account a different criterion: (i) overall popularity (number of rentals in a given location), (ii) distance traveled from a given location, (iii) popularity at a given time of day. To perform these classifications, we compute three descriptive indicators per 200 m cell: (i) trip-start

 https://doi.org/10.3390/electronics15010187

frequency, (ii) average trip distance for trips starting in the cell, and (iii) the dominant time-of-day category of trip starts. For each indicator we visualize the top locations (top-K) and the corresponding spatial distribution. No composite score is formed. The provided top locations visualized in the figures below are results of exploratory, descriptive summaries of location salience under simple, transparent criteria; they are not intended as a statistically validated or causal 'optimal location' model. Because results are derived from a single-operator, one-week sample, the identified hotspots should be interpreted as indicative rather than exhaustive.

According to the first criterion (overall popularity), the top places in the city are where there is generally the highest number of rentals (Figure 9). It is not surprising, therefore, that the areas around the main railway station, which was already identified as an area of high potential, are marked in red. In addition, the areas around the Vatican were identified as the best—another place highlighted in the analyses. It is also worth noting the historic center of the city. There are no red dots there, but there are many orange and yellow ones. This should be interpreted as meaning that there is no single characteristic point in that area, but the whole area is frequently visited by e-scooter users. This is also the result of numerous short rides, which usually take place here (please see the analysis of Figure 6).

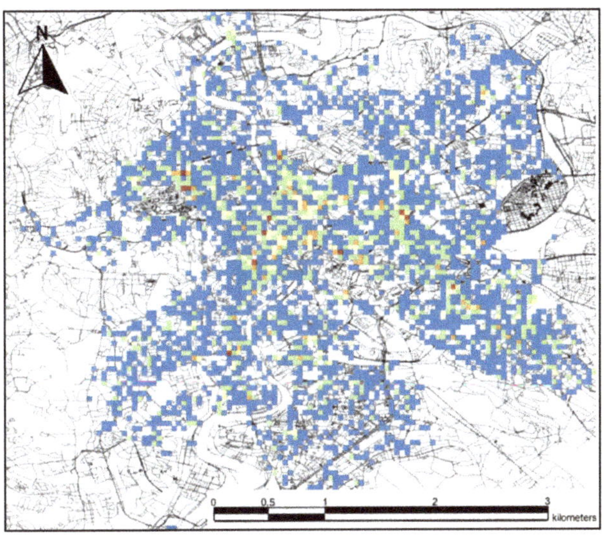


**Figure 9.** Visualization of the top locations in Rome in terms of overall popularity (based on data from 15 to 22 November 2021). The top locations are marked in red.

The next visualization (Figure 10) shows the top locations in the city based on the average distance traveled from them. The top points are primarily located on the outskirts of the city, which is rather obvious—to get anywhere from the edge of the city, one must cover a considerable distance. However, an interesting point is located on St. Peter's Square in the Vatican. It is among the top 10 best points despite being relatively close to the center. Therefore, it can be inferred that e-scooter users usually travel to a completely different part of the city from around the square. Taking into account the analysis of long rides, it can also be concluded that most users move eastward later on.

The last analysis concerns the examination of the most popular time of day in different parts of the city (Figure 11). The histogram indicates colors corresponding to specific time intervals. In addition, yellow dots (most popular in the morning) have been enlarged for better visibility. As the majority of rentals take place in the afternoon and evening hours,

 https://doi.org/10.3390/electronics15010187

most of the points in the city are the most popular during these hours. It is worth paying attention to those points that have been assigned to other times of the day. None of the points popular in the morning are located near the main railway station, the Vatican, or the historic center. These are points that are generally not the most popular but are significant in the morning. On the other hand, points that have peak popularity at night are mainly located in the south of the city. Perhaps in that area, there is no other available means of public transport at night, which is why users most often use e-scooters there.

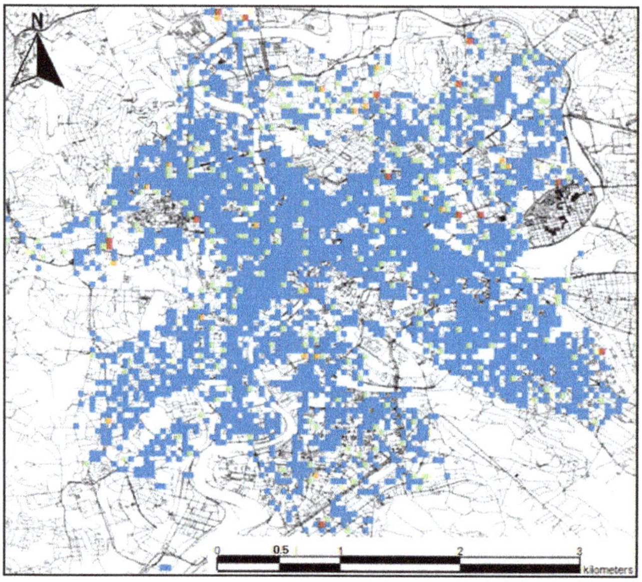


**Figure 10.** Visualization of the top locations in Rome in terms of average distance traveled from them (based on data from 15 to 22 November 2021). The top locations are marked in red.

### 4.3. Beneficiaries of Analysis Results

All the conclusions arising from the analyses shed light on the structure of Rome, but it would be interesting to see how they can be used by real users. In this subsection, a case study is presented on their use in solving real problems for real groups of interested parties. We selected 3 groups of recipients who we believe can benefit from the results of our analyses: (i) rental operators, (ii) city authorities, (iii) owners of local businesses.

#### 4.3.1. Rental Operators

The operator earns the most when their infrastructure is used around the clock, and the devices remain not rented out for as short a time as possible (while taking into account that each e-scooter needs to be charged at the operator's service). Additionally, there are usually several operators in a given city competing for customers. Better positioning of their devices in the city (more tailored to the needs of users) allows for outpacing the competition.

Spatial analyses based on electric scooter data can directly answer the question of where the demand for devices is highest (not only in terms of location, but also time of day and week), and thus where the operator should place the devices so that as many customers as possible can use them.

From the operator's perspective, a key issue is identifying which areas e-scooters should be collected from and where they should be redistributed afterward. Naturally, discharged e-scooters must be retrieved for charging, as they cannot operate without it.

 https://doi.org/10.3390/electronics15010187

However, there may also be locations where it is worth collecting devices before they are fully discharged, for example, in areas with consistently low rental activity. Even more crucial is the question of where to deploy the charged e-scooters, as optimal placement directly impacts usage rates and overall service efficiency.

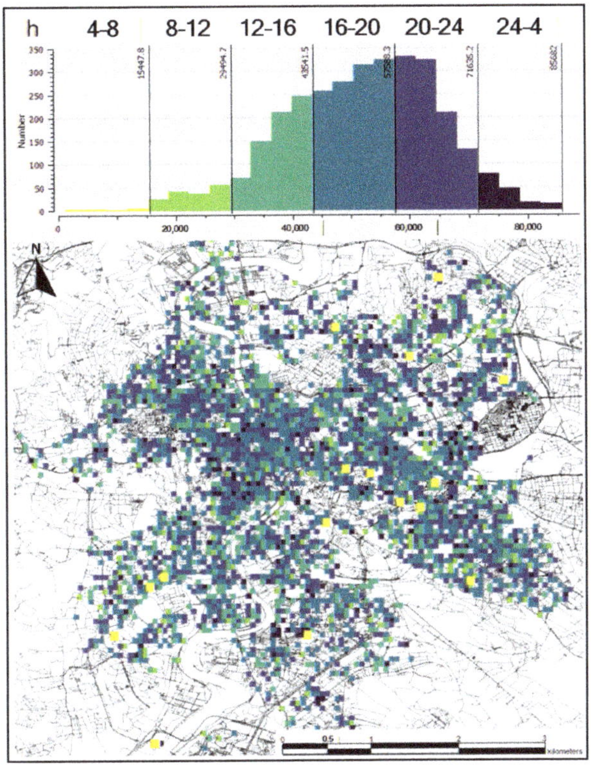


**Figure 11.** Visualization of the most popular time of day in different locations in Rome (based on data from 15 to 22 November 2021). At the top: a histogram showing the number of the most popular locations at different hours. The X axis represents time in seconds since 3:00 a.m.

Based on the available data, it is possible to indicate two types of places: places unfavorable for longer stops and places where e-scooters are sure to be rented again in a short time. The first type of places will be given based on a comparison of the popularity ranking of locations in the city (as discussed in Section 4.2) and the division of locations in the city into clusters (presented in Section 4.1). A combination of the two analyses is used because the first one concerned the analysis of locations based on departures from a given location, and the second one based on arrivals. Places where there are many arrivals but very few departures are potential candidates for locations from which it is worth taking e-scooters (there may be a large number of them gathered there or they may remain unrented for a long time). The characterization of the second type of places is the opposite—in places where many people leave but few arrive, it is worth adding a few e-scooters to balance the rental rate.

The difference between arrivals and departures from a given location is shown in the legend on the left side of Figure 12, representing the range of balance values. In locations with a negative balance, there is a predominance of arrivals, while the situation is reversed for locations with a positive balance (Figure 12). The blue points (with a negative balance)


https://doi.org/10.3390/electronics15010187

in the center are not a big problem—even if there is an accumulation of e-scooters there, it should be noted that there are red and orange points next to them. Users are willing to walk about 200 m to the nearest e-scooter. E-scooters should be removed primarily from locations marked in blue, around which there are no points with a positive balance, especially important are points outside the city center. These places have many arrivals, but few departures, so e-scooters may unnecessarily stand there. An example of such an area is the vicinity of the Colosseum—this location had the lowest balance. Additionally, the locations around the Colosseum also have a negative balance, so no one will even approach to rent an e-scooter from there. As for the second type of places—it is worth placing e-scooters in places marked in red and orange. There may regularly be a shortage of e-scooters there. It is also worth looking at the locations marked in green. There are definitely the most of them. They represent locations that are not very popular, but users leave e-scooters there. Knowing the cost of e-scooter relocation, it would be profitable to move some of them to better locations, but only if such a cost is low (or lower than the potential profit from rentals).

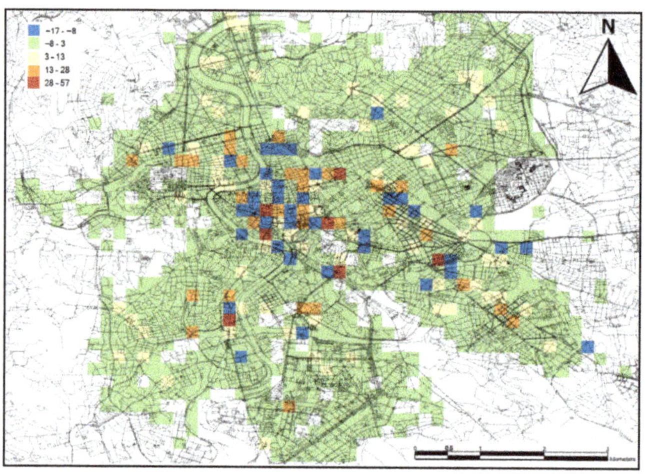


**Figure 12.** The difference between arrivals and departures from a given location after one week (weekly balance (departures − arrivals), per 200 m cell). In the top left corner, the legend shows the range of balance values.

### 4.3.2. City Authorities

The next group of stakeholders considered in our study are city authorities. E-scooters have already become a permanent part of the city landscape, and urban planners are beginning to recognize the need to incorporate them into urban infrastructure design. They need to know which places are particularly frequently visited by e-scooter users so that they can create safe rental zones or adjust other means of public transportation for convenient transfers in these locations.

In most e-scooter systems, the e-scooters can be left anywhere, with the only limitation being the operator's range. However, such a lack of regulations often results in a "mess" in the city. Users leave e-scooters blocking sidewalks or, worse still, sometimes they throw them into the water or even into the trash. The operator can impose penalties on users for damaging equipment, but it is the city's role to provide space in the common area for e-scooters. Therefore, from the point of view of local authorities, an important question is: where should special points for returning e-scooters be located? When a user leaves one e-scooter, there is no need to designate a special zone for it because one e-scooter does

 https://doi.org/10.3390/electronics15010187

not take up much space. Above all, we need to consider locations where there are many e-scooters. When ten e-scooters are left by users in every free space, even a large square can become cluttered. The cost of creating e-scooter parking zones in the city is not high, and it can bring very good results. Although, for example, painting such zones is relatively cheap, it is not possible to place them at every intersection. It does not make sense because as long as e-scooters appear sporadically in a given location, there is no need to designate a special zone for them. In such cases it is enough for users to leave them safely and without disturbing other residents.

Answering the question of where such zones should be placed will be determined based on the popularity ranking of locations (discussed in Section 4.2). Parking areas should only be created where there are large numbers of e-scooters. The proposed locations for e-scooter parking in the city are shown in the visualization on Figure 13. Most of the locations are in the center and surrounding areas; there were too few rentals on the outskirts of the city to create such zones.

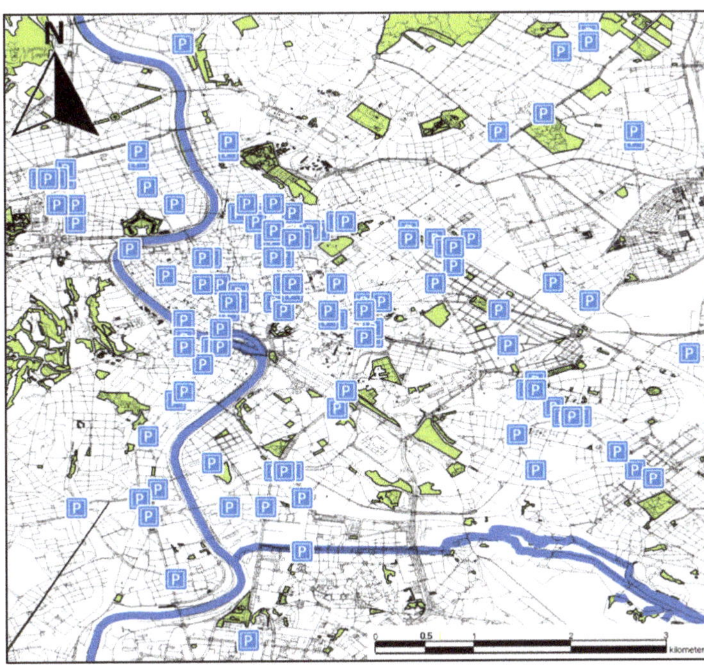


**Figure 13.** Proposed locations for e-scooter drop-off zones (denoted by blue parking signs).

#### 4.3.3. Owners of Local Businesses

The last group of potential stakeholders considered in this paper are owners of local businesses. Based on electric scooter data, they can determine with great accuracy where their potential customers are located in the city. It should be noted that electric scooter users are a specific group—primarily young people (very few older people use this type of transportation). Therefore, the use of electric scooter data will be particularly beneficial for businesses aimed at younger residents. In addition, owners of these businesses can investigate where their customers usually depart from in a particular location and adjust their business profile accordingly.

Here we focus on opening a new bakery. An important question for the investor is: where is the best location for a bakery? Bakeries should be opened in a place that is visited by a large number of users. Even better if these users appear in the morning when the


https://doi.org/10.3390/electronics15010187

demand for bakery goods is the highest. Additionally, the bakery can sell warm products to go, which will also be popular among people who, for example, commute to work and want to buy something for breakfast. The analysis used the ranking of popularity by time of day (discussed in Section 4.2 Exploratory city location scoring) to determine the most popular locations in the morning.

The analysis yielded a dozen or so locations that would be good places for a bakery according to the presented criteria (Figure 14). In the next part, the 4 best points are described in more detail (enlarged on the visualization) in the order from best to worst.

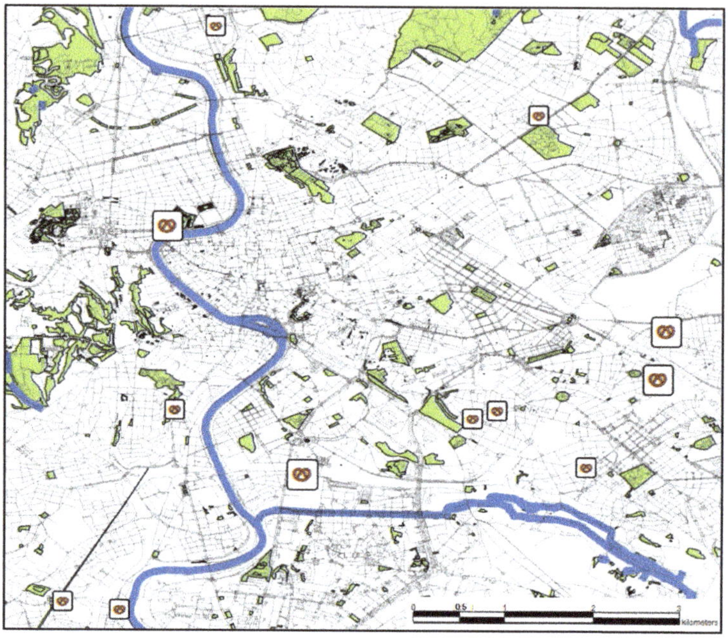

**Figure 14.** Proposed locations for bakeries in Rome (morning-dominant high-demand locations). The larger the symbol, the better the location.

First best location for a bakery is at Piazza Pia (the point on the west by the river)—a very attractive tourist place due to its proximity to St. Peter's Square and Castel Sant'Angelo. In addition, many buses stop here, and it is convenient to transfer to another line. However, this point will have a significant advantage for tourists over the residents of Rome.

The second-best location is a point in a typical residential area (on the east, more southern point). There is Roma Tuscolana railway station in the area, where long-distance and regional trains stop. There is also a school and a theater there. This location, on the other hand, is not attractive for tourists in any way, but many people live there. There are also not many service facilities (especially gastronomy) in the area, so it may be a good place for a new bakery.

The third best location is a point located south of the center of Rome. It is also a less touristy part of the city but is much better connected to the rest of the city. The designated point lies between blocks and a playground, and within a radius of 200 m, there are two railway stations and the Piramide metro station. The area is also characterized by a large number of service facilities and restaurants, so it is an area where people certainly use catering services.

The last point is located north of the second-best point, but it is in a different part of the city. Between the points, there are railway tracks that usually divide the city into

 https://doi.org/10.3390/electronics15010187

distinct parts. This point is located on a fairly busy street, not far from the Pigneto metro station. The surrounding area is similar to that around the third point—mostly blocks of flats and food establishments; however, most of the establishments are located a bit further away from the designated point.

## 5. Discussion

A recurring concern in visualization-driven urban analytics is that actionable insights may appear anecdotal unless the assumptions, robustness, and scope of validity are stated explicitly. In this work, we therefore position the presented outputs as descriptive decision-support visualizations derived from reconstructed mobility traces, rather than as validated prescriptions or causal claims.

The presented analyses depend on reconstructing rentals from high-frequency GBFS snapshots (sampled every 5 s). Rentals are segmented using a continuity rule ($\leq$15 s temporal continuity), and idle episodes are consolidated based on a spatial change threshold (50 m). These choices are intentionally simple and transparent: when snapshots are missing, we avoid interpolating trajectories and instead start a new segment, prioritizing interpretability over aggressive reconstruction. This design reduces the risk that downstream maps (hotspots, corridors) are dominated by artifacts of gap-filling rather than observed e-scooter movement.

At the same time, the reconstructed trajectories should be understood as an approximation of true rides derived from publicly visible availability states. The approach taken is therefore best suited for extracting aggregate patterns (e.g., persistent high-use areas and major movement directions) rather than for fine-grained claims about exact routes or micro-level travel times.

Several parameter choices reflect a trade-off between granularity and interpretability. The paper intentionally uses a compact set of parameters (e.g., continuity threshold tied to sampling frequency; a fixed grid resolution; a small number of clusters for zoning) to keep the workflow reproducible and easy to communicate.

We emphasize that the key visual conclusions are expected to be robust at the level of macro-structures (dominant hotspots and main corridors), while more detailed patterns can vary with choices such as grid size, the short/long trip split, and zoning configuration. For this reason, the results should be interpreted primarily as a structural reading of urban micromobility under the given observation window and assumptions, and not as an attempt to determine a single optimal parameterization.

The section Beneficiaries of analysis results illustrates how the proposed outputs can support practical questions relevant to both operators and city stakeholders (e.g., identifying locations associated with frequent starts, prolonged idle time, or directional flows that may indicate recurrent demand–supply imbalance). However, these examples are not intended as audited policy recommendations; they demonstrate how a stakeholder could translate descriptive outputs into hypotheses and candidate interventions for further validation.

Consistent with this framing, our location scoring is presented as transparent, criterion-based ranking (e.g., frequent starts, higher average trip distance, or time-of-day dominance), explicitly avoiding a composite score that would imply a universally optimal location. This makes the reasoning auditable and allows stakeholders to adjust criteria to their operational context.

The workflow is designed to be transferable to other cities because it relies on GBFS feeds, which are broadly adopted by micromobility operators and are often the only publicly accessible data source. The core steps (snapshot collection, segmentation into rentals/idle episodes, aggregation to a grid, and production of map-based visuals) do not

 https://doi.org/10.3390/electronics15010187

depend on city-specific annotations and can therefore be replicated in other settings where stable e-scooter identifiers and sufficiently frequent snapshots are available.

Nevertheless, substantive interpretation remains conditioned on factors outside the pipeline: operator coverage and fleet management policies, service-area constraints, pricing, seasonality, and short-term events. Accordingly, generalizing from a single-operator, single-week study should be performed cautiously. The most appropriate use of the workflow is as a lightweight, reproducible first step that (i) reveals candidate patterns and (ii) motivates deeper studies using longer periods, multi-operator datasets, or independent mobility indicators when available.

Finally, we clarify that the contribution of this paper is not the general idea of visual storytelling which has a well-established body of prior work, but the operationalization of a GBFS-snapshot-driven pipeline that reconstructs trips and produces a coherent set of interpretable visual outputs under minimal data access constraints. Many existing micromobility studies either rely on operator-provided trip logs or focus on model-driven objectives; by contrast, we demonstrate what can be achieved using only publicly available GBFS snapshots, emphasizing transparency of assumptions and reproducibility of the resulting descriptive products.

The relationship between e-scooter intensity patterns and urban morphology is discussed as an interpretation of persistent hotspots/corridors rather than as a formal land-use validation. Quantitative confirmation (e.g., statistically significant hotspot detection, autocorrelation strength, or correlation with independent land-use/POI density) is feasible but requires additional data integration choices and, in the case of land-use, external reference datasets. We therefore position our morphology discussion as a reproducible descriptive baseline, intended to motivate targeted, metric-based follow-up analyses when such reference data are available.

## 6. Conclusions

Our spatial analysis of electric scooter data in Rome demonstrates how micromobility traces can be used to visually explore and interpret urban dynamics and city structure. Rather than proposing new visualization techniques, the core contribution of this work is methodological and practical: we operationalize a reproducible workflow that turns publicly available GBFS API snapshots into interpretable spatial outputs suitable for urban analysis and stakeholder communication.

Specifically, we describe a transparent GBFS-to-trips reconstruction procedure that infers rentals and idle episodes from high-frequency snapshots using simple continuity rules (without interpolation), and then aggregates the reconstructed mobility to produce a coherent set of map-centered views. These include demand and idle-time hotspots, dominant mobility corridors, complementary short-long trip perspectives, mobility-based zoning on a fixed grid, and criterion-based location ranking. Importantly, the ranking is presented as an auditable summary of observed activity under clearly stated criteria, rather than as a universally best location prescription.

The study's conclusions should be interpreted in light of data representativeness: the dataset covers a single operator and a single week, and the observed patterns may be influenced by operator policies, service-area constraints, fleet management, and short-term conditions. Therefore, the presented outputs are positioned as descriptive decision support and hypothesis generation, most reliable for macro-level structures such as persistent hotspots, main corridors, and broad functional differentiation, rather than as causal inference or externally validated recommendations.

Future work will extend the pipeline to longer observation windows (multi-week and seasonal) and multi-operator/multi-city deployments to assess transferability across


https://doi.org/10.3390/electronics15010187

different operating policies and urban contexts. We also plan to incorporate external reference layers (e.g., POI/land-use proxies and proximity to transport nodes) to support quantitative validation of selected spatial patterns, and to explore optional predictive components (e.g., short-horizon demand or availability forecasting) built on the same grid-based indicators. In addition, while the present study focuses on descriptive visual analytics, future work may explore integrating the workflow with AI-driven urban mobility components (e.g., short-horizon demand or availability forecasting) and considering security and privacy aspects relevant to IoT-enabled micromobility ecosystems (e.g., data integrity, access control, and privacy-preserving aggregation), which are beyond the scope of this paper.

**Author Contributions:** Conceptualization, R.B. and A.D.; methodology, A.D.; software, A.D.; validation, R.B., A.D. and J.C.; investigation, A.D.; resources, A.D.; data curation, A.D.; writing—original draft preparation, R.B.; writing—review and editing, R.B.; visualization, A.D.; supervision, J.C.; project administration, R.B. All authors have read and agreed to the published version of the manuscript.

**Funding:** This research received no external funding.

**Data Availability Statement:** The dataset used in this study was collected from real-time GBFS feed snapshots and processed to reconstruct trip-level records. The collected snapshot archive and the derived datasets are not publicly available.

**Conflicts of Interest:** The authors declare that they have no conflicts of interest.

## References


1. Hu, X. The city as a living organism: Aristotle's naturalness thesis reconsidered. *Hist. Polit. Thought* **2020**, *41*, 517–537.
2. Eremia, M.; Toma, L.; Sanduleac, M. The Smart City Concept in the 21st Century. *Procedia Eng.* **2017**, *181*, 12–19. [CrossRef]
3. Lee, M.; Chow, J.Y.J.; Yoon, G.; He, B.Y. Forecasting e-scooter substitution of direct and access trips by mode and distance. *Transp. Res. Part Transp. Environ.* **2021**, *96*, 102892. [CrossRef]
4. Hollingsworth, J.; Copeland, B.; Johnson, J.X. Are e-scooters polluters? The environmental impacts of shared dockless electric scooters. *Environ. Res. Lett.* **2019**, *14*, 084031. [CrossRef]
5. City of Portland, Oregon. 2018 E-Scooter Findings Report [Online]. 2018. Available online: https://learn.sharedusemobilitycenter.org/wp-content/uploads/PBOT_E-Scooter_01152019.pdf (accessed on 30 January 2022).
6. UPCEA. Micro-Mobility, E-Scooters and Implications for Higher Education. Available online: https://upcea.edu/micro-mobility-e-scooters-and-implications-for-higher-education/ (accessed on 30 January 2022).
7. Yan, X.; Yang, W.; Zhang, X.; Xu, Y.; Bejleri, I.; Zhao, X. Do e-scooters fill mobility gaps and promote equity before and during COVID-19? A spatiotemporal analysis using open big data. *arXiv* **2021**, arXiv:2103.09060. [CrossRef]
8. Fistola, R. Cities between smartness and emergencies: Exploring the role of e-scooter in the "transition era". *Eur. Transp. Eur.* **2021**, *85*, 1–15. [CrossRef]
9. Kegalle, H.; Hettiachchi, D.; Chan, J.; Salim, F.; Sanderson, M. E-Scooter Dynamics: Unveiling Rider Behaviours and Interactions with Road Users through Multi-Modal Data Analysis. In Proceedings of the Augmented Humans International Conference 2024, Melbourne, VIC, Australia, 4–6 April 2024; ACM: New York, NY, USA, 2024; pp. 307–310.
10. Nigro, M.; Comi, A.; De Vincentis, R.; Castiglione, M. A mixed behavioural and data-driven method for assessing the shift potential to electric micromobility: Evidence from Rome. *Front. Future Transp.* **2024**, *5*, 1391100. [CrossRef]
11. Speak, A.; Taratula-Lyons, M.; Clayton, W.; Shergold, I. Scooter Stories: User and Non-User Experiences of a Shared E-Scooter Trial. *Act. Travel Stud.* **2023**, *3*, 4. [CrossRef]
12. Çallı, L.; Çallı, B.A. Value-centric analysis of user adoption for sustainable urban micro-mobility transportation through shared e-scooter services. *Sustain. Dev.* **2024**, *32*, 6408–6433. [CrossRef]
13. Jafarzadehfadaki, M.; Sisiopiku, V.P. Embracing Urban Micromobility: A Comparative Study of E-Scooter Adoption in Washington, D.C., Miami, and Los Angeles. *Urban Sci.* **2024**, *8*, 71. [CrossRef]
14. Wolniak, R.; Turoń, K. The Problems of Scooter-Sharing in Smart Cities Based on the Example of the Silesian Region in Poland. *Smart Cities* **2025**, *8*, 16. [CrossRef]
15. Babapourdijojin, M.; Corazza, M.V.; Gentile, G. Systematic Analysis of Commuting Behavior in Italy Using K-Means Clustering and Spatial Analysis: Towards Inclusive and Sustainable Urban Transport Solutions. *Future Transp.* **2024**, *4*, 1430–1456. [CrossRef]



https://doi.org/10.3390/electronics15010187

16. Dibaj, S.; Hosseinzadeh, A.; Mladenović, M.N.; Kluger, R. Where Have Shared E-Scooters Taken Us So Far? A Review of Mobility Patterns, Usage Frequency, and Personas. *Sustainability* **2021**, *13*, 11792. [CrossRef]
17. Jiao, J.; Bai, S. Understanding the shared e-scooter travels in Austin, TX. *ISPRS Int. J. Geo-Inf.* **2020**, *9*, 135. [CrossRef] [PubMed]
18. Caspi, O.; Smart, M.J.; Noland, R.B. Spatial associations of dockless shared e-scooter usage. *Transp. Res. Part D Transp. Environ.* **2020**, *86*, 102396. [CrossRef] [PubMed]
19. Qu, Y.; Zhang, J. Trade area analysis using user generated mobile location data. In Proceedings of the 22nd International Conference on World Wide Web, Rio de Janeiro, Brazil, 13–17 May 2013; Association for Computing Machinery: New York, NY, USA, 2013; pp. 1053–1064.
20. Alhazzani, M.; Alhasoun, F.; Alawwad, Z.; González, M.C. Urban attractors: Discovering patterns in regions of attraction in cities. *PLoS ONE* **2021**, *16*, e0250204. [CrossRef]
21. Mehzabin Tuli, F.; Mitra, S.; Crews, M.B. Factors influencing the usage of shared E-scooters in Chicago. *Transp. Res. Part A Policy Pract.* **2021**, *154*, 164–185. [CrossRef]
22. Heumann, M.; Kraschewski, T.; Brauner, T.; Tilch, L.; Breitner, M.H. A Spatiotemporal Study and Location-Specific Trip Pattern Categorization of Shared E-Scooter Usage. *Sustainability* **2021**, *13*, 12527. [CrossRef]
23. He, S.; Shin, K.G. Dynamic Flow Distribution Prediction for Urban Dockless E-Scooter Sharing Reconfiguration. In Proceedings of the Web Conference 2020, Taipei, Taiwan, 20–24 April 2020; ACM: New York, NY, USA, 2020; pp. 133–143.
24. Keim, D.; Andrienko, G.; Fekete, J.-D.; Görg, C.; Kohlhammer, J.; Melançon, G. Visual Analytics: Definition, Process, and Challenges. In *Information Visualization*; Kerren, A., Stasko, J.T., Fekete, J.-D., North, C., Eds.; Lecture Notes in Computer Science; Springer: Berlin/Heidelberg, Germany, 2008; Volume 4950, pp. 154–175. ISBN 978-3-540-70955-8.
25. Keim, D.A.; Mansmann, F.; Thomas, J. Visual analytics: How much visualization and how much analytics? *ACM SIGKDD Explor. Newsl.* **2010**, *11*, 5–8. [CrossRef]
26. Andrienko, N.; Andrienko, G. *Exploratory Analysis of Spatial and Temporal Data*; Springer: Berlin/Heidelberg, Germany, 2006; ISBN 978-3-540-25994-7.
27. Andrienko, G.; Andrienko, N.; Bak, P.; Keim, D.; Wrobel, S. *Visual Analytics of Movement*; Springer: Berlin/Heidelberg, Germany, 2013; ISBN 978-3-642-37582-8.
28. Zhang, Y.; Li, B.; Hong, J. Understanding user economic behavior in the city using large-scale geotagged and crowdsourced data. In Proceedings of the 25th International Conference on World Wide Web, Montreal, QC, Canada, 11–15 April 2016; pp. 205–214.
29. Lian, J.; Zhang, F.; Xie, X.; Sun, G. Restaurant survival analysis with heterogeneous information. In Proceedings of the 26th International Conference on World Wide Web Companion, Perth, WA, Australia, 3–7 April 2017; pp. 993–1002.
30. Fu, Y.; Ge, Y.; Zheng, Y.; Yao, Z.; Liu, Y.; Xiong, H.; Yuan, J. Sparse real estate ranking with online user reviews and offline moving behaviors. In Proceedings of the 2014 IEEE International Conference on Data Mining, Shenzhen, China, 14–17 December 2014; IEEE: Piscataway, NJ, USA, 2014; pp. 120–129.
31. Xu, M.; Wang, T.; Wu, Z.; Zhou, J.; Li, J.; Wu, H. Demand driven store site selection via multiple spatial-temporal data. In Proceedings of the 24th ACM SIGSPATIAL International Conference on Advances in Geographic Information Systems, San Francisco, CA, USA, 31 October–6 November 2016; Association for Computing Machinery: New York, NY, USA, 2016; pp. 1–10.
32. Lin, J.; Oentaryo, R.; Lim, E.-P.; Vu, C.; Vu, A.; Kwee, A. Where is the goldmine? Finding promising business locations through Facebook data analytics. In Proceedings of the 27th ACM Conference on Hypertext and Social Media, Halifax, NS, Canada, 10–13 July 2016; pp. 93–102.
33. Yu, Z.; Zhang, D.; Yang, D. Where is the Largest Market: Ranking Areas by Popularity from Location Based Social Networks. In Proceedings of the 2013 IEEE 10th International Conference on Ubiquitous Intelligence and Computing and 2013 IEEE 10th International Conference on Autonomic and Trusted Computing, Vietri sul Mare, Italy, 18–21 December 2013; IEEE: Piscataway, NJ, USA, 2013; pp. 157–162.
34. Yu, Z.; Tian, M.; Wang, Z.; Guo, B.; Mei, T. Shop-type recommendation leveraging the data from social media and location-based services. *ACM Trans. Knowl. Discov. Data TKDD* **2016**, *11*, 1–21. [CrossRef]
35. Liu, Y.; Liu, C.; Lu, X.; Teng, M.; Zhu, H.; Xiong, H. Point-of-interest demand modeling with human mobility patterns. In Proceedings of the 23rd ACM SIGKDD International Conference on Knowledge Discovery and Data Mining, Halifax, NS, Canada, 13–17 August 2017; pp. 947–955.
36. Fu, Y.; Liu, G.; Papadimitriou, S.; Xiong, H.; Ge, Y.; Zhu, H.; Zhu, C. Real estate ranking via mixed land-use latent models. In Proceedings of the 21th ACM SIGKDD International Conference on Knowledge Discovery and Data Mining, Virtual, 10–13 August 2015; pp. 299–308.
37. Zou, Z.; Younes, H.; Erdoğan, S.; Wu, J. Exploratory Analysis of Real-Time E-Scooter Trip Data in Washington, D.C. *Transp. Res. Rec. J. Transp. Res. Board* **2020**, *2674*, 285–299. [CrossRef]
38. Bieliński, T.; Ważna, A. Electric Scooter Sharing and Bike Sharing User Behaviour and Characteristics. *Sustainability* **2020**, *12*, 9640. [CrossRef]


 https://doi.org/10.3390/electronics15010187

39. McKenzie, G. Spatiotemporal comparative analysis of scooter-share and bike-share usage patterns in Washington, D.C. *J. Transp. Geogr.* **2019**, *78*, 19–28. [CrossRef]
40. Chicco, A.; Diana, M. Understanding micro-mobility usage patterns: A preliminary comparison between dockless bike sharing and e-scooters in the city of Turin (Italy). *Transp. Res. Procedia* **2022**, *62*, 459–466. [CrossRef]
41. Li, H.; Yuan, Z.; Novack, T.; Huang, W.; Zipf, A. Understanding spatiotemporal trip purposes of urban micro-mobility from the lens of dockless e-scooter sharing. *Comput. Environ. Urban Syst.* **2022**, *96*, 101848. [CrossRef]
42. Zakhem, M.; Smith-Colin, J. Micromobility implementation challenges and opportunities: Analysis of e-scooter parking and high-use corridors. *Transp. Res. Part D Transp. Environ.* **2021**, *101*, 103082. [CrossRef]
43. Beza, A.D.; Demissie, M.G.; Kattan, L. A Spatiotemporal Analysis of Shared Micromobility Trips in First- and Last-Mile Public Transit Integration. *Transp. Res. Rec. J. Transp. Res. Board* **2025**, *2679*, 762–781. [CrossRef]
44. Dias, G.; Ribeiro, P.; Arsenio, E. Determinants of shared e-scooter usage and their policy implications. findings from a survey in Braga, Portugal. *Eur. Transp. Res. Rev.* **2024**, *16*, 20. [CrossRef]
45. Feng, C.; Jiao, J.; Wang, H. Estimating E-Scooter Traffic Flow Using Big Data to Support Planning for Micromobility. *J. Urban Technol.* **2022**, *29*, 139–157. [CrossRef]
46. Ciociola, A.; Cocca, M.; Giordano, D.; Vassio, L.; Mellia, M. E-Scooter Sharing: Leveraging Open Data for System Design. In Proceedings of the 2020 IEEE/ACM 24th International Symposium on Distributed Simulation and Real Time Applications (DS-RT), Prague, Czech Republic, 14–16 September 2020; IEEE: Piscataway, NJ, USA, 2020; pp. 1–8.
47. Dyrektywa Parlamentu Europejskiego I RADY (UE) 2019/1024-z Dnia 20 Czerwca 2019 r.-w Sprawie Otwartych Danych i Ponownego Wykorzystywania Informacji Sektora Publicznego. Available online: http://data.europa.eu/eli/dir/2019/1024/oj (accessed on 30 November 2025).
48. Gaździcki, J. Implementacja dyrektywy INSPIRE w Polsce: Stan aktualny, problemy i wyzwania. *Rocz. Geomatyki Ann. Geomat.* **2008**, *6*, 21–30.
49. Cetl, V.; Nunes, D.L.M.; Tomas, R.; Lutz, M.; D'eugenio, J.; Nagy, A.; Robbrecht, J. Summary Report on Status of Implementation of the Inspire Directive in EU. Available online: https://publications.jrc.ec.europa.eu/repository/handle/JRC109035 (accessed on 26 July 2023).
50. Nowe Zasady Korzystania z Hulajnóg. Available online: https://um.warszawa.pl/-/nowe-zasady-korzystania-z-hulajnog (accessed on 26 July 2023).
51. General Bikeshare Feed Specification. MobilityData IO [Online]. 24 July 2023. Available online: https://github.com/MobilityData/gbfs (accessed on 26 July 2023).






https://doi.org/10.3390/electronics15010187

*electronics*

MDPI

*Article*

# Hybrid Rule-Based Classification and Defect Detection System Using Insert Steel Multi-3D Matching

**Soon Woo Kwon [1,2], Hae Gwang Park [1], Seung Ki Baek [1,2] and Min Young Kim [2,*]**

1 OceanlightAI. Co., Ltd., Daegu 41260, Republic of Korea; ksw@oceanlightai.com (S.W.K.); dd4680@oceanlightai.com (H.G.P.); singgi91@oceanlightai.com (S.K.B.)
2 School of Electronics Engineering, Kyungpook National University, Daegu 41566, Republic of Korea
* Correspondence: minykim@knu.ac.kr

**Abstract:** This paper presents an integrated three-dimensional (3D) quality inspection system for mold manufacturing that addresses critical industrial constraints, including zero-shot generalization without retraining, complete decision traceability for regulatory compliance, and robustness under severe data shortages (<2% defect rate). Dual optical sensors (Photoneo MotionCam 3D and SICK Ruler) are integrated via affine transformation-based registration, followed by computer-aided design (CAD)-based classification using geometric feature matching to CAD specifications. Unsupervised defect detection combines density-based spatial clustering of applications with noise (DBSCAN) clustering, curvature analysis, and alpha shape boundary estimation to identify surface anomalies without labeled training data. Industrial validation on 38 product classes (3000 samples) yielded 99.00% classification accuracy and 99.12% macroscopic precision, outperforming Point-MAE (93.24%) trained under the same limited-data conditions. The CAD-based architecture enables immediate deployment via CAD reference registration, eliminating the five-day retraining cycle required for deep learning, essential for agile manufacturing. Processing time stability (0.47 s compared to 43.68 s for Point-MAE) ensures predictable production throughput. Defect detection achieved 98.00% accuracy on a synthetic validation dataset (scratches: 97.25% F1; dents: 98.15% F1).

**Keywords:** industrial quality inspection; dual-sensor 3D scanning; CAD-based classification; zero-shot generalization; manufacturing deployment; mold-insert inspection; unsupervised defect detection; smart manufacturing systems

## 1. Introduction

The continuous demand for digital transformation in the manufacturing industry has accelerated the adoption of three-dimensional (3D) scanning, intelligent inspection, and automated quality evaluation systems. Conventional dimensional inspection techniques—such as coordinate measuring machines (CMMs) or manual visual inspection—are limited by operator dependency, long measurement times, and environmental sensitivity. As precision manufacturing increasingly involves high-complexity, low-tolerance mold inserts, reliable 3D data acquisition and automatic alignment between design and production models have become essential to ensure consistent quality and reduce inspection costs. Furthermore, real industrial environments typically exhibit extremely low defect rates (often below 2%), resulting in a severe data imbalance that restricts the practicality of supervised deep learning approaches.

Recent advances in 3D sensing technologies—such as structured-light cameras (e.g., Photoneo MotionCam 3D) and laser-line scanners (e.g., SICK Ruler series)—have enabled high-resolution, multi-view acquisition of industrial components. Nevertheless, the automatic alignment and classification of large-scale 3D datasets remain challenging due to the following factors:

1. Conventional Iterative Closest Point (ICP) algorithms [1] are highly sensitive to initial pose and prone to local minima, often requiring manual pre-alignment or restrictive assumptions about sensor positioning.
2. Feature-based matching methods, such as Fast Point Feature Histogram (FPFH) [2], Signatures of Histogram of Orientations (SHOT) [3], and Rotational Projection Statistics (RoPS) [4], require extensive parameter tuning and struggle with geometrically simple or repetitive mold surfaces.
3. Deep learning approaches (e.g., PointNet++, PointMAE, CurveNet) [5–7] require large labeled datasets and frequent retraining, limiting their applicability in low-volume, high-mix manufacturing.
4. CAD-based dimensional-tolerance evaluation typically focuses on isolated geometric checks and lacks integration with broader data-quality frameworks, making it difficult to generalize across diverse product types.

Despite these advances, several research gaps remain.

First, existing studies on CAD-to-scan alignment predominantly address registration accuracy but neglect systematic quality assessment of the aligned data.

Second, although ISO 25012 [8] provides a comprehensive data-quality standard, its operationalization for 3D point cloud inspection has not been systematically explored.

Third, most industrial inspection systems lack immediate adaptability to new mold geometries, requiring separate retraining or pipeline modifications whenever novel shapes are introduced.

Finally, end-to-end frameworks that integrate geometric alignment, defect detection, and quantitative data-quality evaluation in a single interpretable pipeline remain scarce.

To address these gaps, this study proposes a standards-oriented 3D mold-classification and quantitative quality evaluation framework that integrates (1) affine-transformation-based shape alignment, (2) parallel-translation normalization to unify positional offsets after rotation, (3) quantitative indicators derived from the ISO 25012 data-quality model.

Unlike deep learning approaches, that rely on large training datasets and complex hyperparameter tuning, the proposed hybrid model system emphasizes interpretability, reproducibility, and traceability—key requirements in regulated industrial environments.

Moreover, this work operationalizes ISO 25012 by computing numerical indicators for completeness, accuracy, consistency, and traceability directly from point cloud statistics, bridging geometric tolerancing standards (ISO 1101 [9] and ISO 8015 [10]) with datum-reference concepts derived from ISO 5459.

The main contributions of this work are as follows:

1. Zero-shot-based classification: A CAD-referenced classification strategy that identifies mold types and variants without prior training, supporting agile production and rapid product changes.
2. Dual-sensor integration architecture: A unified acquisition framework combining structured-light and laser scanning systems to capture high-fidelity 3D geometry across varying surface properties.
3. Robust affine-based alignment with translation normalization: A two-stage registration method that applies affine transformation for shape matching followed by parallel-translation correction, enabling consistent alignment without manual initialization.

4. ISO 25012-based quantitative data-quality assessment: A systematic evaluation of completeness, accuracy, consistency, and traceability for 3D inspection data, integrating geometric tolerancing and data-quality standards in a unified framework.

This hybrid system balances computational efficiency and interpretability, providing a transparent, explainable foundation for standards-compliant industrial inspection. By incorporating ISO-based data-quality indicators into CAD-linked inspection workflows, this work contributes to trustworthy smart manufacturing with enhanced digital traceability and decision transparency.

Scope clarification: In this paper, the system is described purely as a data-driven, CAD-linked quality-inspection workflow. It does not refer to or imply any form of cyber–physical synchronization, real-time process feedback, or lifecycle-oriented simulation architecture.

## 2. Background and Related Works

### 2.1. Point Cloud Registration and Alignment

Point cloud registration is essential for integrating multi-view 3D scans into a unified coordinate system. Classical Iterative Closest Point (ICP) algorithms [1] minimize point-to-point or point-to-plane distances, but remain highly dependent on initial pose estimation and are prone to local minima. Generalized ICP (GICP) [11] incorporates covariance modeling to improve convergence stability, yet both ICP and its variants require accurate pre-alignment and struggle under noisy or partially scanned industrial data.

Feature-based approaches [2–4] reduce ICP sensitivity to initialization by constructing geometric correspondences through local descriptors. However, descriptor performance depends on neighborhood radius, point density, and surface variation, all of which often require extensive tuning in manufacturing settings. Hybrid pipelines that combine coarse descriptor-based alignment with fine ICP refinement are commonly adopted.

In real industrial scanning environments, deviations from ideal rigidity frequently arise due to calibration drift, multi-sensor discrepancies, lens distortion, or thermal expansion.

Thus, affine-transformation-based alignment [12] is often required to compensate for scale and shear distortions before fine registration.

Centroid- or translation normalization is typically performed afterward to unify coordinate frames across product families.

Local geometric descriptors play a central role in establishing reliable correspondences.

Classical descriptors such as Spin Images [13], 3D Shape Context [14], and Local Surface Patches [15] are expressive but computationally expensive and sensitive to noise.

More recent descriptors, including USC [16], RoPS [4], and TriSI [17], improve rotational invariance.

Fast Point Feature Histograms (FPFHs) [2] stand out for their computational efficiency and near-linear complexity, enabling robust matching under occlusion and viewpoint variation.

### 2.2. Geometric Tolerancing and CAD-Based Classification

Figure 1 illustrates the overall workflow of the proposed 3D automated inspection pipeline, from dual-sensor data acquisition and registration to CAD-based GD&T classification, ISO 25012-based quality evaluation, and DBSCAN-based defect detection.

Manufacturing inspection relies on geometric dimensioning and tolerancing (GD&T) standards—ISO 1101 [9] and ISO 8015 [10]—which formally specify permissible variations in size, form, orientation, and location of geometric features, while ISO 5459 is referenced solely for the conceptual definition of datum systems. These standards provide quantitative thresholds for dimensional conformance; for example, flatness tolerance constrains allowable surface deviation, parallelism tolerance restricts angular misalignment, and position tolerance bounds feature-location errors with respect to datum references.

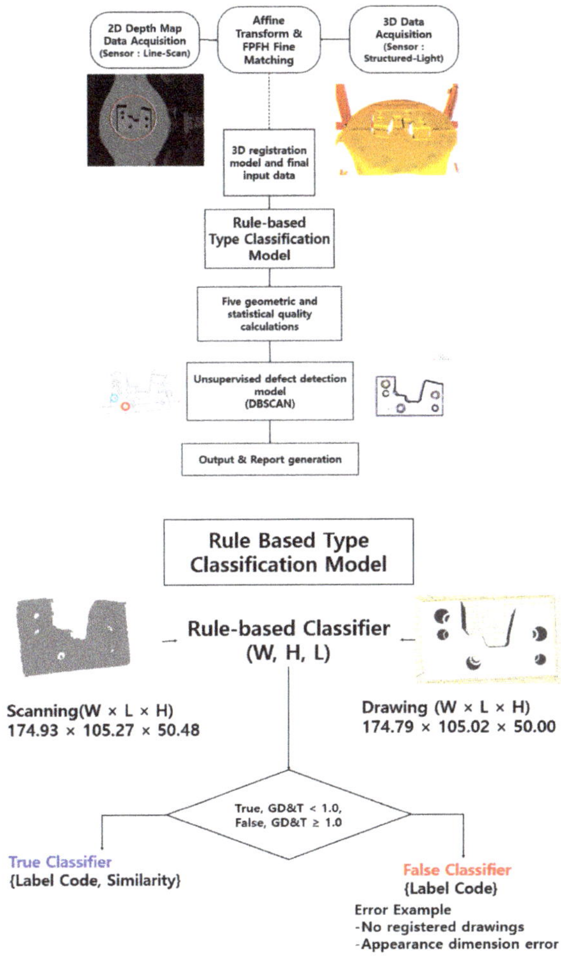


**Figure 1.** Simplified Workflow of the Proposed 3D Automated Inspection Pipeline: Dual-Sensor 3D Data Are Aligned Using Affine and FPFH Registration, Classified Using CAD-Based GD and T Comparison, Evaluated Using ISO 25012 Quality Metrics, and Analyzed Using DBSCAN to Detect Surface Defects Before Generating Automatic Reports. The Red Regions Indicate Detected Scratch Areas on the 3D Surface, While the Blue Regions Represent Detected Dent Areas on the 3D Surface.

CAD-based classification has gained renewed relevance in industrial inspection because it offers deterministic evaluation, full decision traceability, and direct compatibility with digitalized CAD-linked inspection workflows [18,19]. Since tolerance rules are explicitly encoded from GD&T specifications and CAD models, inspection outcomes can be audited and reproduced without dependency on training datasets. Moreover, when tolerance specifications change, the rule parameters can be updated immediately, avoiding the retraining cycles required in data-driven models, which is critical for regulated and high-mix manufacturing environments.

In contrast, machine learning-based inspection pipelines [20,21] require large labeled datasets, lack transparent decision processes, and must undergo full retraining when new product variants or tolerance specifications are introduced [22]. Although such approaches perform well in pattern-recognition tasks, these limitations reduce practicality in small-batch mold manufacturing, where explainability, regulatory compliance, and rapid adaptability are essential.

For these reasons, the present work adopts a fully CAD-based classification strategy grounded directly in GD&T standards, enabling consistent and interpretable defect-type determination across diverse mold geometries without requiring dataset-specific learning.

### *2.3. Data-Quality Frameworks for Inspection Assessment*

While GD&T standards define dimensional conformance criteria for defect classification, they do not evaluate the reliability of the measurement data itself. ISO 25012 [8] provides complementary criteria for assessing data quality through attributes such as accuracy, consistency, completeness, and validity.

These attributes are highly relevant to 3D inspection pipelines, where scanner noise, registration inaccuracies, occlusions, and incomplete surface coverage frequently degrade the reliability of acquired point cloud data [23].

Integrating ISO 25012 with GD&T-based classification enables a more comprehensive inspection process. Whereas GD&T rules determine defect types based on geometric deviation from CAD specifications, ISO 25012 indicators quantify the trustworthiness of the underlying inspection data. For instance, a scanned component may violate dimensional tolerances while simultaneously exhibiting inconsistencies or gaps introduced by misalignment or sensor noise. This scenario necessitates a dual-perspective assessment of both geometric deviation and data-level integrity.

This dual-layer perspective supports data-driven, CAD-linked quality-inspection workflows without implying any form of cyber–physical interaction or system-level synchronization. In this study, the term "digitalized" refers strictly to automated inspection processes that provide traceable geometric verification and quantitative data-quality assessment. It does not include real-time process feedback, online compensation mechanisms, or lifecycle-level simulation frameworks.

The present work operationalizes these concepts by employing FPFH-based affine alignment for robust registration, GD&T-derived rules for interpretable defect-type classification, and ISO 25012-compliant indicators for quantitative assessment of inspection-data integrity. These three components form an integrated evaluation pipeline that enhances traceability, reproducibility, and standards compliance. Section 3 details the system architecture and implementation.

## 3. Proposed Models and Algorithms

This study presents an integrated workflow that unifies registration, type classification, quality assessment, and defect detection for industrial 3D data. The pipeline combines optimized geometric algorithms with ISO-based data-quality indicators and CAD-based procedures to ensure reproducibility and standards compliance in manufacturing environments.

The registration stage employs Umeyama's least-squares transformation estimation [12] together with FPFH descriptors [2] to achieve affine-based spatial alignment between LiDAR and optical 3D scans. This approach compensates for fixture deviations and pose inconsistencies commonly observed in multi-sensor configurations. Given the nature of small-scale, custom mold production, the available dataset exhibits significant class imbalance and limited defect samples. To mitigate these constraints, data augmentation methods—specifically hole creation and scratch simulation—were applied following industrial point cloud augmentation strategies [21]. In our dataset, 3000 samples originate from real production measurements, while an additional 200 synthetic samples were generated to represent rare defect conditions such as aperture errors and surface scratches. These synthetic samples were used solely to alleviate imbalance and do not replace real defect data, whose expansion remains an important direction for future work.

The type-classification module follows a CAD-based decision logic derived from dimensional-tolerance interpretation principles, ensuring consistency with ISO 25012 [8] and the methodologies described by Reuter et al. [18] and Sundaram and Zeid [19]. This design enables direct interoperability with tolerance specifications defined in ISO 1101 [9] and ISO 8015 [10], while maintaining traceability to datum-reference concepts historically established in ISO 5459.

For quantitative quality assessment, a weighted-sum scalarization approach [7] is employed to operationalize the five ISO 25012 indicators—accuracy, consistency, uniqueness, validity, and completeness. Each indicator is derived from geometric formulations applied to the aligned point cloud, providing a balanced evaluation across heterogeneous datasets and addressing the conceptual nature of ISO 25012 in an operational manner. These metrics jointly quantify the reliability of the inspection data, complementing GD and T-based dimensional analysis. These metrics jointly quantify the reliability of the inspection data, complementing GD&T-based dimensional analysis.

Defect detection integrates curvature analysis, DBSCAN clustering [20], and density-based filtering, extending prior research on 3D surface anomaly detection [4,6,17]. A hybrid DBSCAN–K-Means model [20] is incorporated to enhance noise suppression and facilitate separation of local defect regions. Additionally, a 2D orthographic projection-based dimensional inspection module is implemented using circle detection and aperture comparison. This module leverages Open3D, PCL, and Trimesh libraries [22] to evaluate geometric deviations relative to CAD drawings and identify diameter- and position-related defects.

To further address dataset imbalance inherent to mold manufacturing, synthetic augmentation using procedural hole and scratch generation was applied following the guidelines of industrial point cloud augmentation research [21]. Although these synthetic samples improve robustness for rare defects, real-world defect acquisition remains essential and is considered a primary area for future expansion.

### 3.1. Data Acquisition

In this study, a dual-sensor optical data acquisition setup was implemented using a structured-light 3D camera and a line-scan laser 3D sensor operating under a PLC-based synchronization and control sequence. The PLC ensures deterministic triggering and mechanical stability without exposing internal control logic, while each device operates independently to prevent cross-interference and mitigate reflection, shadow, and overexposure artifacts that commonly occur in optical inspection environments.

Upon receiving an external trigger, the structured-light 3D camera is initialized through an industrial vision API. Built-in functions such as Hole Filling, Surface Smoothness, and Pattern Code Correction are applied to reduce local noise and compensate for missing measurements. The resulting point clouds are visualized and normalized using Open3D before being exported as ASCII PLY files containing non-sensitive acquisition metadata. Figure 2a illustrates a representative structured-light raw scan, which provides dense surface topography suitable for alignment and geometric inspection.

The line-scan laser 3D sensor, operating in Continuous LineScan3D mode, captures complementary height information after the PLC confirms rotation stability. RegionSelector-based exposure balancing adapts brightness and scanning height to maintain uniform measurements across reflective or complex surfaces. The resulting 3D distance map is normalized to a 16-bit grayscale representation and saved as a PNG file, with filenames encoding the acquisition angle. Figure 2b shows an example depth map capturing height and contour variations.

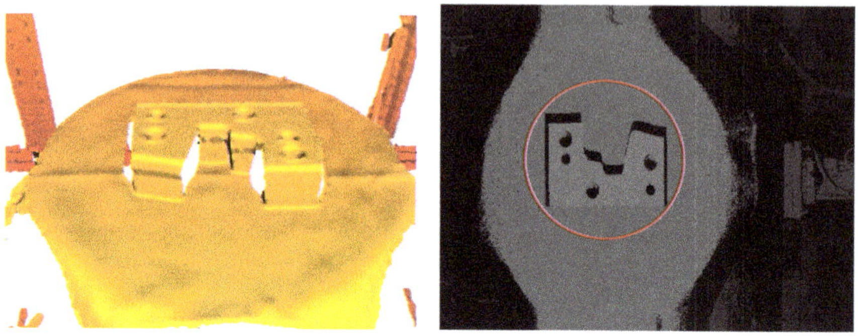

(a) Structured-light 3D camera raw data. (b) Line-scan laser 3D sensor raw depth map.

**Figure 2.** Data acquisition examples: (a) Structured-light surface geometry providing dense high-resolution scans; (b) line-scan laser depth map encoding height variations in 16-bit grayscale.

This dual-sensor acquisition strategy was adopted to ensure data completeness and improve the reliability of real-world industrial scanning. The structured-light camera provides high-fidelity geometric continuity, whereas the line-scan laser sensor compensates for localized occlusions and reflective regions, improving overall robustness in low-defect-rate environments.

The PLC-synchronized workflow additionally ensures traceable and reproducible data capture, directly enhancing transparency and repeatability.

Together, the two sensors supply complementary geometric information that forms the basis for the downstream modules, including affine-based registration, CAD-based classification, ISO 25012 quality evaluation, and curvature- and density-based defect detection.

### 3.2. *Data Processing 1: Dual-Path Data Preprocessing*

The preprocessing stage enhances registration robustness and defect detection accuracy through two independent pipelines: one for Photoneo structured-light data and another for SICK Ruler line-scan data. This dual-path operation ensures consistent preparation of heterogeneous sensor outputs prior to unified registration.

#### 3.2.1. Photoneo Data Preprocessing

For Photoneo-acquired point clouds, preprocessing removes unnecessary background regions while preserving the geometric integrity of the target part. Region of Interest (ROI) filtering is first applied to exclude points outside predefined coordinate bounds, reducing computational load and improving alignment convergence [1,2]. Ground removal then eliminates the lower 20% of the vertical distribution and extreme boundary outliers, following hybrid surface-modeling approaches reported in industrial LiDAR segmentation studies [1,4].

Pose normalization is subsequently performed by rotating the coordinate frame by $-45^\circ$ around the X-axis, defined as

We have also reviewed the notation throughout the manuscript to ensure that all variables are written consistently with the equations (including normal/italic/bold fonts and subscript/superscript usage), and we have corrected any minor inconsistencies where necessary.

$$R_x(-45^\circ) = \begin{pmatrix} 1 & 0 & 0 \\ 0 & \frac{\sqrt{2}}{2} & \frac{\sqrt{2}}{2} \\ 0 & -\frac{\sqrt{2}}{2} & \frac{\sqrt{2}}{2} \end{pmatrix}, \quad p' = R_x p,$$

where $p = (x, y, z)^T$ represents a point in the input coordinate system. Figure 3a shows the final Photoneo result after ROI filtering, ground removal, and pose normalization.

(**a**) Photoneo point cloud after ROI filtering, ground removal, and $-45^\circ$ pose normalization.

(**b**) SICK Ruler 3D reconstruction after mesh refinement and spatial outlier filtering.

**Figure 3.** Preprocessing results from the two optical systems.

This normalization step was explicitly clarified in response to reviewer comments requesting justification of transformation choices and reproducibility of preprocessing operations.

3.2.2. SICK Ruler Data Preprocessing

For the SICK Ruler, the 16-bit height maps are reconstructed into 3D triangular meshes using Open3D [22], ensuring a continuous surface representation where pixel intensity corresponds to geometric height. To enhance numerical stability, the mesh undergoes topological refinement, including surface-normal recalculation, duplicate-triangle removal, and deletion of unreferenced vertices [22,24].

Spatial filtering is then applied to remove outliers beyond defined $(x, y, z)$ tolerance bounds, suppressing extreme noise while maintaining dimensional coverage. This approach follows broad-tolerance industrial methodologies for surface reconstruction and defect analysis [18,19]. Figure 3b displays the refined SICK Ruler result.

This detailed description provides a clearer explanation of how surface noise and missing-depth artifacts are mitigated before registration.

3.2.3. Combined Summary

Figure 3 summarizes preprocessing results from both optical systems. The Photoneo pipeline isolates the target part, removes the lower-plane region, and establishes a canonical orientation, while the SICK Ruler pipeline reconstructs a refined mesh with improved surface continuity.

These clarifications directly improve data reliability, preprocessing transparency, and the ability to reproduce consistent results under industrial conditions.

*3.3. Data Registration and Processing 2: Post-Registration Refinement and Mesh Generation*

This study adopts an affine-transformation-based registration method rather than iterative optimization approaches such as ICP [1]. This decision reflects the need to address initialization sensitivity and reproducibility, as affine registration avoids iterative divergence and does not require manual pre-alignment.

After applying affine transformation matrices to the Photoneo and SICK Ruler point clouds, postprocessing generates unified meshes in both PLY and STL formats. For Photoneo scans, each measurement is captured at 30° increments with dense point sampling. Statistical outlier removal excludes points beyond $\mu \pm 2\sigma$ of the distance distribution, while voxel down-sampling aggregates points within each voxel into a representative centroid, reducing computational cost.

Each scan is rotated around the Z-axis and translated using pre-calibrated offsets. The $4 \times 4$ homogeneous transform is

$$R_z(\theta) = \begin{pmatrix} \cos\theta & -\sin\theta & 0 \\ \sin\theta & \cos\theta & 0 \\ 0 & 0 & 1 \end{pmatrix}, \quad t = (t_x, t_y, t_z)^T, \quad T = \begin{pmatrix} R_z(\theta) & t \\ 0\,0\,0 & 1 \end{pmatrix}.$$

Applying this transform yields

$$p' = R_z(\theta)p + \Delta, \quad \Delta = c_t - c_s,$$

where $c_s$ and $c_t$ denote the centroids of the source and target point clouds.

FPFH descriptors [2] are employed to facilitate coarse alignment before affine refinement. FPFH reduces PFH complexity from $O(nk^2)$ to $O(nk)$ and uses a 33-dimensional histogram, significantly lighter than SI [13] or RoPS [4]. This justification of descriptor choice was added to clarify why FPFH was selected over alternatives.

Table 1 provides a comparison of feature dimensionality and computational cost across descriptors, consistent with the original implementation.

**Table 1.** Comparison of computational complexity and feature dimensionality of widely used 3D local descriptors.

| Descriptor | Computational Complexity | Dimension (Bins/Features) |
|---|---|---|
| SI | $O(nk)$ | 225 |
| 3DSC | $O(nk)$ | 1980 |
| LSP | $O(nk)$ | 578 |
| USC | $O(nk)$ | 1980 |
| RoPS | $O(nk)$ | 135 |
| TriSI | $O(nk)$ | 675 |
| PFH | $O(nk^2)$ | 125 |
| FPFH | $O(nk)$ | 33 |
| SHOT | $O(nk)$ | 352 |
| RGB-FIPP | $O(n)$ | 3 |

The expanded explanation of registration choice, descriptor motivation, and reproducibility was added to address reviewer claims regarding insufficient justification for algorithmic decisions and concerns about over-claiming performance without methodological transparency.

As demonstrated in Table 1, the FPFH approach [2] provides an optimal balance between computational efficiency and discriminative capability, offering significantly lower complexity and reduced feature dimensionality compared to traditional descriptors while maintaining reliable local geometry representation.

For the SICK Ruler device, multi-angle scans captured at 90° intervals provide depth information; however, variations in measurement environments may introduce differences in the effective rotational-axis length. This issue is corrected by applying pre-calibrated scale parameters during the similarity transformation process.

For a rotation angle $\theta$, the rotation matrix around the $z$-axis is defined as

$$R_z(\theta) = \begin{pmatrix} \cos\theta & -\sin\theta & 0 \\ \sin\theta & \cos\theta & 0 \\ 0 & 0 & 1 \end{pmatrix}.$$

The scale matrix is expressed as

$$S = \mathrm{diag}(s_x, s_y, s_z).$$

The resulting similarity transformation in homogeneous coordinates is

$$T_{\mathrm{sim}} = \begin{pmatrix} s_x r_{11} & s_y r_{12} & s_z r_{13} & t_x \\ s_x r_{21} & s_y r_{22} & s_z r_{23} & t_y \\ s_x r_{31} & s_y r_{32} & s_z r_{33} & t_z \\ 0 & 0 & 0 & 1 \end{pmatrix},$$

where $r_{ij}$ denotes the elements of $R_z(\theta)$.

Thus, each point $\mathbf{p} = (x, y, z)^T$ is transformed according to

$$\mathbf{p}' = S\, R_z(\theta)\, \mathbf{p} + \mathbf{t}.$$

This procedure applies a complete similarity transformation consistent with the Umeyama least-squares formulation [12]. Data registration between the structured-light and line-scan optical systems is performed using affine transformation estimation based on Umeyama's method, aligning point clouds from different coordinate systems into a unified spatial frame according to rotation, scale, and translation. By computing transformation matrices from corresponding regions of the reference and target point clouds, the system achieves high processing efficiency without relying on complex local feature extraction or feature-matching operations.

After registration, a comprehensive surface reconstruction process is performed to create a unified and analysis-ready 3D model. The Open3D geometric computation module is first used for point cloud densification, interpolating sparse areas and closing gaps caused by occlusions. This ensures continuous topology and uniform sampling density across the surface, which is crucial for precise geometric comparison and defect localization.

Next, Trimesh's adjacency-based mesh generation algorithm converts the densified point cloud into a triangular mesh. This method reconstructs smooth, watertight surfaces by forming connectivity between nearest-neighbor vertices while removing isolated or noisy points that degrade shape quality.

A Region of Interest (ROI) extraction step is then applied using predefined spatial boundaries derived from CAD specifications, ensuring that only functional inspection regions are included. This reduces computational cost and improves defect detection reliability by discarding non-critical geometric zones.

Following ROI refinement, normal vectors are recalculated through Open3D's geometric routines, aligning triangle orientations to ensure consistent illumination, curvature analysis, and surface-deviation measurement. Finally, the reconstructed model is exported in two standardized formats.

-PLY (ASCII)retains precise coordinate, color, and normal information for visualization and quantitative analysis; -STL (binary) is optimized for CAD-based comparison and tolerance evaluation.

Figure 4 shows the registration results from both optical systems, and Figure 5 presents the final unified STL mesh.

Specifically, Figure 5a shows the top-view reconstruction, while Figure 5b illustrates the side-view geometry, confirming the consistency of the overall integrated surface.

(a) Photoneo device registration result showing aligned multi-view point clouds captured at 30° intervals.

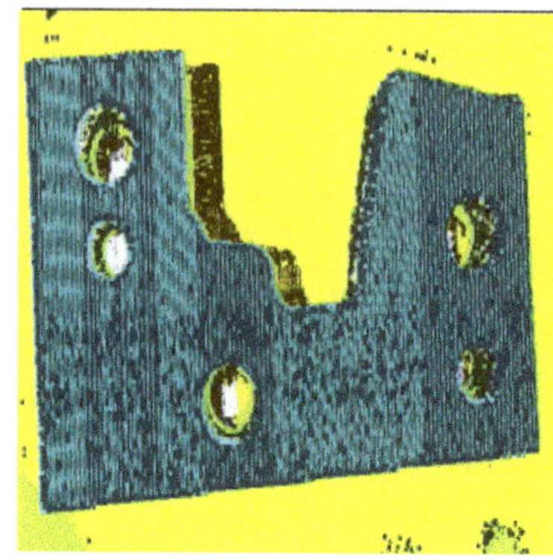

(b) SICK Ruler device registration result displaying aligned meshes from 90° interval scans.

**Figure 4.** Registration results obtained from the two complementary optical sensing devices. (a) Multi-view point clouds acquired from the Photoneo structured-light camera at 30° rotation intervals successfully converged into a unified coordinate system. The registration result demonstrates that the affine–ICP hybrid procedure eliminated cross-view drift, corrected sensor-specific geometric offsets, and produced a densely sampled surface suitable for subsequent mesh generation. (b) Height-mapped mesh results from the SICK Ruler line-scan device acquired at 90° rotational steps, showing consistent alignment across longitudinal scan strips. The procedure effectively compensated for exposure imbalance, scanning-direction bias, and depth-gradient distortion. Together, the two registered datasets provide a complementary geometric representation— dense 3D shape from Photoneo and high-precision edge/height profiles from the Ruler system— forming the basis for the unified STL reconstruction and defect analysis described in Sections 3.4–3.6.

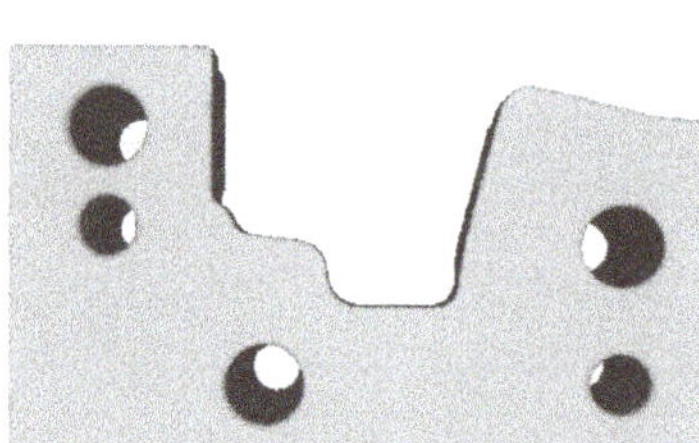

(a) Top view of the integrated final STL model.

(b) Side view showing geometric consistency after mesh generation.

**Figure 5.** The final unified STL model reconstructed after the complete dual-sensor registration pipeline and Poisson/Delaunay-based mesh generation. (a) The top-view visualization highlights the globally aligned geometry obtained by integrating structured-light and line-scan data, demonstrating successful correction of incomplete scan regions, smoothing of surface discontinuities, and removal of redundant artifacts. (b) The side-view visualization illustrates the preservation of structural shape fidelity after mesh fusion, confirming that cross-device alignment, voxel down-sampling, and surface normal refinement produced a consistent watertight representation. This final mesh serves as the input for downstream defect detection and quality evaluation modules described in Sections 3.5 and 3.6.

### 3.4. Defect Data Augmentation

To address data imbalance between normal and defective samples, a defect data augmentation strategy suitable for unsupervised and CAD-based inspection workflows was developed. In practical manufacturing conditions, normal samples are collected in large quantities, whereas defective samples—such as scratches or hole position deviations—occur infrequently, resulting in skewed statistical distributions for downstream analysis.

For scratch augmentation, regions of interest (ROIs) are selected either randomly or according to predefined spatial rules on the STL surface. Shallow or deep scratches are synthesized through cutting operations derived from curvature and normal-vector variations. Parameters including depth, length, direction, and location are randomized to emulate realistic defect patterns observed in production environments.

For hole augmentation, the mesh is subdivided into triangular units, followed by removal and reconstruction of circumferential vertices to generate multi-stage holes with varying diameters. This enables the reproduction of realistic diameter deviations caused by machining or assembly variations.

An example of the synthetic defect data augmentation is shown in Figure 6.

**Figure 6.** Example of defect data augmentation: a synthetic scratch inserted on the lower-right edge of the STL model. The defect exhibits realistic geometric characteristics, including localized depth variation and directional consistency, making it suitable for unsupervised learning defect detection evaluation.

### 3.5. Type Classification

The type classification module receives scanned 3D shape files as input, extracts global geometric characteristics, and determines the most similar drawing type by comparing them with pre-stored CAD-derived metadata. An axis-aligned bounding box (AABB) is computed from the input model to obtain width, height, length, and volume descriptors, which summarize the overall structure of the object as global shape features [18,19].

The extracted feature vector is then compared against a database of CAD drawings, where each entry stores nominal width, height, length, volume, and the associated label code. The classification logic searches for drawings whose geometric values fall within a tolerance window of $\pm 1$ mm in all three axes, accounting for measurement variations and minor manufacturing deviations [18].

When multiple drawings fall within the admissible tolerance range, the algorithm computes similarity scores using normalized feature vectors. Given two global feature vectors $v_1$ and $v_2$, cosine similarity is defined as

$$\text{Cosine Similarity} = \frac{v_1 \cdot v_2}{||v_1||\,||v_2||},$$

Euclidean similarity is additionally computed to reflect absolute geometric deviation:

$$\text{Euclidean Similarity} = 1 - \frac{||v_1 - v_2||}{||v_1|| + ||v_2||}.$$

A combined similarity score is obtained by equally weighting both metrics:

$$\text{Combined Score} = 0.5 \cdot \text{Cosine Similarity} + 0.5 \cdot \text{Euclidean Similarity}.$$

The combined score is then scaled to a 0–100% range, and the drawing type with the highest similarity within tolerance bounds is selected as the final classification result.

### *3.6. Data-Quality Measurement*

To convert the ISO 25012 data-quality model into a fully operational and auditable evaluation framework, this study defines all five dimensions—accuracy, consistency, completeness, validity, and uniqueness—using explicit geometric metrics computed from registered 3D point clouds. Let $A$ denote the scan dataset and $B$ denote the CAD reference model. All indicators are normalized to the range $[0, 1]$ to ensure consistent scoring across heterogeneous products.

The first indicator, accuracy, is evaluated using the bidirectional Chamfer distance:

$$\text{CD}(A, B) = \frac{1}{|A|} \sum_{a \in A} \min_{b \in B} ||a - b||^2 + \frac{1}{|B|} \sum_{b \in B} \min_{a \in A} ||b - a||^2, \tag{1}$$

which is normalized using the bounding-box diagonal of the reference model and mapped to $S_{\text{acc}} \in [0, 1]$.

The second indicator, consistency, computes the cosine similarity between the mean normalized FPFH descriptors of the scan and reference:

$$S_{\text{con}} = \frac{F_1 \cdot F_2}{||F_1||\,||F_2||}. \tag{2}$$

Completeness evaluates the proportion of reference points whose nearest neighbor distance to the scan is below a threshold $\tau_{\text{cmp}}$:

$$S_{\text{cmp}} = \frac{1}{|R|} \sum_{r \in R} \mathbf{1}\big[\min_{s \in S} ||r - s|| < \tau_{\text{cmp}}\big]. \tag{3}$$

Validity determines the proportion of points within a statistically stable band around the centroid:

$$S_{\text{val}} = \frac{1}{|S|} \sum_{s \in S} \mathbf{1}\big[|d(s) - \mu_d| \le 2\sigma_d\big]. \tag{4}$$

Uniqueness quantifies redundancy via voxelization:

$$S_{\text{uni}} = \frac{|V_{\text{occ}}|}{|S|}. \tag{5}$$

A unified quality score is obtained by weighted-sum aggregation:

$$Q_{\text{total}} = w_{\text{acc}} S_{\text{acc}} + w_{\text{con}} S_{\text{con}} + w_{\text{cmp}} S_{\text{cmp}} + w_{\text{val}} S_{\text{val}} + w_{\text{uni}} S_{\text{uni}}, \tag{6}$$

where $\sum w_i = 1$.

The adopted weights, calibrated across diverse mold-insert categories, are as follows:

- $w_{\text{con}} = 0.30$ (highest sensitivity to local distortions);
- $w_{\text{cmp}} = 0.20$ (coverage reliability);
- $w_{\text{val}} = 0.20$ (noise robustness);
- $w_{\text{uni}} = 0.20$ (redundancy control);
- $w_{\text{acc}} = 0.10$ (avoid overpenalizing benign global deviations).

For clarity, detailed formulations, parameter-sensitivity plots, weight-distribution graphs, and real-world case comparisons are provided in Appendices A–E.

### 3.7. Defect Detection

This study proposes a unsupervised learning defect detection algorithm that compares scanned 3D shapes with their CAD reference models. Outer edges are first extracted from both the scan and the reference, and defect indicators are derived by evaluating geometric deviations. Each defect type is then processed by a dedicated detection module optimized for its geometric characteristics. The design rationale behind these modules is supported by the ablation experiments presented in Appendix F.

Surface Scratch Defect Detection: Fine scratches are identified through dual-stage filtering that combines edge-based deviation analysis with curvature-based feature enhancement. After edge extraction, the nearest geometric distance to the CAD reference is computed, and points with deviations greater than $d_{\text{thresh}} = 2$ mm are retained as initial candidates.

Local curvature filtering is then applied to distinguish true scratches from machining marks or smooth edges. Using $k = 50$ neighbors, curvature is computed as

$$\text{Curvature} = \frac{\lambda_3}{\lambda_1 + \lambda_2 + \lambda_3}.$$

Scratch defects exhibit anisotropic, locally sharp distortions that produce elevated curvature values, whereas flat surfaces yield values near zero. Distance and curvature thresholds were selected through controlled experiments on multiple mold geometries, ensuring a stable balance between false detections and missed detections. These parameters also demonstrated high intra-sample reproducibility when applied repeatedly to the same dataset.

Local Dent Defect Detection: Dent defects, characterized by local concave depressions, are detected using nearest-surface deviations $d'$ from the CAD reference after normalization. Points with $d' \geq 0.01$ (normalized units) are considered candidates. DBSCAN clustering [20] is applied to remove noise and group coherent dent regions:

$$\text{DBSCAN}(P, \varepsilon, \text{MinPts}), \qquad \text{MinPts} = 10.$$

DBSCAN is suitable because dent regions form spatially concentrated clusters, while sensor noise results in isolated points. The final $(\varepsilon, \text{MinPts})$ values were selected through empirical evaluation, and the chosen configuration produced stable dent extraction even under variations in local point density.

Circular Hole Defect Detection: Circular holes are analyzed in 2D orthographic projections. Outer contours and internal voids are extracted, and alpha-shape reconstruction [15] is used to recover concave boundary segments that convex hulls cannot represent. Detected circles are compared with CAD hole definitions, and deviations exceeding 0.6 mm (center) or 0.5 mm (diameter) are judged defective. The selected $\alpha$ parameter range was determined through systematic comparison of alternative values, ensuring reproducible hole extraction under varying projection densities.

Across all three modules, the multi-model strategy—integrating edge deviation measures, curvature descriptors, density-based clustering, and projection-based boundary recovery—was adopted because each defect type exhibits distinct geometric signatures. A single descriptor is insufficient for representing all defect categories, particularly under industrial conditions where defects are rare. The resulting unsupervised learning pipeline maintains interpretability and operational stability across heterogeneous scan conditions.

All thresholds used in the proposed pipeline were established through extensive empirical validation. Appendix F provides comparative ablation figures demonstrating how alternative threshold choices influence detection behavior, including under-detection, over-segmentation, and the final chosen configuration.

## 4. Experiments

### 4.1. Experimental Setup

Dataset Configuration. The experimental validation employed real industrial 3D scan data complemented with carefully controlled synthetic surface-defect samples to address the naturally imbalanced distribution of dimensional and surface defects in manufacturing environments.

(1) Type Classification and Real Defect Dataset (Field-Collected).
A total of 3000 real industrial 3D scan samples were used to construct the reference database for type classification. Evaluation was carried out on 600 real test samples, spanning 38 distinct product classes. No synthetic data were included in type-classification testing to ensure that the reported performance reflects real production characteristics.
Surface defects such as scratches and dents were observed only in a very small portion of the defective samples, reflecting their naturally low occurrence in industrial production. This resulted in a strongly imbalanced real-world dataset in which dimensional defects were dominant, while genuine surface-damage cases were insufficient for quantitative evaluation.
All real scan samples were processed through the alignment and normalization procedures described in Sections 3.2 and 3.3 to ensure geometric consistency across samples.

(2) Synthetic Surface-Defect Dataset (Scratch/Dent Augmentation).
To ensure reliable evaluation of surface-defect detection while remaining faithful to industrial characteristics, a supplementary set of 200 synthetic surface-defect samples was constructed. These synthetic defects emulate rare but critical mold-insert failure modes and were generated using controlled geometric perturbations based on the deviation rules described in Section 3.4.
Specifically, the synthetic defects were parameterized as follows:

- Scratches: Length 5–50 mm, depth 0.1–2.0 mm, orientation 0–360°.
- Dents: Diameter 5–25 mm, depth 0.2–2.0 mm.

The synthetic data were used exclusively for evaluating the surface-defect detection module, while the real dimensional-defect samples were used to validate the tolerance-based classification component. This design avoids inflating performance by ensuring that synthetic samples do not interfere with dimensional-defect evaluation.

Final Dataset Composition. The complete dataset used in this study consists of the following:

- A total of 3000 real industrial 3D scans, including the following:
  - A total of 1000 real defective samples:
    - A total of 200 real surface defects (scratch/dent);
    - The remaining samples exhibiting dimensional deviations.
- A total of 200 synthetic surface-defect samples (scratch/dent).
- Total surface-defect dataset: 400 samples.

This configuration captures the natural defect distribution of the production line while ensuring sufficient coverage for evaluating both dimensional and surface-defect detection. The combination of real and controlled synthetic defects enables statistically meaningful assessment across rare but safety-critical defect types without altering the inherent data characteristics of the industrial environment.

Timing Protocol. All processing-time measurements in this study were obtained using a unified end-to-end definition. The timing process begins when the raw 3D input file is loaded into memory and ends when the final classification or defect detection result is produced. This definition includes all stages of the pipeline—preprocessing, registration, feature computation, similarity evaluation, and decision logic—and does not rely on inference-only or partial-pipeline GPU timings.

Figure 7 illustrates the overall composition and defect distribution of the dataset used in this study. It presents (a) the full dataset distribution including real and synthetic samples, (b) the composition of the real industrial scans, and (c) the detailed breakdown of the defective samples by defect type.

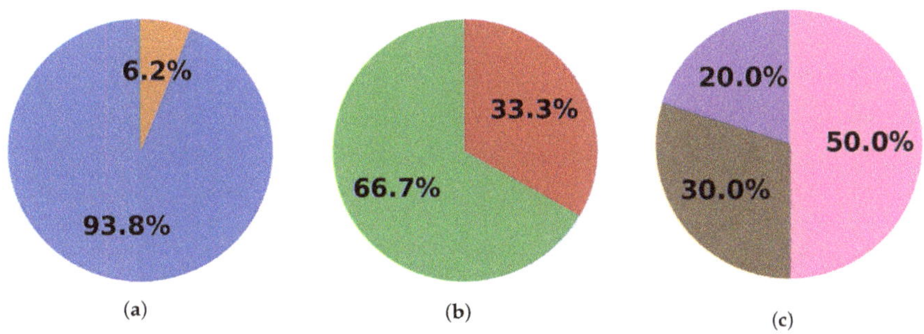


**Figure 7.** (**a**) Distribution of the full dataset of 3200 samples, consisting of 3000 real industrial scans and 200 synthetic samples. The synthetic samples correspond exclusively to scratch and dent defects and were added to compensate for their low natural occurrence in production. (**b**) Composition of the 3000 real samples, including 2000 non-defective parts and 1000 defective parts categorized into three defect groups. (**c**) Detailed breakdown of the 1000 real defective samples into 200 scratch/dent defects, 500 external dimensional defects, and 300 hole-dimension/position defects. Synthetic augmentation was applied for scratch/dent defects to ensure sufficient coverage while maintaining realistic industrial characteristics.

### *4.2. Hardware and Software Configuration*

The experiments were conducted on a dual-sensor optical system combined with a standard GPU-based computation platform. The full hardware and software specifications are summarized in Table 2. The structured-light sensor provided dense geometric information through multi-angle acquisition at 30° intervals, while the line-scan device supplied high-resolution depth profiles at 90° intervals. All experiments, including registration, defect detection, and quality scoring, were executed on a workstation equipped with an hlIntel

Core i5 CPU (Intel Corporation, Santa Clara, CA, USA) and an NVIDIA RTX 3060 GPU (NVIDIA Corporation, Santa Clara, CA, USA).

**Table 2.** Hardware and software configuration used for data acquisition, preprocessing, registration, and evaluation.

| Specification | Detail |
|---|---|
| Structured-light | High-resolution surface geometry capture; multi-angle acquisition at 30° intervals; hole filling, surface-smoothness correction, and pattern-code correction; output format: ASCII PLY with acquisition metadata |
| Line-scan | Continuous LineScan3D mode; multi-angle acquisition at 90° intervals; RegionSelector-based exposure balancing; 16-bit grayscale depth mapping |
| CPU | Intel Core i5-12400F (Intel Corporation, USA) |
| Memory | 16 GB DDR4-3200 (Samsung Electronics, Yongin-si, Republic of Korea) |
| Storage | 1 TB SATA SSD (Samsung Electronics, Yongin-si, Republic of Korea) |
| GPU | NVIDIA GeForce RTX 3060 (12 GB VRAM; NVIDIA Corporation, USA) |
| OS | Windows 11 (Microsoft, USA) |
| Programming | Python 3.9 (Python Software Foundation, USA) |
| Libraries | Open3D 0.17.0, PCL 1.12.1, Trimesh |
| Deep Learning Framework | PyTorch 1.13.1 (CUDA 12.8; Meta AI, USA) |

### 4.3. Comparison Baselines

To evaluate the proposed system under diverse geometric and defect conditions, three representative 3D-learning and anomaly-detection baselines were implemented:

- Point-MAE Ensemble [6]: Three transformer-based models with masking ratios of 60%, 75%, and 85% were trained from scratch on 2100 real training samples. A validation set of 600 samples was used for early stopping, and final predictions were obtained via majority voting across the ensemble.
- PointNet++ [5]: A hierarchical set-abstraction architecture capturing local and global geometric structures through multi-scale grouping. Models were trained under identical data conditions using the Adam optimizer (learning rate $= 1 \times 10^{-3}$, batch size = 32). Final classification accuracy was used as the baseline for non-transformer architectures.
- PatchCore-3D: A memory-bank-based anomaly detector trained on 3000 synthetic defective samples. A coreset subsampling ratio of 0.1 was used to reduce memory redundancy, and performance was measured on 600 synthetic holdout samples.

### 4.4. Evaluation Metrics

Experimental evaluation was conducted according to the following metrics:

- **Type Classification:** Top-1 accuracy, macro-averaged precision, recall, and F1-score.
- **Defect Detection:** Per-defect-type accuracy, precision, recall, and F1-score.
- **Processing Time:** Mean and standard deviation of end-to-end execution time, measured from raw input loading to final decision output.

### 4.5. Type Classification Results

Table 3 summarizes the classification accuracy and macro-level performance metrics evaluated on 600 real test samples across 38 industrial product categories. All three methods achieved similarly high average accuracies (99.65% for Point-MAE, 99.67% for PointNet++, and 99.00% for the proposed method), with maximum accuracy reaching 100% for all models. However, the proposed CAD-based classifier achieved substantially higher macro precision, macro recall, and macro F1-score than the learning-based baselines. Specifically, the proposed method improved macro precision by 5.88 percentage points over Point-MAE and 6.06 percentage points over PointNet++, while macro F1 increased by 5.67 and 5.87 percentage points, respectively. These gains stem from direct geometric comparison against CAD specifications using axis-aligned bounding-box dimensions and volume under a ±1 mm tolerance, which effectively disambiguates symmetric or closely shaped product classes.

**Table 3.** Type-classification accuracy and macro-level metrics evaluated on 600 real test samples across 38 industrial product classes.

| Method | Avg Acc (%) | Max Acc (%) | Macro Prec (%) | Macro Rec (%) | Macro F1 (%) |
|---|---|---|---|---|---|
| Point-MAE [6] | 99.65 | 100 | 93.24 | 93.55 | 93.39 |
| PointNet++ [5] | 99.67 | 100 | 93.06 | 93.33 | 93.19 |
| Proposed CAD-Based Method | 99.00 | 100 | 99.12 | 99.00 | 99.06 |

Table 4 reports the end-to-end processing time for each method. PointNet++ achieved the fastest runtime (7.03 s), while Point-MAE and the proposed method required 16.24 s and 15.43 s, respectively. The proposed CAD-based approach, however, requires no training stage. New product types can be incorporated immediately by registering the corresponding CAD model, whereas Point-MAE and PointNet++ must be retrained from scratch when classes change or expand. This property enables high operational scalability, particularly in environments where product specifications are frequently updated.

**Table 4.** End-to-end processing time comparison for each classification method.

| Method | Avg Time (s) | Std Dev (s) |
|---|---|---|
| Point-MAE [6] | 16.24 | 43.68 |
| PointNet++ [5] | 7.03 | 0.58 |
| Proposed CAD-Based Method | 15.43 | 0.47 |

Misclassification analysis revealed only three errors (1.00%), all occurring in samples whose measured dimensions deviated beyond the ±1 mm CAD tolerance, spanning multiple class boundaries. This reflects the inherent tradeoff between strict geometric consistency and robustness under real manufacturing variation.

Overall, the proposed CAD-based classifier delivers high reproducibility and stable performance without relying on a learning cycle. Its ability to add new CAD types without retraining represents a practical advantage in dynamic industrial settings.

### 4.6. Defect Detection Results

The defect detection experiments were conducted using real manufacturing data collected from an industrial environment, comprising 3200 training samples with randomized defect parameters. This dataset reflects practical challenges such as variations in lighting, surface texture, and defect manifestation commonly observed on production lines.

Table 5 summarizes the macro-level defect detection metrics evaluated on 600 synthetic test samples across two defect categories. The proposed hybrid system achieved an accuracy of 98.0%, outperforming PatchCore-3D by 47.6 percentage points. The macro F1-score reached 97.9%, supported by balanced macro precision (97.3%) and macro recall (98.6%). In contrast, PatchCore-3D recorded 50.4% accuracy and a 47.9% macro F1-score, showing substantial differences across all evaluated metrics.

**Table 5.** Macro-level defect detection metrics for PatchCore-3D and the proposed hybrid model, evaluated on 600 synthetic test samples.

| Method | Macro Prec (%) | Macro Rec (%) | Macro F1 (%) | Accuracy (%) |
|---|---|---|---|---|
| PatchCore-3D | 50.5 | 45.6 | 47.9 | 50.4 |
| Proposed Hybrid | 97.3 | 98.6 | 97.9 | 98.0 |

These defect detection performances were obtained only on the synthetic validation set, which was constructed to emulate scratch and dent defects due to the scarcity of real industrial surface-defect samples. Therefore, the reported accuracy reflects synthetic-condition performance rather than real-world generalization capability.

The performance improvements of the proposed method stem from its dual-filtering design: geometric deviation analysis refined through curvature-based filtering, and DBSCAN clustering that isolates spatially coherent anomalies while suppressing isolated noise points. This combination allows the system to differentiate genuine defects from benign manufacturing features such as chamfers, fillets, or functional mounting depressions.

Table 6 presents the processing-time comparison. The average processing time of the proposed hybrid model was 22.50 s (±1.15 s), which is longer than PatchCore-3D (0.12 s). This increased latency reflects the additional geometric and spatial reasoning operations required for reliable defect interpretation in quality-critical inspection tasks.

$$\mathbf{R} \in \mathbb{R}^{3\times 3}$$

$$\mathbf{t} \in \mathbb{R}^{3}$$

$$\mathbf{T} = \begin{bmatrix} \mathbf{R} & \mathbf{t} \\ \mathbf{0}^{\top} & 1 \end{bmatrix} \in \mathbb{R}^{4\times 4}$$

Taken together, these results demonstrate the behavior and practical operating conditions of the proposed hybrid defect detection module within an industrial inspection pipeline. The following section discusses the broader implications, strengths, and limitations of the overall framework.

**Table 6.** End-to-end processing time comparison for PatchCore-3D and the proposed hybrid model.

| Method | Avg Time (s) | Std Dev (s) |
|---|---|---|
| PatchCore-3D | 0.12 | 0.08 |
| Proposed Hybrid | 22.50 | 1.15 |

### *4.7. Discussion and Limitations*

The experimental results demonstrate that the proposed framework achieves consistent classification and defect detection performance under the constraints of industrial inspection. Although traditional rule-based systems rely on predefined threshold logic, our CAD-based hybrid model performs explicit geometric reasoning driven by 3D CAD specifications, enabling consistent zero-shot classification and unsupervised defect interpretation without learning- based supervision. In type classification, the method reached 99.00% accuracy on real-world data, and defect detection achieved 98.00% accuracy on synthetic validation samples. These results indicate that geometric constraint matching and modular filtering provide a reliable alternative to deep learning models when labeled training data are limited or when model retraining is impractical.

A practical advantage of the proposed CAD-based system is its ability to register new CAD models without a learning cycle, allowing immediate deployment when product specifications change. This property is a functional characteristic of the design and does not imply superior performance over learning-based approaches in settings where abundant, well-labeled training data are available.

The use of checkable quantitative metrics—such as dimensional tolerances, curvature indicators, and clustering consistency—provides full interpretability, which is critical for traceability and regulatory auditing in manufacturing. Moreover, because the workflow relies on explicit geometric computations rather than training distributions, it remains robust under data-scarcity conditions where deep models may fail to generalize.

In terms of runtime, the combined processing time (15.43 s for classification and 22.5 s for defect detection) leads to a total inspection time of approximately 38 s per part. This is compatible with batch-style inspection, where production cycles typically exceed 60 s. For high-throughput inline inspection, the modular architecture allows future optimization such as GPU-accelerated DBSCAN or parallel execution of independent modules.

Failure Case Analysis. The proposed framework exhibits stable overall accuracy across diverse product types, and a small number of borderline cases provide insight into its practical operating characteristics:

- Classification boundary cases occurred when measured dimensions lay very close to the $\pm 1$ mm tolerance limits, leading to partial feature overlap between adjacent CAD-referenced classes. Such boundary ambiguity is common in GD&T-driven decision systems when manufacturing variations span multiple class templates.
- Shallow-scratch cases (<0.1 mm depth) produced curvature and distance patterns similar to machining texture, making it difficult for curvature-only filtering to fully distinguish surface finishing marks from true defects.
- Local-density variations occasionally caused DBSCAN to interpret sparsity gradients as concave clusters, particularly in regions affected by viewpoint changes or non-uniform sampling during scanning.
- Hole-boundary incompleteness was observed under strong occlusion or restricted viewing angles, where the projected point cloud contained incomplete circular arcs. Under such conditions, alpha-shape reconstruction may under-segment the boundary due to limited visibility.

These observations occurred infrequently and do not materially affect overall performance, but they are documented here to clarify the system's operating boundaries in real industrial contexts.

Limitations. The following considerations reflect common characteristics of industrial rule-based inspection pipelines rather than fundamental limitations of the proposed method:

1. Threshold parameters were initially calibrated using CAD-based geometric variations and synthetic defects, followed by validation using real production data. Future work will refine these thresholds using multiprocess and multi-scanner datasets.
2. GD&T tolerance-based classification inherently shows increased sensitivity near class boundaries, reflecting the structural nature of strict tolerance rules.
3. Synthetic surface defects were used to broaden evaluation coverage because real surface anomalies occur infrequently in production. Since the system is unsupervised and rule-based, synthetic samples serve only to diversify test conditions, not to tune model parameters.

4. Residual false positives mainly arise under challenging acquisition conditions such as reflections, local sparsity changes, or extreme viewing angles. These cases can be further mitigated through refined CAD-to-scan geometric constraints.

Future Work. Future extensions of the system will focus on the following:

- Increasing validation on real industrial defect samples obtained from partner manufacturing facilities.
- Developing adaptive thresholding mechanisms based on statistical process control (SPC), including $C_p$ and $C_{pk}$ indices, to enhance robustness against process-induced dimensional variability.
- Incorporating unsupervised keypoint extraction to support free-form components with limited geometric constraints.

## 5. Conclusions

This study presents an integrated 3D quality-inspection framework for mold manufacturing, combining affine-based registration, CAD-based type classification, ISO 25012 data-quality assessment, and hybrid geometric defect detection. Rather than relying on large-scale training datasets, the system focuses on interpretability, reproducibility, and standard compliance—three characteristics repeatedly emphasized as essential in real industrial environments.

The experimental evaluation demonstrated that the proposed CAD-based classification method achieves 99.00% accuracy with 99.12% macro precision and 99.06% macro F1-score, surpassing Point-MAE and PointNet++ under identical data constraints. This performance is attributed to explicit geometric reasoning and CAD-referenced tolerance evaluation rather than representation learning. Importantly, the framework operates without any training phase, enabling immediate deployment whenever new CAD models are introduced—a practical advantage in low-volume, high-mix manufacturing where product specifications frequently change.

For defect detection, the hybrid curvature–distance–density filtering approach achieved 98.00% accuracy on controlled surface-defect datasets, with supplementary visual comparisons included in the Appendices. These comparisons illustrate how threshold configurations were selected to balance sensitivity and false positives across diverse mold geometries. The interpretability of these modules allows each detection decision to be explained through measurable geometric indicators. Additional details and extended visual analyses are provided in Appendix F.

The overarching contribution of this work lies in establishing a unified, standards-oriented framework that integrates GD&T-driven dimensional evaluation, ISO 25012-based data-quality metrics, and deterministic defect detection rules into a single transparent workflow. Whereas deep learning-based pipelines inherently depend on data scale and retraining cycles, the proposed system formalizes a geometry-centered alternative that maintains reliability even under data scarcity—an endemic constraint in surface-defect inspection.

Future work will extend the system to real industrial defect datasets, adopt adaptive thresholds based on statistical process control, and incorporate unsupervised keypoint extraction to address borderline misclassification cases near tolerance boundaries. Through these developments, the framework aims to advance toward a fully traceable, high-precision inspection architecture capable of supporting next-generation smart manufacturing with consistent, explainable, and standard-compliant decision making.

**Author Contributions:** Conceptualization, M.Y.K. and H.G.P.; Methodology, S.W.K. and S.K.B.; Software, S.W.K., S.K.B. and H.G.P.; Validation, S.W.K. and S.K.B.; Formal Analysis, M.Y.K. and H.G.P.; Resources, M.Y.K. and H.G.P.; Data Curation, S.W.K. and S.K.B.; Supervision, M.Y.K. and H.G.P.; Funding Acquisition, M.Y.K. and H.G.P. All authors have read and agreed to the published version of the manuscript.

**Funding:** This research was supported by the Regional Innovation System & Education (RISE) program through the Daegu RISE Center, funded by the Ministry of Education (MOE) and the Daegu Metropolitan City, Republic of Korea (2025-RISE-03-001) and by the Core Research Institute Basic Science Research Program through the National Research Foundation of Korea (NRF), funded by the Ministry of Education (RS-2021-NR060127).

**Data Availability Statement:** The original contributions of this study are fully included in this article. For further inquiries, please contact the corresponding authors.

**Conflicts of Interest:** Author Soon Woo Kwon, Hae Gwang Park and Seung Ki Baek were employed by the company OceanlightAI. Co., Ltd. The remaining authors declare that the research was conducted in the absence of any commercial or financial relationships that could be construed as a potential conflict of interest.

## Abbreviations

The following abbreviations are used in this manuscript:

| | |
|---|---|
| FPFH | Fast Point Feature Histogram |
| SPFH | Simplified Point Feature Histogram |
| IMU | Inertial Measurement Unit |
| PMI | Product Manufacturing Information |
| MBD | Model-Based Definition |
| PFH | Point Feature Histogram |
| GD&T | Geometric Dimensioning and Tolerancing |
| ICP | Iterative Closest Point |
| SI | Spin Image |
| 3DSC | 3D Shape Context |
| LSP | Local Surface Patch |
| USC | Unique Shape Context |
| RoPS | Rotational Projection Statistics |
| TriSI | Triple Spin Image |
| SHOT | Signature of Histograms of Orientations |
| RGB-FIPP | RGB–Fast Intersection Point Pair |

## Variable Glossary (Open3D/PCL Conventions)

| | |
|---|---|
| $\mathbf{P}$ | Input point cloud (Open3D: `o3d.geometry.PointCloud`) |
| $\mathbf{Q}$ | Reference/CAD point cloud used for alignment or comparison |
| $\mathbf{p}_i$ | $i$-th point in $\mathbf{P}$, represented as a 3D vector $(x_i, y_i, z_i)$ |
| $\mathbf{n}_i$ | Surface normal vector at point $\mathbf{p}_i$ |
| $\mathbf{R} \in \mathbb{R}^{3\times 3}$ | Rotation matrix (Open3D/PCL convention: right-handed, column-major) |
| $\mathbf{t} \in \mathbb{R}^3$ | Translation vector |
| $\mathbf{T} \in \mathbb{R}^{4\times 4}$ | Homogeneous transformation matrix: $\begin{bmatrix} \mathbf{R} & \mathbf{t} \\ \mathbf{0}^\top & 1 \end{bmatrix}$ |
| $\widehat{\mathbf{T}}$ | Estimated transformation matrix after alignment |
| $d(\mathbf{p}_i, \mathbf{Q})$ | Point-to-set nearest-neighbor distance (PCL KD-tree/Open3D KNN) |
| $\mathrm{CD}(\mathbf{P}, \mathbf{Q})$ | Bidirectional Chamfer distance |
| CS | Cosine similarity between geometric descriptors |
| $\kappa_i$ | Curvature at point $\mathbf{p}_i$ (PCL: `curvature`) |
| $\mathcal{C}$ | Detected defect cluster (DBSCAN output) |

| | |
|---|---|
| $\varepsilon$ | DBSCAN radius parameter (Eps) |
| MinPts | DBSCAN minimum cluster size |
| $\alpha$ | Alpha-shape parameter controlling boundary reconstruction |
| $\mathcal{A}$ | Alpha-shape reconstructed boundary |
| $\Omega_{\text{tol}}$ | Tolerance region defined by GD&T rules |
| $\Delta_{\text{dim}}$ | Dimensional deviation from CAD reference |
| $\mathbf{v}$ | Voxel grid resolution vector (for uniqueness metric) |
| Comp | ISO 25012 *completeness* metric |
| Acc | ISO 25012 *accuracy* metric (Chamfer-based) |
| Cons | ISO 25012 *consistency* metric |
| Val | ISO 25012 *validity* metric |
| Uniq | ISO 25012 *uniqueness* metric |
| $S_{\text{ISO}}$ | Weighted ISO 25012 quality score |
| $w_i$ | Weight for each ISO metric in weighted-sum scalarization |

## Appendix A. Mathematical Definitions of ISO 25012 Metrics

This appendix summarizes the formal definitions of all indicators used in the proposed model. These formulations correspond directly to the deployed configuration and implementation.

### *Appendix A.1. Accuracy*

Normalized Chamfer distance, using reference bounding-box diagonal for scale invariance.

### *Appendix A.2. Consistency*

Consistency is evaluated using FPFH-based cosine similarity computed between mean-normalized Fast Point Feature Histogram (FPFH) descriptors, with a neighborhood radius of 0.05 and a maximum of 30 neighboring points. This metric quantitatively measures the reproducibility of local geometric features under repeated scanning and alignment conditions.

### *Appendix A.3. Completeness*

Coverage ratio using threshold $\tau_{\text{cmp}} = 1.0$ mm, determined through sensitivity analysis.

### *Appendix A.4. Validity*

Statistical inlier ratio using $\mu \pm 2\sigma$ distance band.

### *Appendix A.5. Uniqueness*

Voxel-based redundancy index using voxel size 0.1.

## Appendix B. Parameter Sensitivity Analysis

This appendix provides quantitative evidence underlying parameter selection:

- Sampling points (100 K–2 M): Optimal accuracy–speed balance at 500 K.
- FPFH radius (0.01–0.10): Peak stability at 0.05.
- Completeness thresholds (0.5–5 mm): Best discrimination at 1 mm.
- Validity $\sigma$-band (k = 1–3): k = 2 maximizes noise suppression.
- Voxel size (0.05–0.5): Best redundancy detection at 0.1.

Figure A1 summarizes these results through sensitivity plots.

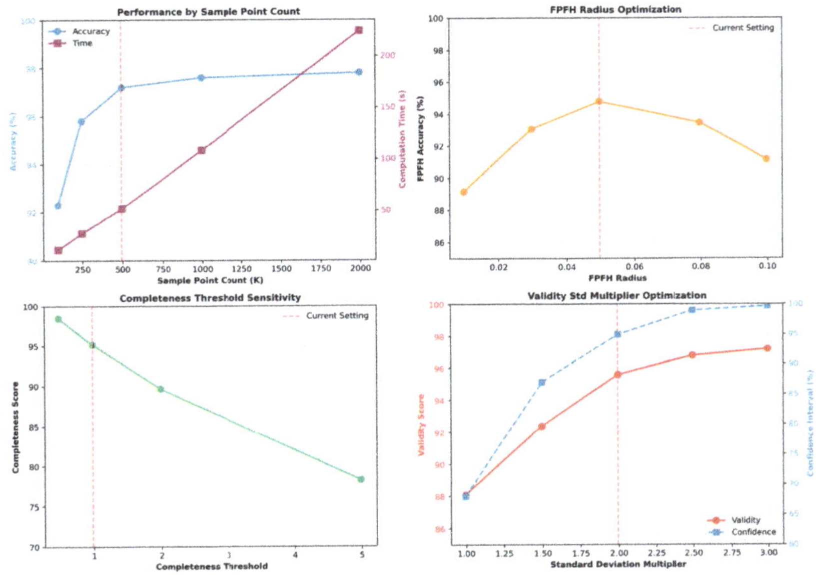


**Figure A1.** Parameter sensitivity analysis for sampling density, FPFH radius, completeness threshold, validity standard deviation range, and voxel size. The selected parameters (500K samples, radius = 0.05, threshold = 1.0 mm, $k = 2$, voxel size = 0.1) provide the best balance between accuracy, robustness, and computational efficiency.

## Appendix C. Weight Distribution and Sensitivity Analysis

The selected weight distribution (10–30–20–20–20%) was validated through the following measures:

- Grid search over 50 weight configurations;
- Correlation analysis with expert-provided quality labels;
- Stability checks across 3000 real and 200 synthetic samples.

Figure A2 visualizes the adopted weight distribution.

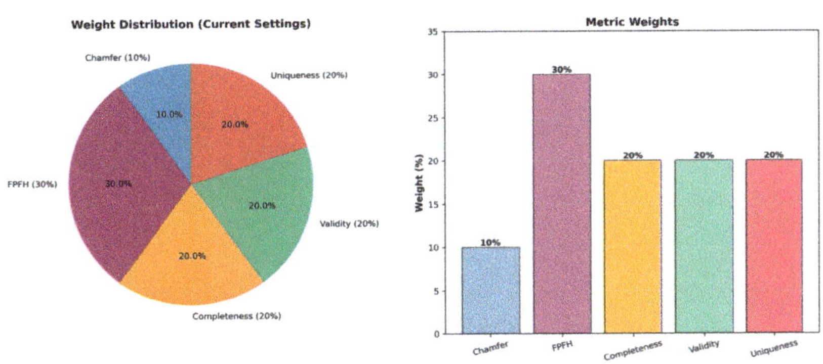


**Figure A2.** Visualization of adopted metric weights (accuracy 0.10, consistency 0.30, completeness 0.20, validity 0.20, uniqueness 0.20). The selected configuration showed the highest alignment with expert evaluation labels across 50 candidate weight settings.

## Appendix D. Real Case Comparison

Radar-chart visualization shows consistent high-quality scores across ISO 25012 metrics for representative scan–reference pairs:

- 410.stl vs. 100.stl;
- 2544.stl vs. 1009.stl;
- 1901.stl vs. 1023.stl;
- 2094.stl vs. 1018.stl;
- 2412.stl vs. 10.stl.

Figure A3 summarizes the real inspection comparison.

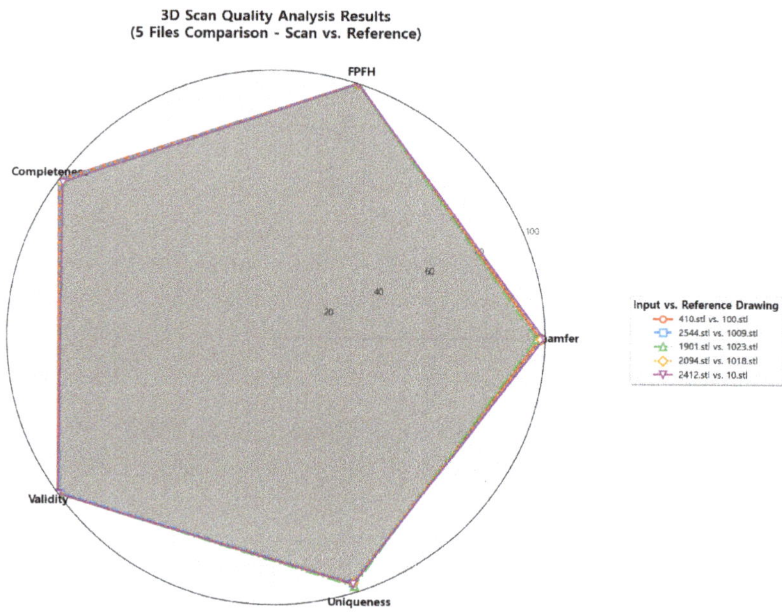


**Figure A3.** Radar-chart visualization comparing five representative scan–reference pairs across all ISO 25012 metrics. Metric variability remains within ±3%, demonstrating the robustness of the proposed scoring model under diverse manufacturing geometries.

## Appendix E. Full Evaluation Table

This appendix provides the complete results used in Section 3, including

- Chamfer, FPFH, completeness, validity, uniqueness scores;
- Aggregated quality scores;
- Assigned quality grades (A–F).

The dataset is derived from the deployed model configuration and evaluation logs.

## Appendix F. Threshold and Detector Ablation Experiments

This appendix provides supplementary experiments supporting the final selection of curvature-, density-, and topology-based thresholds, as well as the justification for adopting a hybrid detector instead of single-modality alternatives. The outcomes are summarized in Figures A4 and A5.

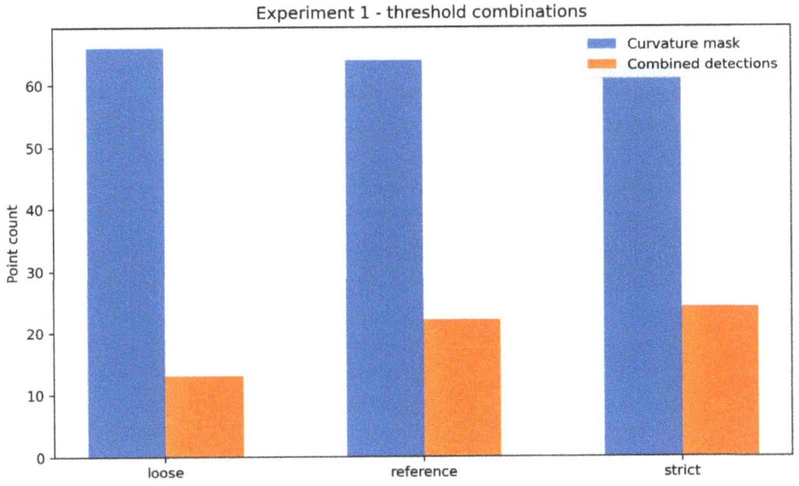


**Figure A4.** Experiment 1: Comparison of loose, reference, and strict threshold configurations. The reference setting preserves stable DBSCAN clustering (60 clusters) and a consistent alpha-shape area, avoiding both the merging observed in the loose setting (28 clusters) and the fragmentation observed in the strict setting (107 clusters).

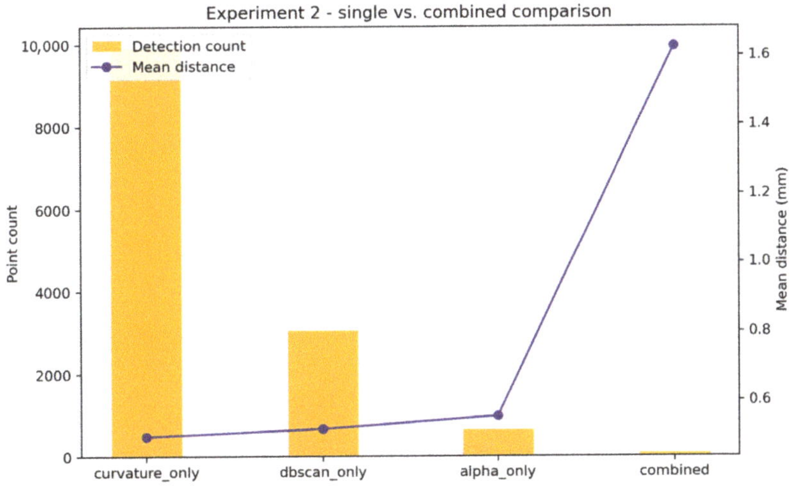


**Figure A5.** Experiment 2: Comparison of single detectors with the hybrid detector. The hybrid method significantly reduces false positives (66 points vs. 9924 for curvature-only) while emphasizing structurally meaningful deviations (mean distance 1.626 mm).

*Appendix F.1. Experiment 1: Threshold Combination Study*

To evaluate the stability of curvature-, density-, and topology-based features under different parameter configurations, three joint threshold settings were examined: a loose configuration that prioritized higher recall, a strict configuration that enforced aggressive pruning, and a balanced reference configuration.

The loose setting produced 66 curvature-mask points but only 28 DBSCAN clusters, indicating under-segmentation due to merging of structurally distinct regions. The strict configuration retained 63 curvature-mask points but resulted in 107 DBSCAN clusters, fragmenting coherent areas into many small subregions. In contrast, the reference configuration maintained 60 stable clusters and produced 22 combined detections while keeping the alpha-shape area nearly constant (13,730.64 $mm^2$). These results demonstrate that the chosen thresholds avoid over-merging and over-fragmentation while preserving geometric fidelity.

*Appendix F.2. Experiment 2: Single vs. Hybrid Detector Comparison*

A second experiment compared three single-modality detectors—curvature-only, DBSCAN-only, and alpha-only—against the proposed hybrid detector integrating curvature cues, density clustering, and topology-based boundary features.

The curvature-only detector produced 9924 detections, yielding excessive false positives; the DBSCAN-only detector yielded 3042 detections due to local density sensitivity; and the alpha-only detector produced 635 detections but failed to capture surface-type anomalies because it relies solely on boundary topology.

In contrast, the hybrid detector retained only 66 high-confidence detections, representing a nearly 150× reduction relative to curvature-only, while increasing the mean deviation to 1.626 mm. This demonstrates that the hybrid approach effectively suppresses false positives while isolating structurally meaningful regions outside tolerance. Additionally, the DBSCAN cluster count remained stable at 60, showing that geometric structure is preserved during the filtering process.

## References


1. Besl, P.J.; McKay, N.D. A method for registration of 3-D shapes. *IEEE Trans. Pattern Anal. Mach. Intell.* **1992**, *14*, 239–256. [CrossRef]
2. Rusu, R.B.; Blodow, N.; Beetz, M. Fast Point Feature Histograms (FPFH) for 3D registration. In Proceedings of the 2009 IEEE International Conference on Robotics and Automation (ICRA), Kobe, Japan, 12–17 May 2009; pp. 3212–3217. [CrossRef]
3. Salti, S.; Tombari, F.; Di Stefano, L. SHOT: Unique signatures of histograms for surface and texture description. *Comput. Vis. Image Underst.* **2014**, *125*, 251–264. [CrossRef]
4. Guo, Y.; Sohel, F.; Bennamoun, M.; Lu, M.; Wan, J. Rotational Projection Statistics for 3D Local Surface Description and Object Recognition. *Int. J. Comput. Vis.* **2013**, *105*, 63–86. [CrossRef]
5. Qi, C.R.; Yi, L.; Su, H.; Guibas, L.J. PointNet++: Deep Hierarchical Feature Learning on Point Sets in a Metric Space. *arXiv* **2017**, arXiv:1706.02413.
6. Younes, R.; Yaacoub, C.; El Khoury, G.; Possik, J.; Abi Zeid Daou, R. Evaluation of Point-MAE for Robust Point Cloud Classification Across Diverse Datasets. In Proceedings of the 2024 International Conference on Smart Systems and Power Management (IC2SPM), Beiruit, Lebanon, 28–29 November 2024. [CrossRef]
7. Muzahid, A.A.M.; Wan, W.; Sohel, F.; Wu, L.; Hou, L. CurveNet: Curvature-based multitask learning deep networks for 3D object recognition. *IEEE/CAA J. Autom. Sinica* **2021**, *8*, 1177–1187. [CrossRef]
8. *ISO 25012:2008*; Software Product Quality Requirements and Evaluation—Data Quality Model. ISO: Geneva, Switzerland, 2008.
9. *ISO 1101:2017*; Geometrical Product Specifications (GPS)—Geometrical Tolerancing—Tolerances of Form, Orientation, Location and Run-Out. ISO: Geneva, Switzerland, 2017.
10. *ISO 8015:2011*; Geometrical Product Specifications (GPS)—Fundamentals—Concepts, Principles and Rules. ISO: Geneva, Switzerland, 2011.
11. Segal, A.; Haehnel, D.; Thrun, S. Generalized ICP. In *Robotics: Science and Systems*; MIT Press: Cambridge, MA, USA, 2009. [CrossRef]
12. Umeyama, S. Least-Squares Estimation of Transformation Parameters Between Two Point Patterns. *IEEE Trans. Pattern Anal. Mach. Intell.* **1991**, *13*, 376–380. [CrossRef]
13. Johnson, A.E.; Hebert, M. Using Spin Images for Efficient Object Recognition in Cluttered 3D Scenes. *IEEE Trans. Pattern Anal. Mach. Intell.* **1999**, *21*, 433. [CrossRef]
14. Frome, A.; Huber, D.; Kolluri, R.; Bülow, T.; Malik, J. Recognizing Objects in Range Data Using Regional Point Descriptors. *Lect. Notes Comput. Sci.* **2004**, *3023*, 224–237. [CrossRef]
15. Chen, Y.; Medioni, G. Object modelling by registration of multiple range images. *Image Vis. Comput.* **1992**, *10*, 145–155. [CrossRef]
16. Tombari, F.; Salti, S.; Di Stefano, L. Unique Shape Context for 3D Data Description. In Proceedings of the 3D Object Retrieval (3DOR'10), Firenze, Italy, 25 October 2010. [CrossRef]

17. Choi, H.; Kim, E. New Compact 3-Dimensional Shape Descriptor for a Depth Camera in Indoor Environments. *Sensors* **2017**, *17*, 876. [CrossRef] [PubMed]
18. Reuter, L.; Denkena, B.; Wichmann, M. Adaptive inspection planning using a digital twin for quality assurance. *Procedia CIRP* **2023**, *120*, 3–8. [CrossRef]
19. Sundaram, S.; Zeid, A. Artificial Intelligence-Based Smart Quality Inspection for Manufacturing. *Micromachines* **2023**, *14*, 570. [CrossRef]
20. Escudero, P.A.; López González, M.C.; García Valldecabres, J.L. Optimising Floor Plan Extraction: Applying DBSCAN and K-Means in Point Cloud Analysis of Valencia Cathedral. *Heritage* **2024**, *7*, 5787–5799. [CrossRef]
21. Liu, S.; Ni, H.; Li, C.; Zou, Y.; Luo, Y. DefectGAN: Synthetic Data Generation for EMU Defects Detection With Limited Data. *IEEE Sens. J.* **2024**, *24*, 17638–17652. [CrossRef]
22. Rusu, R.B.; Cousins, S. 3D is here: Point Cloud Library (PCL). In Proceedings of the 2011 IEEE International Conference on Robotics and Automation, Shanghai, China, 9–13 May 2011; pp. 1–4. [CrossRef]
23. Soudarissanane, S.; Lindenbergh, R.; Menenti, M.; Teunissen, P. Scanning geometry: Influencing factor on the quality of terrestrial laser scanning points. *ISPRS J. Photogramm. Remote Sens.* **2011**, *66*, 389–399. [CrossRef]
24. Li, P.; Wang, R.; Wang, Y.; Gao, G. Fast Method of Registration for 3D RGB Point Cloud with Improved Four Initial Point Pairs Algorithm. *Sensors* **2020**, *20*, 138. [CrossRef]

electronics

MDPI

*Article*

# End-to-End Camera Pose Estimation with Camera Ray Token

**Jin-Woo Kim [1,2] and Jong-Eun Ha [3,*]**

1 Graduate School of Automotive Engineering, Seoul National University of Science and Technology, Seoul 01811, Republic of Korea; kjwkch@seoultech.ac.kr
2 Technology Research Lab, Ways1, Uiwang Si 16006, Gyeonggi-do, Republic of Korea
3 Department of Mechanical and Automotive Engineering, Seoul National University of Science and Technology, Seoul 01811, Republic of Korea
* Correspondence: jeha@seoultech.ac.kr

**Abstract:** This paper proposes an end-to-end method for estimating camera poses using ray regression, a diffusion model-based ray inference approach. The conventional ray regression model outputs moments and directions, which are then converted into the final pose through traditional methods; however, this conversion process can introduce errors. In this work, we replace the conversion process with a deep learning network to achieve more stable pose estimation performance. Furthermore, the proposed model incorporates an additional rendering network for image reconstruction, demonstrating not only camera pose estimation but also the scalability to scene reconstruction. Leveraging the learned features, the model enables image rendering from novel viewpoints. Experimental results demonstrate that the proposed end-to-end method outperforms the conventional ray regression approach under the same training conditions, achieving approximately a 16% improvement in camera pose estimation and a nearly 30% gain in translation accuracy.

**Keywords:** camera pose estimation; end-to-end; ray; point cloud

## 1. Introduction

As technology advances, the use of robots is becoming increasingly common in tasks that involve risk or require simple repetitive operations. In the near future, it is expected that robots capable of handling more complex tasks will replace a significant portion of human labor [1,2]. To carry out their tasks, robots must perceive and localize their surroundings using sensors within their working environment. Commonly used sensors include cameras, LiDAR, and RADAR. Among these, cameras differ from the others in that they cannot directly capture 3D information, and the quality of information varies significantly depending on lighting conditions. Nevertheless, cameras are relatively inexpensive, provide color information, and can capture more information at once, making them an essential sensor for the widespread adoption of robots. The advantages of camera sensors, such as low cost and rich information content, make them indispensable in modern robotics. Consequently, the use of camera-only robots is expected to increase. Therefore, achieving accurate pose estimation and real-time performance with cameras is critical, and this challenge is becoming easier to overcome with advances in hardware and the emergence of deep learning.

Ray diffusion [3] is a method based on diffusion models, a class of generative models that have recently demonstrated outstanding performance in image and audio synthesis. However, diffusion models are inherently slow due to their reliance on iterative denoising processes to learn data distributions, which makes real-time performance challenging. The authors of ray diffusion also discussed the performance of ray regression, which uses only a single denoising step. They demonstrated that ray regression achieves strong performance and is well-suited for real-time applications. Ray regression outputs rays characterized by their moments and directions—information that precedes the final pose estimation—and employs traditional methods to infer camera poses [3].

In this study, we adopt the ray regression model, replacing the traditional pose estimation step with a deep learning-based approach. The replacement deep learning architecture is designed to mimic the structure of the conventional method. The concept of rays, originating from NeRF [4], refers to virtual lines that pass through a 3D space and convey information about scene color or depth. Building upon this concept, we extend the model by incorporating a rendering network for additional image reconstruction. Our approach demonstrates stable pose estimation performance, strong generalization ability, and the potential for scalability toward image reconstruction. In particular, accurate and stable camera pose estimation is crucial for visual odometry (VO) and Simultaneous Localization and Mapping (SLAM) in the field of autonomous driving, to which our stable method can make a significant contribution.

## 2. Related Works

Traditional methods for inferring each camera's pose using multiple images involve extracting features from images, performing matching across individual images, and then verifying the matches geometrically to remove noise, thereby enabling accurate pose estimation. HF-Net [5] utilizes a feature-extraction network to extract image features, which are then globally matched, followed by local refinement, enabling robust pose estimation across large-scale environments. RelPose [6] extracts features using a CNN and combines the features of two images with a probabilistic relative rotation matrix. From this, a three-layer MLP predicts pose values, enabling the probabilistic evaluation of energy-based symmetry and uncertainty, thereby allowing for accurate pose estimation even with a limited number of images. Pose diffusion [7] employs a diffusion model to progressively optimize camera parameters, leveraging epipolar geometry for fine-tuning. This enables the estimation of both intrinsic and extrinsic camera parameters, regardless of the number of images. RelPose++ [8] extends RelPose to handle multiple images simultaneously and introduces a transformer to estimate camera poses jointly. In particular, instead of normalizing relative to the first camera, it uses the optical centers of all cameras as the reference for translation estimation, thereby improving inference stability. GeoNeRF [9] encodes multiple images using FPNs, applies homography transformations to generate tokens, and combines these tokens with those of the target view for information exchange via a transformer. The density is calculated using the target view tokens from the exchanged tokens, and color values are derived from source image tokens. Rendering is performed through volume rendering, as in NeRF, using the computed density and color values. The performance improves with the addition of more source images, and the approach demonstrates the feasibility of a generalized model that does not require environment-specific training. GNT [10] generalizes NeRF by employing two transformers: a view transformer to define space from source views and a ray transformer for rendering. However, during image reconstruction, it searches for features from sources based on epipolar geometry, which results in slower performance.

## 3. Method

Ray diffusion [3] divides an image into patches, where the center of each patch is represented as a ray. From the generated rays, the camera's intrinsic and extrinsic matrices are estimated using an optimization method. In this paper, however, we observed an issue where the intrinsic parameters were estimated differently for the same camera, even though they should remain consistent. Since the intrinsic parameters are already known in most SLAM applications, we proceed under the assumption that they are given. Moreover, since ray diffusion is unsuitable for real-time applications, we base our study on ray regression, which was also discussed in the paper on ray diffusion. Ray regression removes the diffusion process from ray diffusion, achieving approximately 83 times faster inference speed while retaining about 94% of its performance, making it more suitable for real-time systems.

### 3.1. Pose Estimation Network

In the ray regression, the input image is divided into 16 × 16 patches, and the center ray of each patch is represented in the Plücker coordinate system. According to Plücker coordinates [11], a line can be expressed as $r = \langle d, m \rangle$, which is known to represent an infinite line uniquely. For the central ray of an image patch, the moment is computed as $m = p \times d$, where $p \in \mathbb{R}^3$ denotes the camera center and $d \in \mathbb{R}^3$ denotes the ray direction. The conventional model calculates the camera center $c$ from the output rays using Equation (1).

$$c = \operatorname{argmin}_{p \in \mathbb{R}^3} \sum_{\langle d,m \rangle \in R} ||p \times d - m||^2 \tag{1}$$

The rotation matrix $R$ and the camera intrinsic matrix $K$ are obtained by first computing the optimal homography matrix using the DLT method [12], and then applying QR decomposition, where $K$ corresponds to the upper triangular matrix $R$, and $R$ corresponds to Q. Using the computed RRR, the translation matrix $t$ is then calculated as $t = -R^T c$.

However, a discrepancy arises when examining the actual computation of the camera center. Specifically, while the ground truth is given as $m = p \times d$ with $p = c$, when inferring from the predicted $\langle d, m \rangle$ of the trained model and recomputing the camera center $c$ as $p' = d \times m$, the resulting $p'$ may differ from the original $p$. Consequently, the calculated camera center $c$ inevitably contains some error compared to the true value.

In conclusion, since $R, t, K$ can be computed from $m, d$ through a minimization process, they can reasonably be replaced by a deep learning approach. To address the error occurring in the translation $t$ computed in the ray regression, we introduce an additional network that directly estimates $R$ and $t$.

Figure 1 illustrates the original ray regression architecture and the modified design. In the original ray regression, the moment and the direction were simultaneously computed from the Diffusion Transformer (DiT) [13]. However, both the moment and the direction were used for translation estimation when inferring camera pose using traditional methods. In contrast, only the direction was used for rotation estimation, comparing it against the patch-center direction in the NDC coordinate system.

In the modified architecture, the features for computing the moment and direction are separated, allowing each feature to calculate the moment and direction independently. Furthermore, the features extracted before the head are stored and utilized in an additional network designed to estimate the camera pose parameters $R, t$.

Figure 2 presents the proposed network architecture for estimating $R, t$. The moment features and direction features used as inputs are taken from the outputs of Figure 1b, with the same color coding. Figure 2a illustrates the architecture constructed using the input format of ray regression: for estimating $R$, the inferred ray directions and the patch rays are used, while for estimating $t$, the inferred ray moments and directions are employed. Here, a patch ray refers to the direction vector of a ray expressed in the NDC coordinate system at the center of each patch. Figure 2b, in contrast, shows the architecture that uses only the inferred ray information as input to estimate $R, t$ without providing patch center information.

### 3.2. Image Rendering Network

When training the pose estimation network, the feature representation that infers the central ray of each image patch is obtained. This feature can infer the central ray based on the information within the patch and thus can be regarded as a compressed representation of the rays that constitute the patch. By using the compressed image features as keys and values in rendering, and applying the inferred $R, t$ it becomes possible to generate the ray of a specific pixel, which is then used as the query in rendering. In this way, the patch-center ray of a specific ray provides the association needed to retrieve the most relevant feature, allowing the color to be synthesized.

Figure 3 illustrates the architecture of the rendering network. The DiT features are derived from the outputs shown in Figure 1b, which are indicated with the same color coding.

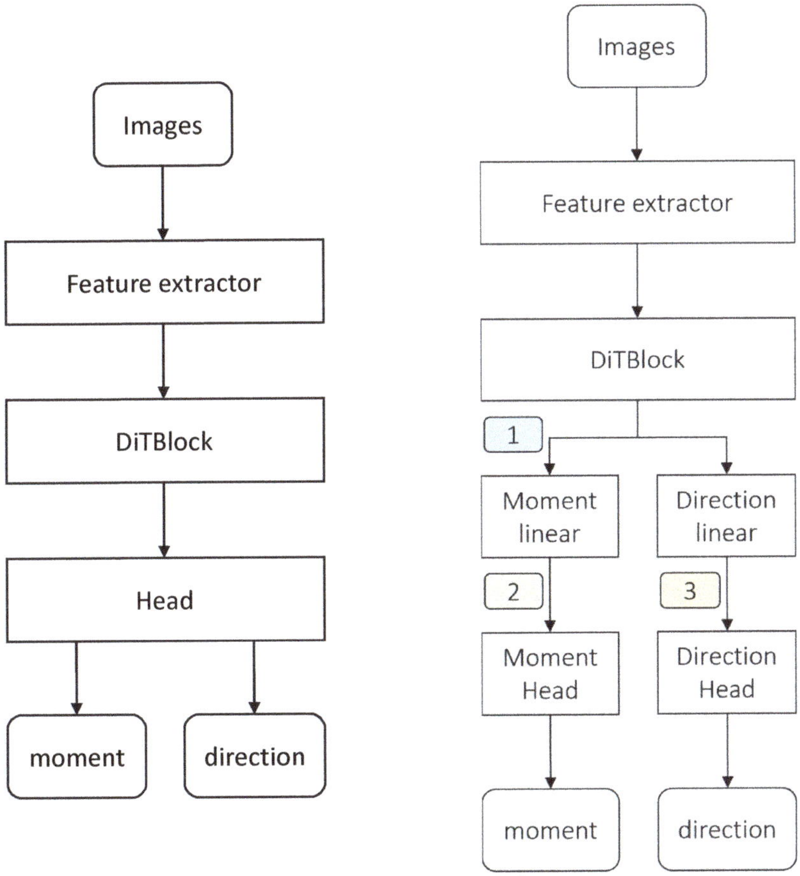


(a) (b)

**Figure 1.** Ray prediction network architectures (**a**) ray regression prediction architecture (**b**) our prediction architecture (detailed network structure is represented in Figure 2, and the color of the rectangle is related to Figure 2).

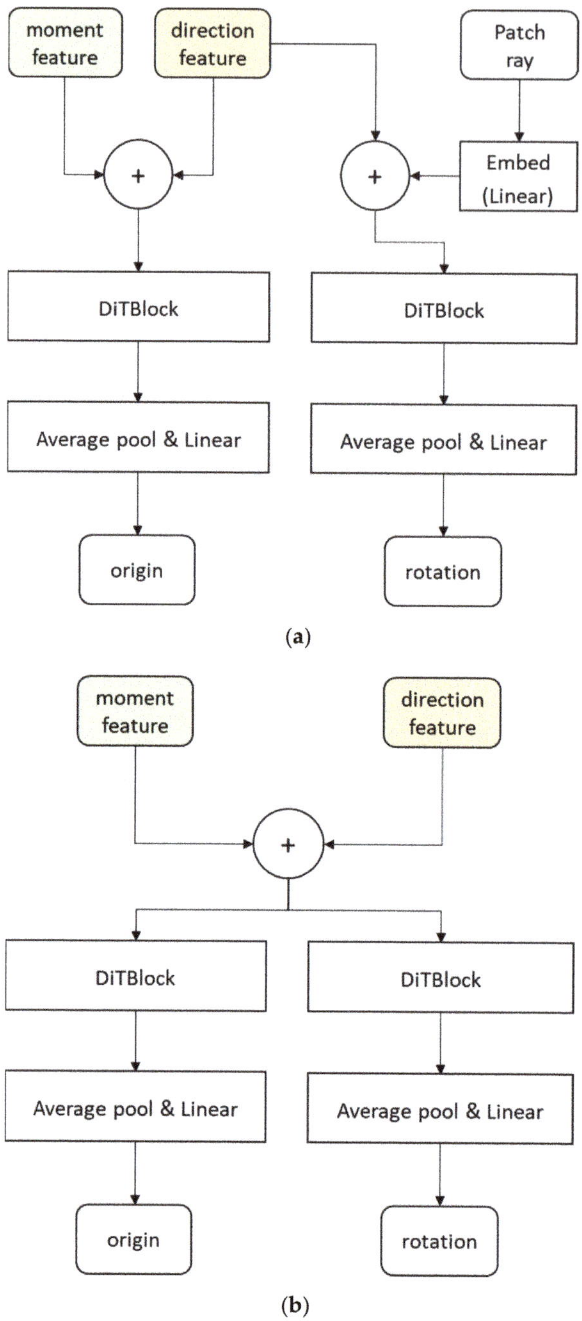


**Figure 2.** The proposed network architecture for estimating pose (**a**) block 1: with patch center information; (**b**) block 2: without patch center information. The moment feature input is utilized from 2 in Figure 1b, and the direction feature input is utilized from 3 in Figure 1b.

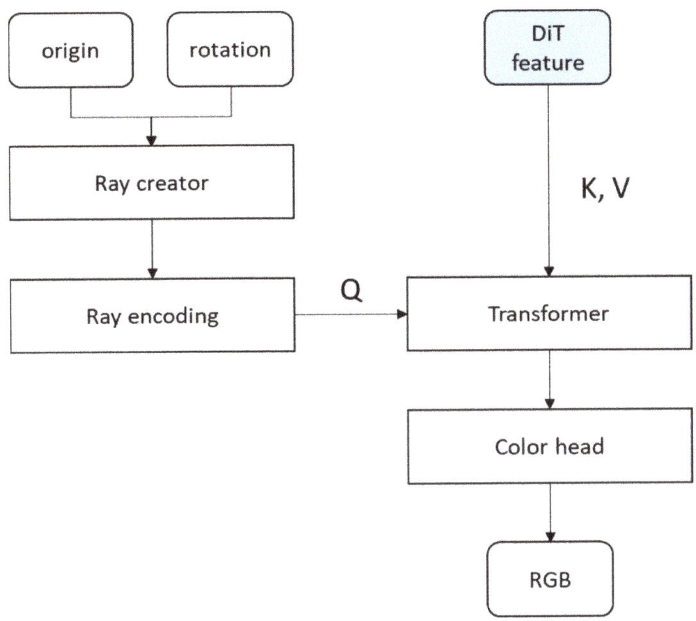


**Figure 3.** Rendering network with patch features. The DiT feature used here is illustrated as 1 in Figure 1b.

### 3.3. Loss Terms

Equation (2) represents the loss function used for training. $L_{ray}$ is a modified version of the loss function employed in ray regression, while $L_{geo}$ is the loss function used to estimate the camera pose directly.

$$L = L_{ray} + L_{geo} + L_{render} \tag{2}$$

Although ray regression was described as using an L2 loss function defined as the L2 error divided by the number of rays in the set, its actual implementation employed a loss function based on the mean L2 error. In this paper, we revise this by adopting an L2 loss function divided by the total number of rays, as expressed in Equation (3). Here, $N_r$ denotes the total number of rays, $\hat{r}_i$ represents the predicted ray vector, and $r_i$ denotes the ground-truth ray vector.

$$L_{ray} = \frac{1}{N_r}\sum_{i=1}^{N_r} \|\hat{r}_i - r_i\|_2^2 \tag{3}$$

Equation (4) defines the loss function for camera pose. $\hat{R}$ denotes the predicted quaternion, $R$ the ground-truth quaternion, $\hat{t}$ the predicted translation, $t$ the ground-truth translation, and $N_C$ the number of cameras. $L_S$ represents the Smooth L1 loss.

$$L_{geo} = \frac{1}{N_C}\sum_{i=1}^{N_C} \left(L_S(\hat{R}, R) - L_S(\hat{t}, t)\right) \tag{4}$$

Equation (5) defines the loss function for rendering. The loss function commonly used in NeRF-based methods is employed. Here, $N_R$ denotes the number of training rays generated using $R$, $t$. $\hat{C}$ represents the predicted color, and $C$ is the ground-truth color.

$$L_{render} = \frac{1}{N_R}\sum_{i=1}^{N_R} \|\hat{C} - C\|_2^2 \tag{5}$$

## 4. Experimental Results

### 4.1. Datasets and Implementation Details

Based on ray diffusion, we implemented an additional network for estimating camera pose using PyTorch [14]. The training data was taken from CO3Dv2 [15], and training was conducted for 300,000 iterations each on four NVIDIA RTX 3090 GPUs (24GB) and four NVIDIA A5000 GPUs (24GB). CO3D [15] is a video dataset comprising approximately 200 consecutive images of 51 specific object categories, where the ground-truth camera information is provided as estimates obtained using COLMAP. However, this dataset contains some samples with large errors. In the original ray regression, invalid COLMAP estimates were filtered out by discarding data where the ground-truth translation vector exceeded $1 \times 10^5$, or the determinant of the rotation matrix was smaller than 0.99 or larger than 1.01. The data sampling method employed the same strategy as the ray diffusion baseline.

In this paper, in addition to those conditions, we further excluded data where (1) the focal length in the NDC coordinate system was larger than 10, which indicates cases where only part of the object was captured, and (2) the size of the principal axis obtained through PCA analysis exceeded 20, to remove biased data. The learning rate was fixed at $1 \times 10^{-4}$, the same as in the original, and the batch size was set to 4 per GPU.

Furthermore, in ray regression, the input images were masked to crop only the region containing the object and resized into square images with a 1:1 aspect ratio. In contrast, for potential integration with NeRF in this work, we did not apply masking and instead used the full images, resized to a 1:1 ratio.

The feature extractor used is DINOv2 [16], which is identical to the one employed in ray diffusion. The DiT [13] was also set up with the same architectural specifications as ray diffusion, utilizing 8 layers, 16 multi-heads, and a 1152 hidden layer dimensions.

### 4.2. Experimental Results and Discussions

Figure 4 visualizes the input images and the results of the inferred rays. Similar to ray regression, the camera pose estimation network computes the camera pose parameters $R, t$ from the ray moments and directions; therefore, both the moments and directions were trained in the same manner. It can be observed that the predicted ray moments and directions are learned in the same form as the inferred rays produced by ray regression, and that $R, t$ are estimated close to the ground truth. The dotted lines indicate the ground truth, while the solid lines represent the visualized predicted $R, t$. Since the full images were used without masking and resized to an aspect ratio of 1, black zero-padding can be observed in the inputs. In the second and fourth columns, failures in predicting patch-center rays occur in the padded regions, which are presumed to cause a degradation in rotation estimation performance.

Table 1 presents the performance evaluation of the rotational component using CO3D, and Table 2 presents the evaluation of the translational component. The evaluation follows the same protocol as in the ray regression. Seen categories refer to object classes included in training, while unseen categories denote object classes not used during training. In addition, since the filtering conditions of the CO3D dataset were modified, the pretrained parameters of ray diffusion and ray regression were used for performance evaluation. Ray regression* denotes the evaluation results obtained when ray regression was retrained under the same conditions, including training iterations, batch size, and additional dataset filtering, as our method. The masking strategy was kept identical to that in the ray diffusion paper. Bold values indicate the best performance compared to ray regression, and underlined values indicate the best performance compared to ray diffusion.

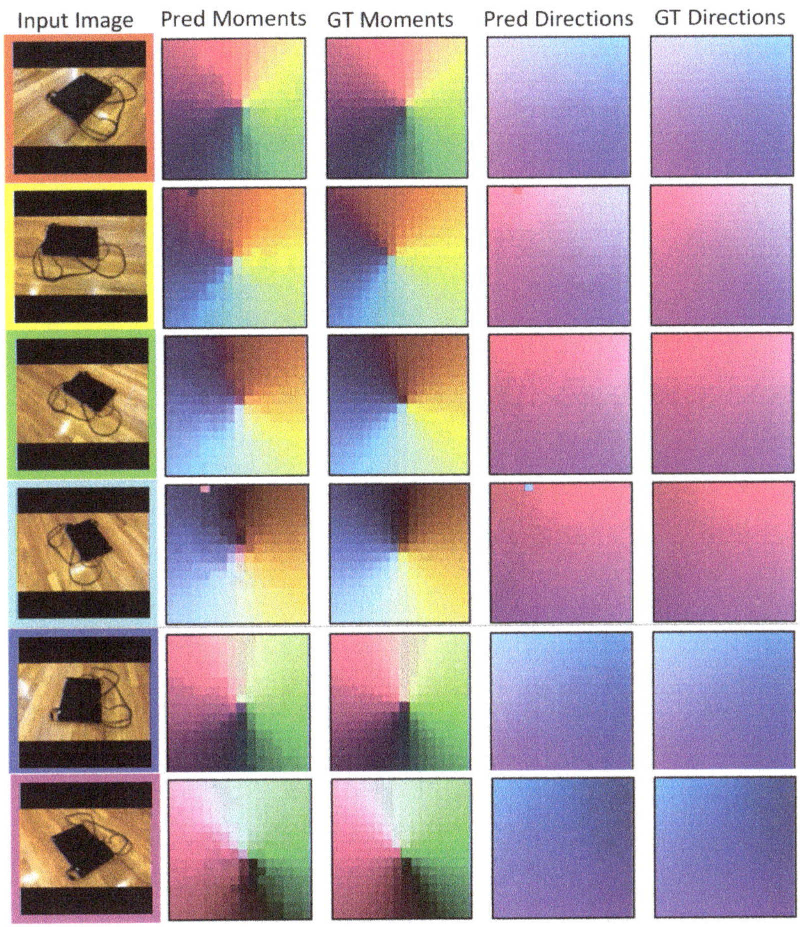


(a)

(b)

**Figure 4.** Results of the proposed algorithm (**a**) visualization of ray moments and direction (**b**) visualization of computed pose (each color corresponds to the color of the input image, where the dashed lines represent the ground truth and the solid lines represent the prediction).

**Table 1.** CO3D camera rotation inference accuracy (@ 15°).

| Number of images | 2 | 3 | 4 | 5 | 6 | 7 | 8 |
|---|---|---|---|---|---|---|---|
| | | | Seen Categories | | | | |
| Ray Diffusion [3] | 92.9 | 93.7 | 94.0 | 94.2 | 94.4 | 94.5 | 94.7 |
| Ray Regression [3] | **90.2** | **90.3** | **90.5** | **90.9** | **91.2** | **91.2** | **91.1** |
| Ray Regression* | 79.1 | 80.3 | 80.4 | 80.9 | 80.5 | 80.5 | 80.5 |
| Ours (R + T) | 87.4 | 86.7 | 86.5 | 86.7 | 86.7 | 86.7 | 86.5 |
| Ours (R + T + Render) | 80.9 | 81.3 | 80.8 | 80.7 | 80.7 | 80.7 | 80.3 |
| | | | Unseen Categories | | | | |
| Ray Diffusion [3] | 84.8 | 87.3 | 88.4 | 89.0 | 89.0 | 89.4 | 89.6 |
| Ray Regression [3] | 81.2 | 82.7 | **83.4** | **84.0** | **84.1** | **84.4** | **84.5** |
| Ray Regression* | 64.4 | 65.1 | 64.0 | 64.3 | 64.2 | 64.9 | 65.0 |
| Ours (R + T) | **84.0** | **83.3** | 83.3 | 83.2 | 83.1 | 83.0 | 82.7 |
| Ours (R + T + Render) | 79.2 | 78.2 | 78.3 | 77.8 | 77.5 | 77.2 | 76.5 |

**Table 2.** CO3D camera translation inference accuracy (@ 0.1).

| Number of images | 2 | 3 | 4 | 5 | 6 | 7 | 8 |
|---|---|---|---|---|---|---|---|
| | | | Seen Categories | | | | |
| Ray Diffusion [3] | 100 | 95.0 | 91.5 | 88.9 | 87.5 | 86.3 | 85.3 |
| Ray Regression [3] | 100 | 92.3 | 86.8 | 83.2 | 81.0 | 79.0 | 77.4 |
| Ray Regression* | 100 | 85.5 | 75.4 | 69.5 | 65.3 | 63.2 | 60.5 |
| Ours (R + T) | 100 | 99.7 | 99.6 | 99.6 | 99.5 | 99.5 | 99.4 |
| Ours (R + T + Render) | 100 | **99.8** | **99.6** | **99.6** | **99.5** | **99.5** | **99.4** |
| | | | Unseen Categories | | | | |
| Ray Diffusion [3] | 100 | 88.5 | 83.1 | 79.0 | 75.7 | 74.6 | 72.4 |
| Ray Regression [3] | 100 | 85.5 | 76.7 | 72.4 | 69.1 | 66.1 | 64.9 |
| Ray Regression* | 100 | 72.9 | 58.5 | 51.8 | 48.1 | 45.1 | 43.9 |
| Ours (R + T) | 100 | 99.3 | 98.9 | 98.9 | 98.5 | 98.3 | 98.2 |
| Ours (R + T + Render) | 100 | **99.4** | **98.9** | **98.8** | **98.5** | **98.4** | **98.3** |

The comparison model in this paper uses block1 and applies a tanh activation function at the final stage of rotation estimation. The proposed method demonstrates superior accuracy in camera translation estimation compared to ray regression and ray diffusion, regardless of whether the evaluation is conducted on unseen categories. In particular, as the number of camera images increases from 3 to 8, ray regression exhibits a performance drop of approximately 15% even within the seen categories. In contrast, our method shows only a decrease of about 0.3%, demonstrating more stable performance.

On the other hand, the accuracy of camera rotation estimation is measured to be about 4% lower than that of ray regression on seen categories. However, in unseen categories, it shows comparable performance to ray regression, suggesting that our method offers better generalization. When the rendering network is also included, the translation estimation performance improves slightly, whereas the rotation estimation performance decreases by approximately 5%. This appears to result from the fact that camera rays are represented in the normalized NDC coordinate system, which lacks sufficient information about the kinematic transformation relationships necessary to accurately describe spatial relations across images. Furthermore, compared to ray regression*, the proposed method achieves, on average, about 16% higher performance in rotation estimation and about 30% higher performance in translation estimation, demonstrating superior accuracy and faster convergence than existing approaches.

### 4.3. Ablation Studies

Tables 3 and 4 present the results under various training conditions. In Table 4, Model 1 corresponds to the baseline with block1, while Model 2 additionally applies a tanh activation function for rotation estimation. Using the activation function yields an improvement of about 3% for both seen and unseen categories.

**Table 3.** CO3D camera rotation inference accuracy in ablation studies (@ 15°).

| Number of images | 2 | 3 | 4 | 5 | 6 | 7 | 8 |
|---|---|---|---|---|---|---|---|
| | | | Seen Categories | | | | |
| 1.—Our block1 (R + T) | 84.5 | 83.7 | 83.6 | 83.7 | 83.9 | 83.9 | 83.9 |
| 2.—Rotation w/tanh | 87.4 | 86.7 | 86.5 | 86.7 | 86.7 | 86.7 | 86.5 |
| 3.—ConvNext encoder all freeze * | 59.5 | 58.9 | 59.0 | 58.9 | 59.1 | 58.7 | 58.6 |
| 4.—ConvNext encoder all freeze | 50.6 | 49.5 | 49.4 | 49.4 | 49.6 | 49.8 | 49.7 |
| 5.—ConvNext encoder 0, 1 freeze | 60.8 | 60.3 | 60.6 | 60.9 | 61.0 | 60.9 | 60.8 |
| 6.—Our block1 (R + T + Render) | 80.9 | 81.3 | 80.8 | 80.7 | 80.7 | 80.7 | 80.3 |
| 7.—Our block2 (R + T) | 87.8 | 87.2 | 86.9 | 86.9 | 86.8 | 86.7 | 86.7 |
| 8.—Our block2 (R + T + Render) | 85.9 | 85.3 | 85.7 | 85.5 | 85.6 | 85.5 | 85.3 |
| | | | Unseen Categories | | | | |
| 1.—Our block1 (R + T) | 82.1 | 80.7 | 80.4 | 80.6 | 80.2 | 80.3 | 80.3 |
| 2.—Rotation w/tanh | 84.0 | 83.3 | 83.3 | 83.2 | 83.1 | 83.0 | 82.7 |
| 3.—ConvNext encoder all freeze * | 45.0 | 43.4 | 42.0 | 42.0 | 41.9 | 41.3 | 40.8 |
| 4.—ConvNext encoder all freeze | 26.0 | 24.5 | 24.5 | 24.4 | 24.1 | 23.8 | 23.5 |
| 5.—ConvNext encoder 0, 1 freeze | 51.2 | 51.1 | 51.8 | 52.3 | 52.7 | 52.8 | 52.9 |
| 6.—Our block1 (R + T + Render) | 79.2 | 78.2 | 78.3 | 77.8 | 77.5 | 77.2 | 76.5 |
| 7.—Our block2 (R + T) | 84.6 | 83.3 | 82.6 | 81.6 | 81.8 | 81.5 | 81.8 |
| 8.—Our block2 (R + T + Render) | 82.3 | 81.2 | 81.5 | 81.0 | 81.1 | 81.0 | 80.6 |

Models 3, 4, and 5 in Table 4 replace the image encoder from DINOv2 [16]'s ViT-S/14 distilled model with the ConvNeXt-T, a tiny version of ConvNeXt [17]. Model 3 utilizes an input resolution of 224 × 224 and processes the output of stage 2, resulting in a 14 × 14 feature map that is similar in size to that of DINOv2. Models 4 and 5 instead employ a doubled input resolution of 448 × 448, which allows stage 3 to also output a 14 × 14 feature map. Compared to Model 1, Model 3 exhibits a performance drop of approximately 50%, and Model 4 shows a drop of about 71%. Model 5, which partially fine-tunes parts of the encoder while following the same configuration as Model 4, reduces the performance degradation to about 38% relative to Model 1.

Although ConvNeXt-T has a comparable computational cost and parameter size to DINOv2 ViT-S/14, it outperforms DINOv2 ViT-S/14 on ImageNet-1k but exhibits poor transfer learning performance. These results indicate that CNN-based encoders require partial fine-tuning during transfer learning to achieve competitive results. Moreover, despite using a deeper encoder, Model 4 performs worse than Model 3, indicating that encoders optimized for the classification domain may be unsuitable when transferred to other tasks.

**Table 4.** CO3D camera translation inference accuracy in ablation studies (@ 0.1).

| Number of images | 2 | 3 | 4 | 5 | 6 | 7 | 8 |
|---|---|---|---|---|---|---|---|
| | | | Seen Categories | | | | |
| 1.—Our block1 (R + T) | 100 | 99.7 | 99.6 | 99.6 | 99.5 | 99.5 | 99.4 |
| 2.—Rotation w/tanh | 100 | 99.7 | 99.6 | 99.6 | 99.5 | 99.5 | 99.4 |
| 3.—ConvNext encoder all freeze * | 100 | 99.7 | 99.3 | 99.1 | 98.9 | 98.7 | 98.6 |
| 4.—ConvNext encoder all freeze | 100 | 99.6 | 99.2 | 98.9 | 98.6 | 98.4 | 98.2 |
| 5.—ConvNext encoder 0, 1 freeze | 100 | 99.4 | 99.0 | 98.7 | 98.4 | 98.3 | 98.1 |
| 6.—Our block1 (R + T + Render) | 100 | 99.8 | 99.6 | 99.6 | 99.5 | 99.5 | 99.4 |
| 7.—Our block2 (R + T) | 100 | 99.8 | 99.7 | 99.6 | 99.4 | 99.5 | 99.5 |
| 8.—Our block2 (R + T + Render) | 100 | 99.6 | 99.2 | 98.9 | 98.6 | 98.4 | 98.2 |
| | | | Unseen Categories | | | | |
| 1.—Our block1 (R + T) | 100 | 99.3 | 98.9 | 98.9 | 98.5 | 98.3 | 98.2 |
| 2.—Rotation w/tanh | 100 | 99.7 | 99.6 | 99.6 | 99.5 | 99.5 | 99.4 |
| 3.—ConvNext encoder all freeze * | 100 | 98.8 | 98.2 | 97.6 | 97.2 | 99.5 | 99.4 |
| 4.—ConvNext encoder all freeze | 100 | 98.6 | 97.3 | 96.7 | 95.9 | 95.5 | 94.9 |
| 5.—ConvNext encoder 0, 1 freeze | 100 | 99.0 | 98.1 | 97.7 | 96.8 | 96.8 | 96.5 |
| 6.—Our block1 (R + T + Render) | 100 | 99.4 | 98.9 | 98.8 | 98.5 | 98.4 | 98.3 |
| 7.—Our block2 (R + T) | 100 | 99.1 | 98.6 | 98.6 | 98.5 | 98.4 | 98.2 |
| 8.—Our block2 (R + T + Render) | 100 | 99.1 | 98.9 | 99.0 | 98.6 | 98.5 | 98.4 |

Another possible reason is that DINOv2 was trained using multiple pretraining datasets with masked autoencoding (MAE), making it more generalizable and less domain-specific than encoders tailored strictly for classification. On the other hand, replacing the encoder with ConvNeXt reduces the memory requirement by approximately 4 GB, and even when the input resolution is doubled, the memory usage remains almost unchanged. This suggests an advantage in handling high-resolution images. Furthermore, ConvNeXtV2 has been reported to guarantee improved performance when pretrained with MAE in a CNN-appropriate manner, indicating a promising direction for future improvements.

### 4.4. Rendering Quality Analysis

Figure 5 presents the results rendered to the original resolution image via the rendering network. This demonstrates the feasibility of scene rendering by incorporating the rendering network, which takes the DiT features and rays generated by the camera pose estimation network as input.

Figure 6 shows the PSNR curve when the model is trained using Block 2 and the rendering loss. It can be observed that the performance improvement becomes significantly slower after approximately 5000 training iterations. This suggests that the current network architecture is insufficient for effectively reconstructing detailed color information.

This limitation in rendering performance is considered to be associated with the lower overall pose estimation performance seen in Tables 3 and 4 when the rendering loss is applied. Therefore, we anticipate that the scalability aspect can be further complemented by research focused on enhancing the network's rendering performance.

**Figure 5.** Results of rendering network.

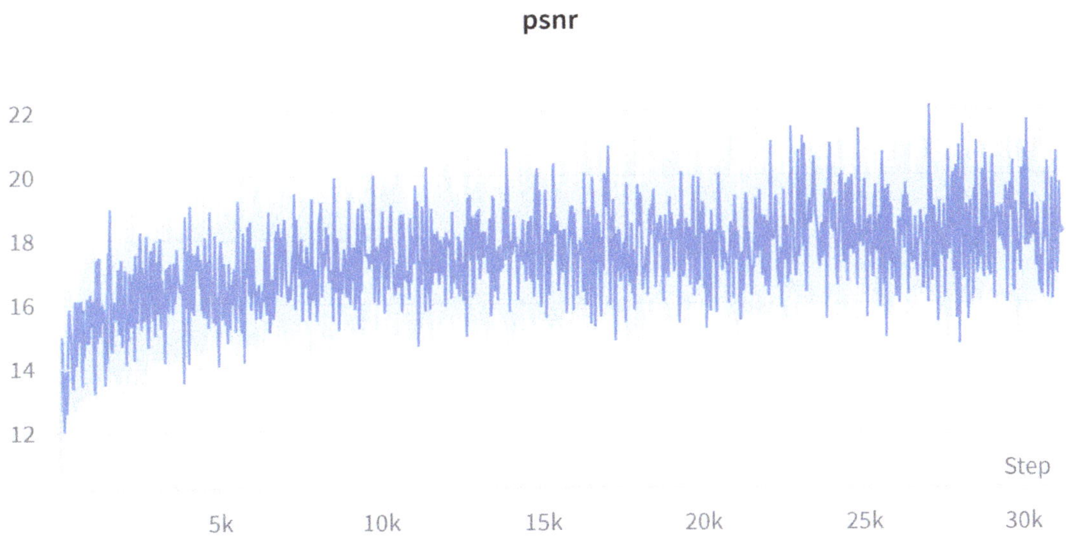


**Figure 6.** PSNR performance curve during training with rendering loss and Block 2.

## 5. Conclusions

In this paper, we improved the ray regression method—which estimates camera pose by inferring rays from images and computing the pose parameters using traditional methods—by incorporating a deep learning-based network to directly assess the camera pose, thereby enabling more stable inference. Under the same training conditions, the proposed method achieves approximately 16% higher accuracy in rotation estimation and 30% higher in translation estimation, with faster convergence than ray regression. Furthermore, unlike ray regression, which relies on masked images that focus only on regions around the object, our method uses the entire image, resulting in more stable translation estimation performance. However, since the input images are converted to a square aspect ratio (1:1), the added padding regions lack comparable features, which appears to cause a drop of approximately 2% in rotation estimation performance compared to ray regression. We expect that this limitation can be overcome by using unpadded images and incorporating image size information to improve the estimation of patch-center rays, thereby enhancing rotation matrix estimation.

When adding a rendering network to the pipeline, we observed a decrease in rotation estimation performance compared to when the rendering network was not included. This is likely due to discrepancies between the normalized NDC coordinate system, in which the camera pose is computed, and the non-normalized coordinate system in which query rays are represented. This issue could be resolved by requesting queries in the normalized coordinate system or by introducing an additional deep learning module for coordinate transformation for each camera [18,19].

Moreover, as shown by Deformable-DETR [20], comparing only a subset of highly correlated tokens in a transformer decoder yields faster training and inference, as well as higher accuracy, compared to comparing all tokens. Since rays generated from compressed features can appear only in limited views of other cameras, comparing candidate features with higher correlation would be more effective than comparing all image features. Finally, high-resolution images are required to detect small objects such as traffic signs or lights. Since CNN-based features enable scaling to higher resolutions without significantly increasing computational cost, future research should also explore leveraging such features to improve performance. Crucially, the enhanced stability in camera pose inference demonstrated by our End-to-End deep learning network lays a robust foundation for future work, and we intend to proceed with research focused on Simultaneous Localization and Mapping (SLAM).

**Author Contributions:** Conceptualization, J.-W.K. and J.-E.H.; methodology, J.-W.K. and J.-E.H.; software, J.-W.K.; validation, J.-W.K.; formal analysis, J.-W.K.; investigation, J.-W.K.; resources, J.-W.K.; data curation, J.-W.K.; writing—original draft preparation, J.-W.K.; writing—review and editing, J.-E.H.; visualization, J.-W.K.; supervision, J.-E.H.; project administration, J.-E.H.; funding acquisition, J.-E.H. All authors have read and agreed to the published version of the manuscript.

**Funding:** This work was supported by the National Research Foundation of Korea (NRF) through the Korean Government (MSIT) under Grant 2023R1A2C1005870.

**Data Availability Statement:** The authors do not have permission to share data.

**Acknowledgments:** This paper is based in part on the author's Ph.D. dissertation [21].

**Conflicts of Interest:** The authors declare no conflicts of interest.

## References

1. Zhang, Q.-N.; Zhang, F.-F.; Mai, Q. Robot adoption and laber demand: A new interpretation from external completion. *Technol. Soc.* **2023**, *74*, 102310. [CrossRef]
2. Kojima, T.; Zhu, Y.; Iwasawa, Y.; Kitamura, T.; Yan, G.; Morikuni, S.; Takanami, R.; Solano, A.; Matsushima, T.; Murakami, A.; et al. A comprehensive survey on physical risk control in the era of foundation model-enabled robotics. *arXiv* **2025**, arXiv:2505.12583v2. [CrossRef]
3. Zhang, J.Y.; Lin, A.; Kumar, M.; Yang, T.-H.; Ramanan, D.; Tulsiani, S. Camera as rays: Pose estimation via ray diffusion. In Proceedings of the International Conference on Learning Representations (ICLR), Vienna, Austria, 7–11 May 2024.
4. Mildenhall, B.; Srinivasan, P.; Tancik, M.; Barron, J.T.; Ramamoorthi, R.; Ng, R. NeRF: Representing scenes as neural radiance fields for view synthesis. In Proceedings of the European Conference on Computer Vision (ECCV), Glasgow, UK, 23–28 August 2020.
5. Sarlin, P.-E.; Cadena, C.; Siegwart, R.; Dymczyk, M. From coarse to fine: Robust hierarchical localization at large scale. In Proceedings of the IEEE/CVF Conference on Computer Vision and Pattern Recognition, Long Beach, CA, USA, 15–20 June 2019; pp. 12716–12725.
6. Zhang, J.Y.; Ramanan, D.; Tulsiani, S. Relpose: Predicting probabilistic relative rotation for single objects in the wild. In Proceedings of the European Conference on Computer Vision, Tel Aviv, Israel, 23–27 October 2022; pp. 592–611.
7. Wang, J.; Rupprecht, C.; Novotny, D. Posediffusion: Solving pose estimation via diffusion-aided bundle adjustment. In Proceedings of the IEEE/CVF International Conference on Computer Vision, Paris, France, 1–6 October 2023; pp. 9773–9783.

8. Lin, A.; Zhang, J.Y.; Ramanan, D.; Tulsiani, S. Relpose++: Recovering 6d poses from sparse-view observations. In Proceedings of the 2024 International Conference on 3D Vision (3DV), Davos, Switzerland, 18–21 March 2024; pp. 106–115.
9. Johari, M.M.; Lepoittevin, Y.; Fleuret, F. Geon erf: Generalizing nerf with geometry priors. In Proceedings of the IEEE/ CVF Conference on Computer Vision and Pattern Recognition, New Orleans, LA, USA, 18–24 June 2022; pp. 18365–18375.
10. Wang, P.; Chen, X.; Chen, T.; Venugopalan, S.; Wang, Z. Is attention all that nerf needs? *arXiv* **2022**, arXiv:2207.13298.
11. Plücker, J. *Analytisch-Geometrische Entwicklungen*, 2nd ed.; GD Baedeker: Essen, Germany, 1828.
12. Abdel-Aziz, Y.I.; Karara, H.M.; Hauck, M. Direct linear transformation from comparator coordinates into object space coordinates in close-range photogrammetry. *Photogramm. Eng. Remote Sens.* **2015**, *81*, 103–107. [CrossRef]
13. Peebles, W.; Xie, S. Scalable diffusion models with transformers. In Proceedings of the IEEE/CVF International Conference on Computer Vision, Paris, France, 1–6 October 2023; pp. 4195–4205.
14. Paszke, A. Pytorch: An imperative style, high-performance deep learning library. *arXiv* **2019**, arXiv:1912.01703.
15. Reizenstein, J.; Shapovalov, R.; Henzler, P.; Sbordone, L.; Labatut, P.; Novotny, D. Common objects in 3d: Large-scale learning and evaluation of real-life 3d category reconstruction. In Proceedings of the IEEE/CVF International Conference on Computer Vision, Montreal, QC, Canada, 10–17 October 2021; pp. 10901–10911.
16. Oquab, M.; Darcet, T.; Moutakanni, T.; Vo, H.; Szafraniec, M.; Khalidov, V.; Fernandez, P.; Haziza, D.; Massa, F.; El-Nouby, A.; et al. Dinov2: Learning robust visual features without supervision. *arXiv* **2023**, arXiv:2304.07193.
17. Liu, Z.; Mao, H.; Wu, C.-Y.; Feichtenhofer, C.; Darrell, T.; Xie, S. A convnet for the 2020s. In Proceedings of the IEEE/CVF Conference on Computer Vision and Pattern Recognition, New Orleans, LA, USA, 18–24 June 2022; pp. 11976–11986.
18. Shi, S.; Wang, X.; Li, H. Pointrcnn: 3d object proposal generation and detection from point cloud. In Proceedings of the IEEE/CVF Conference on Computer Vision and Pattern Recognition, Long Beach, CA, USA, 15–20 June 2019; pp. 770–779.
19. Wang, P.; Liu, Y.; Chen, Z.; Liu, L.; Liu, Z.; Komura, T.; Theobalt, C.; Wang, W. F2-nerf: Fast neural radiance field training with free camera trajectories. In Proceedings of the IEEE/CVF Conference on Computer Vision and Pattern Recognition, Vancouver, BC, Canada, 17–24 June 2023; pp. 4150–4159.
20. Zhu, X.; Su, W.; Lu, L.; Li, B.; Wang, X.; Dai, J. Deformable detr: Deformable transformers for end-to-end object detection. *arXiv* **2020**, arXiv:2010.04159.
21. Kim, J.W. Intergrated Enhancement of SLAM Components Using Deep Learning and Its Applicability. Ph.D. Thesis, Seoul National University of Science & Technology, Seoul, Republic of Korea, August 2025.

*electronics*

MDPI

*Article*

# Contactless Estimation of Heart Rate and Arm Tremor from Real Competition Footage of Elite Archers

**Byeong Seon An [1,†], Song Hee Park [1,†], Ji Yeon Moon [2,*] and Eui Chul Lee [3,*]**

1 Department of AI & Informatics, Graduate School, Sangmyung University, Hongjimun 2-Gil 20, Jongno-Gu, Seoul 03016, Republic of Korea; 202433029@sangmyung.kr (B.S.A.); 202432031@sangmyung.kr (S.H.P.)
2 Department of Sports ICT Convergence, Sangmyung University, Hongjimun 2-Gil 20, Jongno-Gu, Seoul 03016, Republic of Korea
3 Department of Human-Centered Artificial Intelligence, Graduate School, Sangmyung University, Hongjimun 2-Gil 20, Jongno-Gu, Seoul 03016, Republic of Korea
* Correspondence: jiyeon@smu.ac.kr (J.Y.M.); eclee@smu.ac.kr (E.C.L.)
† These authors contributed equally to this work.

**Abstract:** This study investigates the effects of heart rate and arm tremor on performance in elite archery, using non-contact physiological monitoring from real Olympic competition footage. A total of 50 video segments were extracted from publicly available international broadcasts, comprising athletes of various backgrounds. From these, heart rate signals were estimated via remote photoplethysmography (rPPG) from facial regions, and micro-movements were quantified from right and left arm regions using feature point tracking. Ordinal logistic regression was employed to evaluate the relationship between biometric variables and archery scores (10, 9, $\leq$8 points). Results showed that elevated heart rate ($\beta = -0.1166$; $p < 0.001$) and greater right-arm movement ($\beta = -6.1747$; $p = 0.008$) were significantly associated with lower scores. Athletes scoring 10 points exhibited significantly lower heart rate ($p < 0.001$) and reduced right-arm tremor ($p = 0.010$) compared to others. These findings support the hypothesis that physiological arousal and biomechanical instability impair performance, and they further demonstrate the feasibility of contactless monitoring in real competition environments. The proposed method enables objective, in-game performance evaluation and supports the development of personalized training systems for precision sports.

**Keywords:** archery biometric analysis; heart rate variability; micro-movement; non-contact; statistical analysis

## 1. Introduction

Since the Tokyo Olympics, monitoring athletes' tension through heart rate evaluation has emerged as an innovative element in sports broadcasting [1]. During the 2024 Paris Olympics, the Korean archery team captured global attention by winning gold medals in all events [2]. To prepare for such competitions, the Korean athletes focused on simulating diverse scenarios they might face during matches. For this year's preparations, the team implemented non-contact heart rate monitoring technology, allowing real-time tracking of heart rate fluctuations during training [3]. This method significantly enhanced athletes' psychological stability by providing an objective understanding of their physiological responses. Heart rate is a critical biomarker in archery, directly influencing an athlete's performance [4,5]. Fluctuations in heart rate reflect tension, stress, and psychological states, all of which can significantly impact results. For instance, with elevated heart rates, it is hypothesized that reduced stability can lead to lower scores. However, some athletes have demonstrated high performance even under such conditions. This discrepancy suggests that heart rate fluctuations do not always correlate with performance declines [6,7]. Such outcomes likely stem from the complex interaction of factors including physical fitness, mental focus, and heart rate regulation. In addition to physiological signals such as heart rate and tremor, behavioral and biochemical factors—such as anxiety, hormonal fluctuations, and neurotransmitter activity—may also influence performance in precision sports. Although not directly measured in this study, these factors form part of the broader psychophysiological context. Hand tremors have also been identified as a critical factor influencing athletic performance [8,9]. Micro-tremors during the shooting phase may stem from psychological tension but can also represent a physiological mechanism aimed at achieving precise targeting of the bullseye. A quantitative examination of the effects of these tremors on performance scores offers valuable insights for developing biometric-based psychological and physical training strategies.In particular, this study proposes heart rate variability and micro-tremor patterns as statistically significant indicators that can serve as novel metrics for evaluating athletes' readiness and performance potential. By adopting a non-contact, real-time physiological monitoring approach, the proposed method enables objective assessment without interfering with athletes' movements and concentration. This framework not only enhances training feedback but also holds strong potential for in-game application, offering actionable insights during live competitions. Moreover, by overcoming the limitations of controlled lab settings through the analysis of actual Olympic footage, this research lays a practical foundation for expanding physiological monitoring to sports such as shooting, golf, and other precision-dependent disciplines. Ultimately, this study provides essential groundwork for developing field-applicable, data-driven, personalized training systems that integrate biometric and performance analytics.This research analyzed actual Olympic match footage, ensuring accurate biometric data collection within realistic competitive settings without relying on additional equipment. Unlike traditional laboratory-based methods, this approach strives to deliver more reliable results by utilizing biometric data gathered directly from real-world competition environments. Thus, this study aims to investigate the effects of heart rate and body tremors on archery performance outcomes by applying non-contact physiological analysis to real Olympic footage. Specifically, the relationship between hand movements, heart rate, and performance scores is quantitatively evaluated using ordinal logistic regression and group-based comparisons. This study hypothesizes that elevated heart rate and excessive right-arm tremor negatively affect archery performance. While previous studies have largely relied on laboratory experiments or wearable devices, few have examined these associations in real-world competition settings. By analyzing Olympic-level footage using non-contact methods, this work contributes novel evidence on how physiological stability and biomechanical precision impact elite performance.

## 2. Related Works

Table 1 summarizes previous studies by categorizing them into two groups: psychological response analysis and biometric data-based analysis. Psychological response analysis focuses on HR, HRV, and attention, with limitations such as controlled indoor environments and limited data diversity. Biometric data-based analysis investigates factors such as postural sway, aiming time, and cardiopulmonary metrics but is constrained by the reliance on contact sensors and the predominance of novice participants in these studies.

**Table 1.** Summary of studies on archery performance and analysis.

| Method | Author(s) | Summary | Limitation(s) |
|---|---|---|---|
| Psychological Responses and Performance Analysis | Dal et al. [10] | Analyzed psychophysiological differences between VR and real archery by evaluating HR, HRV, and respiration rate. Found higher HRV in real archery and greater proportional changes in VR archery. | Conducted in a controlled environment, limiting generalization to real competition settings. |
| | Accardo et al. [11] | Investigated the relationship between HR and shooting performance in elite athletes, finding no significant differences in scores despite elevated HR levels. | Limited to indoor conditions and relied on traditional measurements like lactate levels, lacking data diversity. |
| | Vrbič et al. [12] | Compared HR, attention, relaxation levels, and arrow scores between recurve and compound archers, showing higher performance and attention in compound archers. | EEG data collected using a single channel, limiting detailed analysis of brainwave activity. |
| Analysis Based on Biometric and Movement Data | Keast et al. [13] | Explored the relationship between postural sway, aiming time, cardiac cycle, and arrow quality. Identified increased sway with poorer arrow quality. | Relied on contact-based sensors, restricting real-time analysis and applicability in competitive environments. |
| | Eswaramoorthi et al. [14] | Analyzed the relationship between cardiopulmonary metrics and performance, classifying athletes into HOCA and LOCA groups using PCA and HACAA. | Relied on contact-based equipment and focused only on cardiopulmonary metrics, lacking integrated analysis with other data. |
| | Quan et al. [15] | Investigated the relationship between aiming patterns and scores in novice archers using DTW and regression analysis, achieving moderate prediction accuracies. | Focused on novice participants and use of contact-based sensors, limiting relevance to elite competition settings. |
| | Ogasawara et al. [16] | Proposed a feedback system using accelerometers to quantify and suppress postural tremors, enhancing scores. | Depended on contact-based technology, restricting real-time application and lacking statistical approaches for deeper analysis. |

### *2.1. Psychological Responses and Performance Analysis*

Dal et al. investigated the psychophysiological differences between virtual reality (VR) archery and real archery by comparing heart rate (HR), heart rate variability (HRV), and respiration rate, along with psychological and performance differences between the two methods. Their study involved 22 participants (8 females, aged 20–24) shooting 10 arrows from an 18-m distance. Results indicated that RMSSD (a time-domain HRV measure) was significantly higher in real archery, although the proportional change was greater in the VR setting. Participants perceived real archery as more physically and mentally demanding, and they demonstrated better performance in VR archery. However, these findings are limited by their controlled experimental settings and may not fully generalize to actual competition scenarios. In contrast, our study overcomes these limitations by analyzing biometric and fine movement indicators derived from real competition data, allowing for a more accurate assessment of how these factors impact performance outcomes.

Açıkada et al. examined the impact of HR on shooting performance among 13 international-level elite athletes (7 females, 6 males). The study followed a standardized indoor protocol, where participants performed a 3-minute shuttle run to elevate physiological stress, including heart rate. Then they shot three arrows from an 18-meter distance. Blood lactate (BL) levels and HR were measured during rest and post-exercise conditions, with average resting HR of 119 bpm and BL of 1.72 mmol/L; post-exercise values were 168 bpm and 4.21 mmol/L, respectively. Despite the physiological stress, no statistically significant differences in shooting scores were observed between resting and post-exercise conditions ($p > 0.05$). While this study provided valuable insights into the physiological aspects of archery, it relied on invasive blood lactate measurements and controlled laboratory environments, limiting its applicability to real-world competitions. Our research addresses these limitations by employing a non-invasive, camera-based biometric data extraction method that enables real-time physiological monitoring in actual training and competition settings.

Vrbik et al. analyzed HR and single-channel EEG recordings in eight expert archers, comparing recurve and compound archers' scores. Their results revealed that compound archers scored higher and exhibited greater HR and attention levels before, during, and after shooting, compared to recurve archers, while relaxation levels remained consistent. ANOVA analysis confirmed significant differences in scores, HR, and attention levels ($p < 0.01$) but no differences in relaxation levels. Although this study integrated HR data with EEG measurements, its small sample size and limit the generalizability of its findings. By contrast, the present research leverages real Olympic competition footage, combining HR data with fine motion analysis to provide a comprehensive understanding of biometric indicators' effects on performance. By focusing on real-world data, we deliver more reliable and actionable insights applicable to competitive environments.

### 2.2. *Analysis Based on Biometric and Movement Data*

Keast et al. examined the relationships between postural sway, aiming time, cardiac cycle, and the timing of the first finger movement during the ECG cycle with arrow quality, categorized as good, moderate, or poor based on predefined scoring criteria. Their analysis of 240 arrows showed that postural sway significantly increased as arrow quality worsened ($p < 0.05$–$0.001$), while aiming time remained consistent among athletes but varied by arrow quality. High-quality arrows were associated with a significant increase in the cardiac cycle immediately before release ($p < 0.05$–$0.01$), and the first finger movement consistently occurred during the ST phase of the ECG cycle ($p < 0.0001$). While the study provided valuable insights, it was conducted in controlled environments, limiting its applicability to competitive settings. Our study addresses this limitation by analyzing data from actual Olympic-level competitions, offering a more realistic assessment of the impact of postural sway and cardiac cycles on performance.

Eswaramoorthi et al. identified key cardiopulmonary parameters influencing archery scores and analyzed their impact using PCA, HACA, and DA methods. Data were collected from 32 archers (mean age: 17), and seven key parameters (FVC, MVV, PEFR, IRV, RRR, RSBP, RDBP) were identified. HACA classified participants into high-optimal-capacity (HOCA) and low-optimal-capacity (LOCA) groups, with DA achieving classification accuracies between 90.63% and 96.88%. Despite its comprehensive approach, this study focused primarily on cardiopulmonary measurements without integrating data on fine motor movements or real competition data. In contrast, our research combines biometric data, such as HR, with movement analysis, providing a holistic perspective on the factors influencing performance in elite-level competitions.

Quan et al. investigated the relationship between aiming patterns and archery scores using accelerometer data from four novice middle school archers. Dynamic Time Warping (DTW) was used to analyze points of interest (POIs), with stepwise multiple regression models explaining scores with prediction accuracies ranging from 27.93% to 72.02%. However, the study's reliance on contact-based sensors and novice participants limits its applicability to elite athletes in competitive scenarios. Our research overcomes these limitations by employing contactless camera-based biometric data collection for Olympic-level athletes, offering a more precise and practical understanding of aiming patterns and performance.

Ogasawara et al. proposed a feedback system to reduce postural tremors in archery using accelerometer-based measurements. The system automatically detected shooting phases (aiming, release, follow-through) and quantified tremors during aiming to predict scores, achieving a classification accuracy of 0.72 and a correlation coefficient of 0.74. While effective, this approach relied on contact-based sensors attached to the bow, limiting its practicality in high-level competition. Unlike this feedback-focused study, our research employs statistical methods to analyze the relationship between fine movements and scores, integrating HR data to explore the potential of biometric indicators for enhancing performance.

## 3. Method

To enhance clarity and transparency of the study design, we provide a flowchart following the STROBE guidelines (Figure 1). This diagram summarizes the overall research process, including data sources, screening and exclusion criteria, final dataset composition, and subsequent analysis steps. As shown in the figure, the study began with nine YouTube videos of elite archers. After screening and excluding background-only scenes, low-quality or blurred footage, missing face/body visibility, and clips with camera movement, a total of 50 valid video segments were retained. These segments were then categorized into three groups according to performance scores (score of 10: $n = 20$; score of 9: $n = 20$; score $\leq 8$: $n = 10$). Subsequently, rPPG-based heart rate extraction (Section 3.2.1) and micro-movement analysis (Section 3.2.2) were performed, followed by statistical analyses (Section 3.2.3).

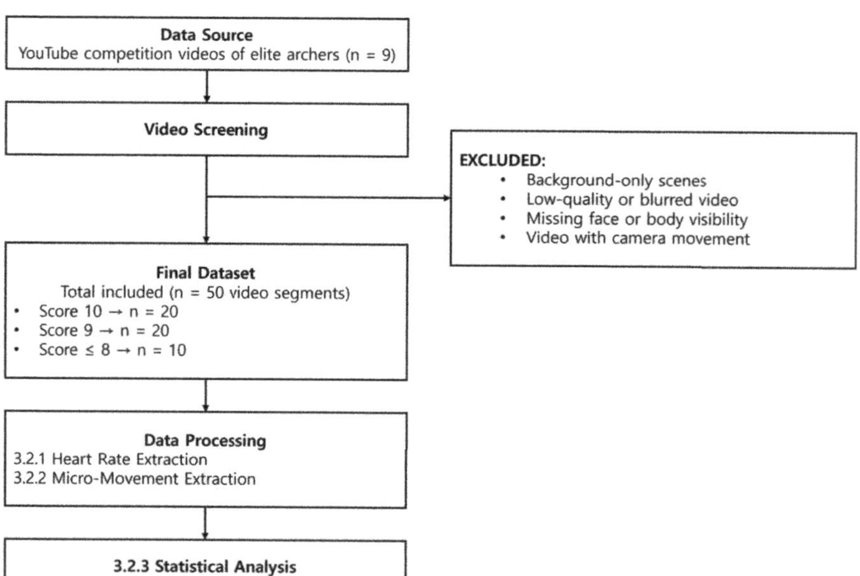


**Figure 1.** Study flowchart following STROBE guidelines, summarizing the overall research process.

### 3.1. Dataset

This study investigates the correlation between heart rate and arm movement data in relation to archery performance. Simple and multiple regression analyses were conducted to assess both the individual and interactive effects of these variables. The dataset was compiled from official match footage of the World Archery Championships available on YouTube, comprising 50 high-reliability observational data points. The sample included athletes of diverse genders and backgrounds, ensuring a representative and heterogeneous dataset. Figure 2 presents sample frames from the dataset used in this study. To ensure compliance with privacy protection and copyright regulations, all identifiable elements—such as athlete faces, broadcaster logos, and graphical overlays—were anonymized through blurring or masking.

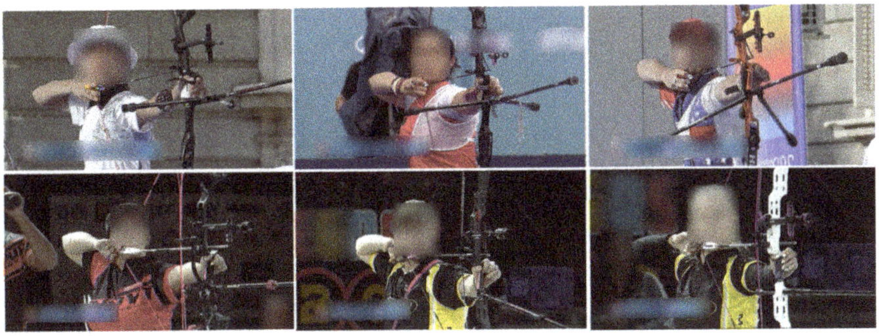

**Figure 2.** Representative sample frames extracted from official World Archery Championships footage used in this study.

Similar dataset sizes have been employed in previous studies. For instance, Eswaramoorthi et al. analyzed heart rate and athletic performance using 32 data points, while Ogasawara et al. predicted archery scores with only 11 data points.To assess the adequacy of the sample size from a statistical perspective, a post hoc power analysis was conducted based on the effect size (log-odds coefficient) of the movement variable obtained from the full ordinal logistic regression model that included both movement and average heart rate as predictors. The resulting statistical power was 0.9486, indicating that the sample size of 50 was sufficient to detect meaningful effects.

Each data point corresponded to a 10-second video segment recorded at 25 fps. Heart rate data were extracted from PPG signals obtained from the athlete's facial region. Arm movement data were measured from the start of the aiming phase to the release of the bowstring. To ensure data reliability, only heart rate values with a confidence score of 0.7 or higher were included. For movement analysis, micro-movements within a 5-pixel threshold were considered. Average values across each 10-second segment were calculated for all variables to standardize the analysis.

### 3.2. Extraction of Biometric Indicators

#### 3.2.1. BPM

In this study, we focused on extracting the rPPG signal from the facial region of interest (ROI) using a systematic approach. The facial region was identified and tracked using a deep learning-based model to enable continuous user monitoring. Since blood absorbs light more effectively than surrounding tissues, periodic changes in skin color occur as blood flows through the vessels. We used these fluctuations to derive the rPPG signal. Figure 3 illustrates the overall process of rPPG feature extraction.

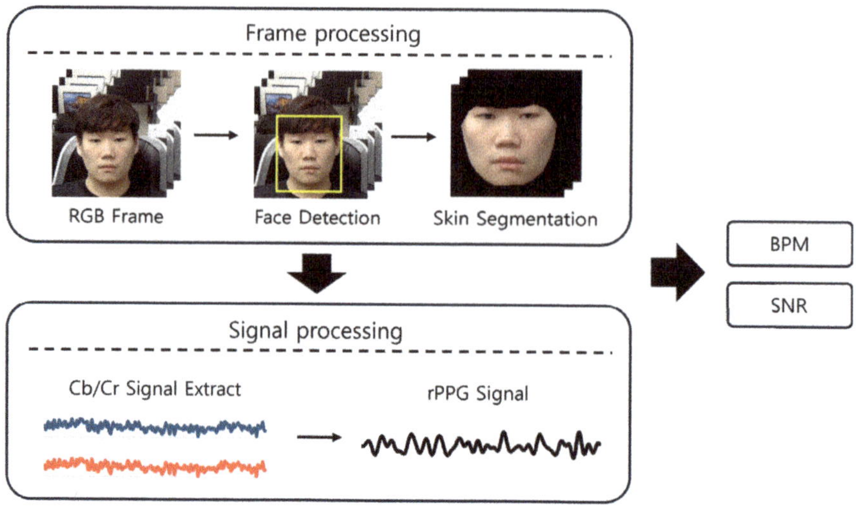


**Figure 3.** Overall process of rPPG signal extraction from facial video.

The extraction process was carried out in several steps. Initially, the face was detected in each frame using a Face Detection model. To isolate the skin pixels, filtering was performed in the YCbCr color space, which is more resilient to variations in skin tone and lighting conditions compared to RGB. Pixels were classified as skin if their Cb and Cr values fell within the ranges of 133 to 177 and 77 to 127, respectively. The RGB frames were converted to YCbCr using Equation (1), and any out-of-range pixel values were clipped to the nearest valid boundary. Here, R′, G′, and B′ denote normalized values of the respective color channels [17].

$$\begin{aligned} \mathrm{Y} &= 16 + (65.481 \cdot R' + 128.553 \cdot G' + 24.966 \cdot B') \\ \mathrm{Cb} &= 128 + (-37.797 \cdot R' - 74.203 \cdot G' + 112.0 \cdot B') \\ \mathrm{Cr} &= 128 + (112.0 \cdot R' - 93.786 \cdot G' - 18.214 \cdot B') \end{aligned} \tag{1}$$

Once the skin pixels were isolated using the threshold-based mask, the raw rPPG signal was extracted by analyzing the chrominance components of the skin region. Specifically, we focused on the Cr (red-difference) and Cb (blue-difference) channels, which are known to exhibit subtle yet periodic changes associated with blood volume pulses beneath the skin. To quantify this chrominance-based variation, the average value of the Cr and Cb channels over all skin pixels was computed for each frame, as expressed in Equation (2). This value served as a frame-wise scalar representation of the rPPG signal:

$$\mathrm{rPPG}_{\mathrm{frame}} = \frac{1}{N}\sum_{i=1}^{N}(\mathrm{Cr}_i + \mathrm{Cb}_i) \tag{2}$$

where $N$ denotes the total number of skin pixels. By aggregating this value across successive frames, we obtained a temporal rPPG signal encoding the physiological pulse rhythm.

To improve the quality of the extracted signal, detrending and bandpass filtering were applied to remove motion-related noise, such as respiration artifacts, and to isolate frequencies within the human heart rate range (42 bpm to 180 bpm) [18]. This filtering step ensured that meaningful physiological signals were preserved while reducing noise interference.

Subsequently, the processed rPPG signal was transformed into the frequency domain using the Fast Fourier Transform (FFT). The dominant frequency within the filtered range was identified and used to calculate the heart rate in beats per minute (bpm), following the formula described in Equation (3).

$$bpm = dominantfrequency(Hz) * 60 \quad (3)$$

Lastly, the confidence level of the extracted heart rate was assessed using the signal-to-noise ratio (SNR). The SNR was determined by comparing the power of the dominant frequency, representing the heart rate, to the power of noise frequencies within the rPPG signal. A higher SNR value indicated a more reliable signal, and the confidence score was calculated as outlined in Equation (4).

$$\text{Confidence} = \frac{\text{Power of Dominant Frequency}}{\text{Total Power of Noise Frequencies}} \quad (4)$$

3.2.2. Micro-Movement

To extract feature points within the object, an object recognition process was first performed. For this, a deep learning-based model, YOLO v8, was utilized, enabling efficient detection of target objects for analysis [19]. Once the object detection was complete, the skeleton of the detected object was extracted. The skeleton represented the primary body structure of the object and was used to define the regions of the left and right arms [20]. Figure 4 illustrates the process for defining the arm areas in an image.

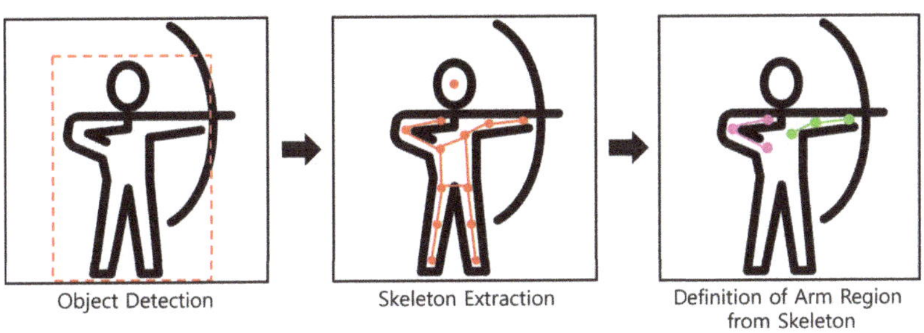


**Figure 4.** Definition of left and right arms for micro-movement detection.

Once the skeleton extraction was completed, an automated feature extraction model was applied to detect and define various feature points on the object. Among these detected points, those closest to the defined body regions (left and right arms) were selectively filtered. These filtered feature points served as key reference points in the subsequent tracking process.

Feature point tracking was then performed to analyze the continuous movement of the object. The X and Y coordinates of the selected feature points were recorded for each frame, and their displacement was calculated based on the changes in coordinate values across consecutive frames. This process enabled the collection of detailed movement data specific to the object's body parts. The detailed process is shown in Figure 5.

This study effectively combined deep learning-based object detection technology, YOLO v8, with automated feature extraction methods to analyze body regions and movements of objects.

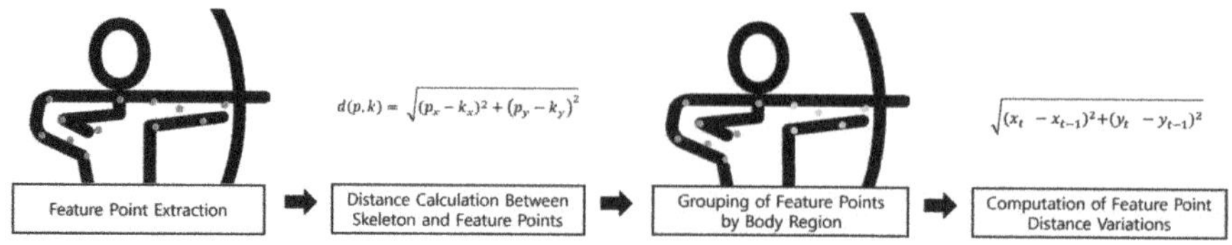


**Figure 5.** Calculation of distance variations in micro-movements by body region through feature point tracking.

### 3.2.3. Statistical Analysis

Continuous variables were summarized as the mean ± standard deviation (SD) when normally distributed and as the median with the interquartile range (IQR) when non-normally distributed. Categorical variables were presented as counts and percentages.

The normality of the continuous variables was assessed using the Shapiro–Wilk test, and the homogeneity of variances was examined with Levene's test. For group comparisons between the 10-point group and the below-10-point group, an independent two-sample *t*-test was conducted when assumptions of normality and homoscedasticity were satisfied. When these assumptions were violated, the Mann–Whitney U test was applied instead. A schematic overview of this statistical testing process is presented in Figure 6.

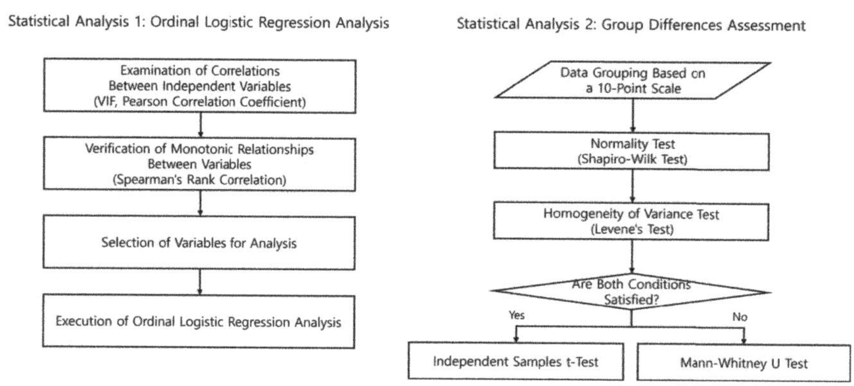


**Figure 6.** Diagram of the statistical analysis process.

Correlation analyses were performed to examine the relationships among independent variables and to prevent potential multicollinearity in the regression model. Specifically, the variance inflation factor (VIF) [21] was calculated, as shown in Equation (5), with values close to 1 indicating no multicollinearity. A threshold of 10 or higher was considered indicative of multicollinearity.

$$VIF_i = \frac{1}{1 - R_i^2} \tag{5}$$

Since the VIF does not provide the direction or strength of associations, Pearson correlation coefficients [22] were also computed, as defined in Equation (6).

$$r = \frac{\sum_{i=1}^{n}(x_i - \bar{x})(y_i - \bar{y})}{\sqrt{\sum_{i=1}^{n}(x_i - \bar{x})^2}\sqrt{\sum_{i=1}^{n}(y_i - \bar{y})^2}} \tag{6}$$

Pearson's correlation quantifies the linear relationship between two variables, with values ranging from $-1$ to 1. A value near 1 indicates a strong positive correlation, while a value near $-1$ signifies a strong negative correlation.

In addition, Spearman correlation analysis [23] was conducted to evaluate monotonic relationships, which was useful when the variables exhibited non-linear associations.

For regression modeling, ordinal logistic regression was employed to examine the effects of movement and heart rate on performance scores. The dependent variable, score, was defined as an ordinal outcome with three categories (10 points, 9 points, and 8 points or less). The independent variables, average heart rate and average movement values extracted from 10-second video segments, were treated as continuous predictors. Ordinal logistic regression was selected because it preserved the ordinal nature of the outcome variable while enabling an effective evaluation of the association between predictors and scores [24]. All statistical analyses were performed using Python (version 3.7.12), with the SciPy and statsmodels packages.

## 4. Results

Before presenting the statistical analyses, the characteristics of the analyzed dataset are summarized. A total of 50 valid data points were extracted from international archery competition footage, including athletes of diverse genders and backgrounds. After preprocessing, the dataset comprised 10 entries for 8 points, 20 entries for 9 points, and 20 entries for 10 points. This distribution provided a heterogeneous and representative sample for subsequent analyses.

This study analyzed the effects of heart rate and movement variables on archery scores. To better understand the biometric data used in this study, an example image illustrating the process of extracting physiological signals is presented in Figure 7. This example demonstrates the use of camera-based remote photoplethysmography (rPPG) technology to capture heart rate and variability, as well as the extraction of micro-movement feature points of archers during their performance. The visualized data illustrates the process of extracting biometric indicators from video.

Written informed consent was obtained from the individual depicted in Figure 7 for the publication of their image in this manuscript.

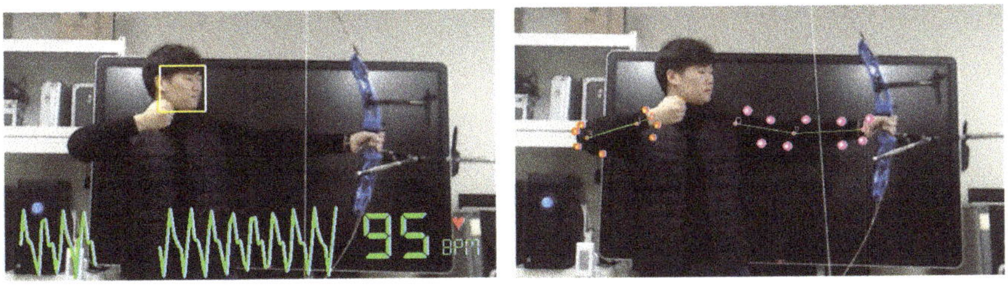


(a) (b)

**Figure 7.** Examples of biometric data extraction: (**a**) heart rate extraction using rPPG; (**b**) micro-movement feature points.

The scores were categorized into three groups: 10 points, 9 points, and 8 points or lower. Scores below 8 points were preprocessed and grouped as 8 points. After preprocessing, the dataset consisted of 10 entries for 8 points, 20 entries for 9 points, and 20 entries for 10 points.

To assess multicollinearity, the VIF (variance inflation factor) values were calculated. The VIF for heart rate and total movement was 1.0313, that for heart rate and right-arm movement was 1.0471, and that for heart rate and left-arm movement was 1.0131. All VIF values were close to 1, indicating no multicollinearity issues. Pearson correlation coefficients were also analyzed, revealing a correlation of 0.1741 between heart rate and total movement, 0.2113 between heart rate and right-arm movement, and 0.1138 between heart rate and left-arm movement. These low correlation coefficients indicate weak linear relationships among the variables. Detailed analysis results are presented in Table 2.

**Table 2.** Results of variance inflation factor (VIF) and Pearson correlation coefficient analysis among heart rate and movement variables. Abbreviations: VIF = variance inflation factor. *p*-values are reported with three decimal places (values below 0.001 are presented as $p < 0.001$).

| Variable 1 | Variable 2 | VIF | Pearson Correlation Coefficient |
|---|---|---|---|
| Heart Rate | Movement (Overall) | 1.0313 | 0.174 |
| | Movement (Right Arm) | 1.0471 | 0.211 |
| | Movement (Left Arm) | 1.0131 | 0.114 |

Spearman correlation analysis revealed a strong negative monotonic relationship between heart rate and scores, indicating that higher heart rates were associated with lower scores. Similarly, a statistically significant negative monotonic relationship was observed between movement and scores, except for left-arm movement, which showed no significant correlation. However, no statistically significant relationship was found between heart rate and movement. Based on these findings, heart rate and movement variables were independently included in the regression model. The Spearman correlations reported in Table 3 were computed on the full dataset across all three score categories.

**Table 3.** Results of Spearman correlation analysis between heart rate, movement variables, and archery performance scores. Abbreviations: $\rho$ = Spearman's rank correlation coefficient. *p*-values are reported with three decimal places (values below 0.001 are presented as $p < 0.001$).

| Variable 1 | Variable 2 | Spearman Correlation | *p*-Value |
|---|---|---|---|
| Heart Rate | Score | −0.6183 | $p < 0.001$ |
| Movement (Overall) | Score | −0.3249 | 0.021 |
| Movement (Right Arm) | Score | −0.3931 | 0.004 |
| Movement (Left Arm) | Score | −0.1364 | 0.345 |
| Heart Rate | Movement (Overall) | 0.1603 | 0.266 |
| Heart Rate | Movement (Right Arm) | 0.1710 | 0.235 |
| Heart Rate | Movement (Left Arm) | 0.0512 | 0.724 |

Figure 8 visualizes the Spearman correlation coefficients between biometric variables and archery scores. Heart rate showed the strongest negative correlation with score ($\rho = -0.618$; $p < 0.001$), followed by right-arm movement ($\rho = -0.393$; $p = 0.005$) and overall movement ($\rho = -0.325$; $p = 0.021$). In contrast, left-arm movement did not show a statistically significant relationship with score ($\rho = -0.136$; $p = 0.345$).

The results of the ordinal logistic regression analysis showed that the regression coefficient for heart rate was −0.1166, with a *p*-value of less than 0.05, indicating statistical significance. Similarly, the regression coefficient for total movement was −4.5968 ($p = 0.033$), and for right-arm movement, it was −6.1747 ($p = 0.008$), both of which were also statistically significant. However, the regression coefficient for left-arm movement was −1.7256, with a *p*-value of 0.364, indicating a lack of statistical significance. When movement and heart rate were simultaneously included as independent variables in the regression model, statistically significant outcomes were observed only when heart rate and right-arm movement were analyzed together ($p = 0.031$). In contrast, overall movement became less influential when considered alongside heart rate, and left-arm movement remained unrelated to performance.

Taken together, these results highlight that physiological arousal (heart rate) and fine motor control of the right arm are the primary determinants of shooting performance. The detailed regression results are summarized in Table 4.

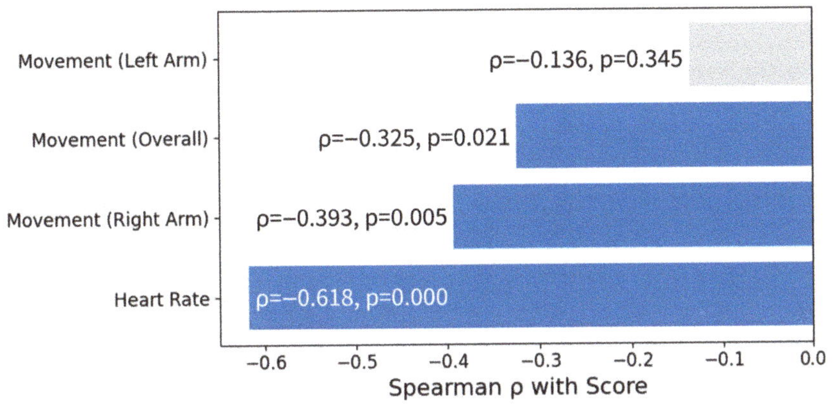


**Figure 8.** Spearman correlation coefficients (ρ) between biometric variables and scores. Bars indicate the strength and direction of associations, with statistically significant results ($p < 0.05$) shown in blue and non-significant results in gray.

**Table 4.** Statistical analysis results of ordinal logistic regression based on independent variables.

| Independent Variable 1 (x1) | Independent Variable 2 (x2) | Coefficient (x1) | Coefficient (x2) | *p*-Value (x1) | *p*-Value (x2) |
|---|---|---|---|---|---|
| Heart Rate | – | −0.1166 | – | $p < 0.001$ | – |
| Movement (Overall) | – | −4.5968 | – | 0.033 | – |
| Movement (Right Arm) | – | −6.1747 | – | 0.008 | – |
| Movement (Left Arm) | – | −1.7256 | – | 0.364 | – |
| Heart Rate | Movement (Overall) | −1.5645 | −0.5568 | $p < 0.001$ | 0.061 |
| Heart Rate | Movement (Right Arm) | −1.5322 | −0.7183 | $p < 0.001$ | 0.031 |
| Heart Rate | Movement (Left Arm) | −1.5641 | −0.1637 | $p < 0.001$ | 0.577 |

To analyze differences in movement and heart rate between the 10-point group and other groups, appropriate statistical tests, determined by normality and homoscedasticity assumptions, were conducted. The analysis revealed a significant difference in heart rate and right-arm movement between the groups, with the 10-point group showing lower values. In contrast, no significant differences were observed in overall or left-arm movement. Detailed statistical results, including test types and significance levels, are summarized in Table 5. In the context of elite-level competition, achieving a perfect score of 10 is a critical indicator of performance; therefore, we dichotomized the scores into 10 and below 10 for analysis.

In addition to the statistical tests, graphical analyses were conducted to provide a more intuitive understanding of the differences between groups. Violin plots (Figure 9) illustrate the distribution of heart rate and movement variables across the 10-point and non-10-point groups. Consistently with the statistical test results in Table 5, the violin plots demonstrate that the 10-point group exhibited markedly lower heart rates and reduced right-arm movement, while distributions of total and left-arm movement showed considerable overlap between groups.

**Table 5.** Results of normality and homogeneity of variance tests, applied statistical methods, and corresponding test statistics and $p$-values for differences in heart rate and movement between 10-point and below-10-point groups. Statistical analyses included Shapiro–Wilk test, Levene's test, independent $t$-test, and Mann–Whitney U test. $p$-values are reported to three decimal places (values below 0.001 are reported as $p < 0.001$).

| Variable | Normality Test | | Homogeneity of Variance Test | Test Method | Test Results | |
|---|---|---|---|---|---|---|
| | 10-Point Group | Below-10-Point Group | | | Statistic | $p$-Value |
| Heart Rate | 0.0006 | 0.0007 | 0.0304 | Mann–Whitney U Test | 120.5000 | $p < 0.001$ |
| Movement (Overall) | 0.0523 | 0.5505 | 0.2329 | Independent two-sample $t$-test | 1.8905 | 0.065 |
| Movement (Right Arm) | 0.2355 | 0.3242 | 0.1383 | Independent two-sample $t$-test | −2.6871 | 0.010 |
| Movement (Left Arm) | 0.3710 | 0.2843 | 0.7740 | Independent two-sample $t$-test | −1.1408 | 0.260 |

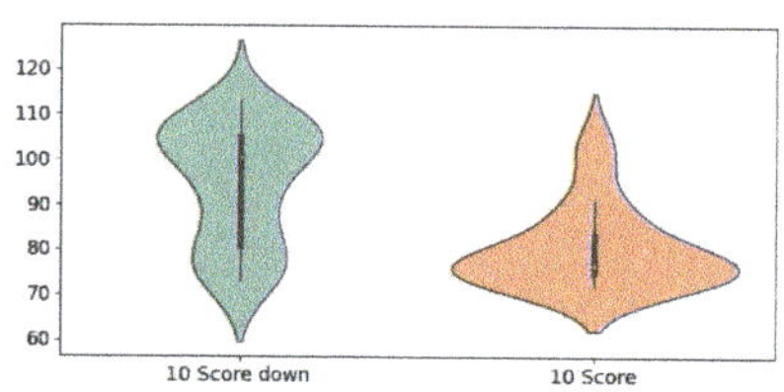


(**a**) Heart rate.

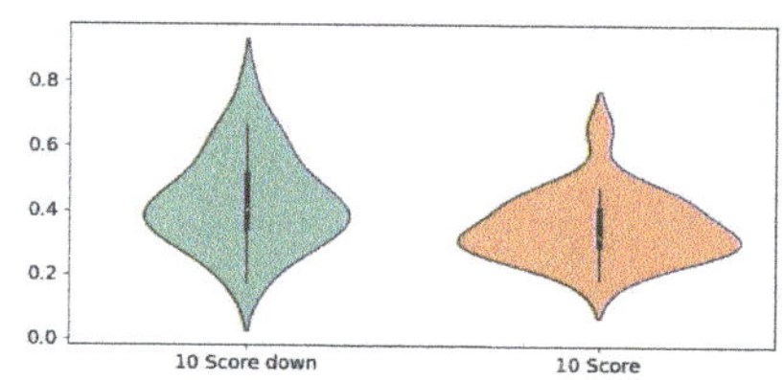


(**b**) Overall movement.

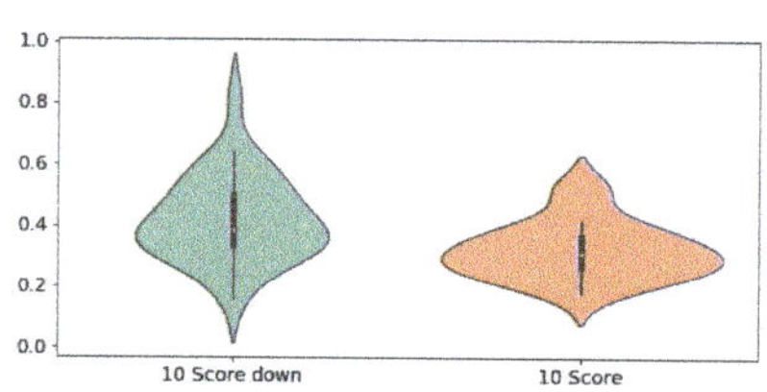


(**c**) Right-arm movement.

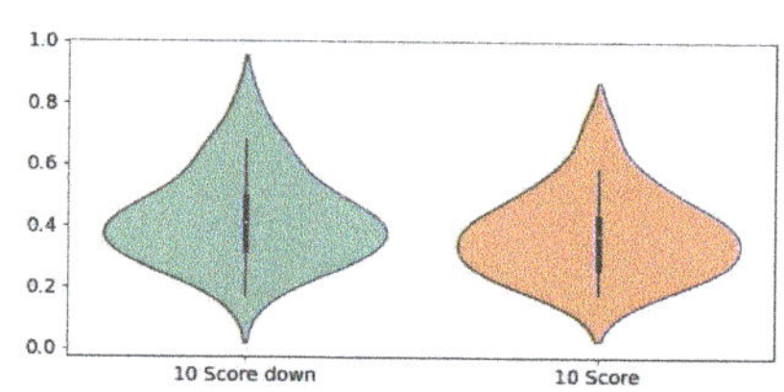


(**d**) Left-arm movement.

**Figure 9.** Violin plots comparing biometric indicators between score groups: (**a**) heart rate, (**b**) overall movement, (**c**) right-arm movement, and (**d**) left-arm movement. The distributions visualize both density and summary statistics (median and interquartile range).

Histograms with kernel density estimation (Figure 10) further highlight the differences in distribution. The heart rate distribution of the 10-point group was concentrated in the lower range (around 70–80 bpm), whereas the non-10-point group showed a broader distribution centered at higher values (90–110 bpm). A similar pattern was observed for right-arm movement, with the 10-point group clustered at lower values compared to the non-10-point group.

Finally, scatter plots (Figure 11) depicting the joint relationship between heart rate and movement reveal that archers in the 10-point group are predominantly located in the lower-left quadrant, representing both lower heart rates and smaller movement values. This visualization supports the conclusion that reduced physiological arousal and motor instability are associated with higher performance in archery.

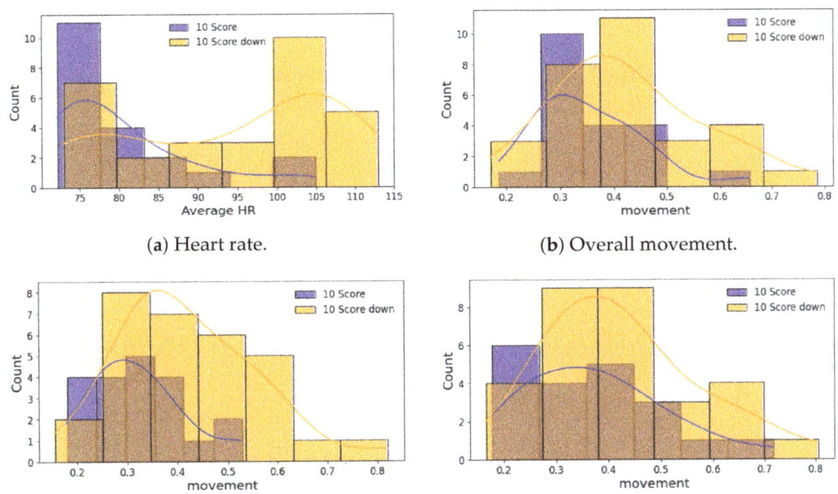


(**a**) Heart rate. (**b**) Overall movement.

(**c**) Right-arm movement. (**d**) Left-arm movement.

**Figure 10.** Histogram plots comparing biometric indicators between score groups: (**a**) heart rate, (**b**) overall movement, (**c**) right-arm movement, and (**d**) left-arm movement. The histograms, overlaid with kernel density estimation (KDE) curves, illustrate the distributional differences between the 10-point and below-10-point groups.

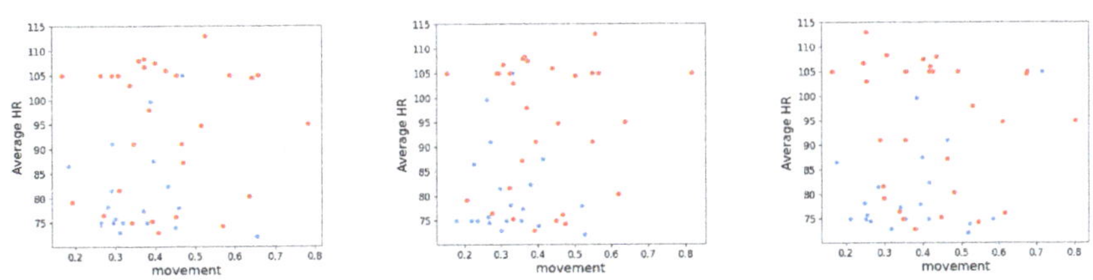


(**a**) (**b**) (**c**)

**Figure 11.** Scatter plots of heart rate versus movement variables across score groups: (**a**) heart rate vs. overall movement, (**b**) heart rate vs. right-arm movement, and (**c**) heart rate vs. left-arm movement. Blue dots represent the 10-point group, while red dots represent the below-10-point group. These plots illustrate the joint distribution of biometric variables, highlighting that archers achieving 10 points tend to cluster in the lower-heart-rate and lower-movement regions.

## 5. Discussion

This study provides important insights into how heart rate and movement variables influence archery performance. Multicollinearity evaluation confirmed that all VIF values were near 1, indicating low correlations among independent variables and no multicollinearity issues. This supports the reliability of the regression analysis and allows the independent effects of these variables on performance scores to be analyzed without redundancy.

These findings are consistent with Lu and Zhong [4], who reported that lower heart rates predicted higher performance scores among Olympic-level archers. In contrast, Accardo et al. [11] found no significant association between elevated heart rate and performance, suggesting that factors such as individual fitness or adaptation to pressure may moderate this relationship. Similarly, Keast et al. [13] emphasized the role of postural sway in performance, but their reliance on contact-based sensors distinguishes their work from our contactless, video-based approach. By analyzing biometric data directly from real-world competition footage, our study offers an alternative methodology that complements and extends prior laboratory-based research. Correlation analyses further clarify these relationships. Pearson's correlation revealed only weak linear associations between heart rate and movement variables, indicating limited predictive value. However, Spearman's rank correlation identified a strong negative monotonic relationship between heart rate and performance scores, suggesting that elevated heart rate—often linked with tension or stress—may impair precision. This interpretation is consistent with prior studies highlighting the detrimental effects of heightened arousal on accuracy in precision-based sports. Finally, the increase in the second predictor's $p$-value when both variables were included in the regression model is best interpreted not as multicollinearity but as the result of larger standard errors caused by shared variance between predictors.

Ordinal regression analysis identified heart rate, total movement, and right-arm movement as significant predictors of performance scores. From a practical perspective, the regression coefficient for heart rate (−0.1166) indicates that a one-unit decrease in heart rate was associated with an increase of approximately 0.12 points in performance score. Similarly, the coefficient for right-arm movement (−6.1747) suggests that reducing tremor in the dominant arm by one unit could improve the score by more than six points. These effect sizes underscore the substantial influence of physiological and biomechanical control on archery outcomes, reinforcing their importance in athlete training and performance evaluation. In contrast, the non-significant coefficient for left-arm movement suggests its limited contribution to performance. Consistently with previous findings, movements of the non-dominant limb appear to play only a minor role in outcome variability, though further studies are needed to confirm this across different techniques and competition formats.

Group analysis further demonstrated that athletes scoring 10 points or higher exhibited significantly lower heart rates and reduced right-arm movement compared to those scoring below 10 points. Taken together, these findings underscore the critical role of physiological regulation and biomechanical precision in achieving elite performance. From both clinical and practical standpoints, they suggest that interventions targeting heart rate regulation—such as breathing techniques, meditation, and biofeedback—may directly enhance competitive outcomes by promoting physiological stability. Similarly, biomechanical training that reduces right-arm tremor can yield substantial performance gains. Notably, the adoption of non-contact, video-based monitoring enables such evaluations to be conducted seamlessly during both training and competition, without disrupting athlete performance. This approach paves the way for real-time, data-driven feedback systems that support individualized training strategies and optimize performance.

Importantly, this study not only validates the feasibility of non-contact physiological monitoring in real competitive settings but also demonstrates its practical applicability without interfering with athletes' performance. By analyzing biometric data extracted from actual Olympic footage, the study overcomes the limitations of controlled laboratory environments and establishes a realistic, field-based evaluation framework. This approach holds strong potential for broader applications in other precision-demanding sports such as shooting and golf, where physiological stability and fine motor control are crucial. Ultimately, the proposed methodology offers a foundation for real-time, data-driven training strategies and performance optimization systems tailored to individual athletes.

The insignificant relationship for left-arm movement may indicate its lesser role in performance, though future research should investigate this across different techniques, competition formats, and experience levels. Real-time feedback systems, including wearable devices and motion capture technologies, could also enhance training by providing precise data for performance optimization.

Future research should investigate how heart rate and movement interact under varying conditions, such as elevated stress or environmental changes. Such analyses would offer deeper insights into the interplay between physiological and biomechanical factors, thereby broadening the understanding of archery performance. In addition, clarifying the neural and psychological mechanisms underlying heart rate regulation and movement stability may provide new directions for improving precision and consistency in archery.

## 6. Conclusions

This study analyzed the effects of heart rate and movement variables on archery performance using real-world data collected from actual competition footage. The findings highlight that heart rate and right arm movement significantly influence performance scores, with higher heart rates and excessive right arm movements being associated with lower scores. These results underline the critical importance of physiological stability and biomechanical precision for achieving success in precision-based sports like archery.

The multicollinearity analysis confirmed that the independent variables—heart rate, total movement, and right arm movement—could be analyzed independently without redundancy. Spearman's rank correlation analysis showed a strong negative relationship between heart rate and performance scores, while ordinal regression analysis identified right arm movement as a key biomechanical factor affecting performance. Group analysis further revealed that athletes scoring 10 points or higher consistently exhibited lower heart rates and reduced right arm movements compared to those scoring below 10 points. This underscores the importance of physiological regulation and biomechanical precision in achieving elite performance.The results of this study support our hypothesis that elevated heart rate and excessive right-arm tremor negatively affect archery performance. These findings confirm that physiological stability and biomechanical control are critical determinants of success in precision-based sports.

This study also demonstrated the practicality of non-contact biometric data collection methods. By eliminating the need for intrusive equipment, this approach enables real-time monitoring and feedback during training and competition, overcoming the limitations of traditional contact-based methods.

Based on the statistical evidence, this study proposes heart rate and right-arm micro-movements as novel and objective indicators for athlete evaluation. These metrics provide quantifiable insight into an athlete's physiological state and biomechanical control under pressure, making them suitable for integration into data-driven performance monitoring and personalized training systems.

The regression-based effect sizes also provide valuable insight into performance improvement strategies. Even small reductions in heart rate or right-arm tremor can yield measurable gains in scoring. These findings suggest that targeted physiological and biomechanical training may result in quantifiable performance benefits.

In conclusion, this research contributes to the growing field of sports science by providing empirical evidence on the relationship between heart rate, movement variables, and athletic performance. The findings not only inform tailored training programs in archery but also offer insights applicable to other precision-based sports. However, this study has several limitations, including the small sample size, variability in video quality, lack of athlete metadata, and influence of uncontrolled environmental factors, which should be addressed in future research. In particular, the imbalanced distribution of score categories (10 entries for 8 points, 20 for 9 points, and 20 for 10 points) introduces a moderate risk of selection bias, which may affect the representativeness and generalizability of the findings. Therefore, future studies should aim to include a larger and more balanced dataset. Furthermore, while this study does not involve direct clinical or training interventions, the proposed strategies may have indirect applications in athletic training. Pilot validation studies are recommended before large-scale implementation. Future studies should explore the interactions between physiological and biomechanical variables under diverse conditions and integrate advanced technologies to further enhance athletic success. Ultimately, this study fulfills its objective by demonstrating that heart rate and right-arm micro-movements are decisive factors in archery performance, validating the effectiveness of non-contact monitoring in real competitive settings.

**Author Contributions:** Conceptualization, J.Y.M. and E.C.L.; Methodology, B.S.A. and E.C.L.; Software, B.S.A. and S.H.P.; Validation, B.S.A. and S.H.P.; Formal analysis, S.H.P.; Investigation, J.Y.M.; Data curation, B.S.A. and S.H.P.; Writing—original draft preparation, B.S.A. and S.H.P.; Writing—review and editing, J.Y.M. and E.C.L.; Supervision, E.C.L. All authors have read and agreed to the published version of the manuscript.

**Funding:** This research received no external funding.

**Data Availability Statement:** The data supporting the findings of this study were obtained from publicly available YouTube videos. The specific videos analyzed in this study include: Sara Lopez v Jesse Broadwater—Legends Match (exhibition) | Vegas Shoot 2020 (Available online: https://www.youtube.com/watch?v=NlYCHenpTj4, accessed on 11 September 2025); 2023 USA Archery Indoor National Finals | Men's Compound Gold Medal Match (Available online: https://www.youtube.com/watch?v=hB3INnmDyhw, accessed on 11 September 2025); Full session: Compound Men's Finals | Samsun 2018 Hyundai Archery World Cup Final (Available online: https://www.youtube.com/watch?v=G2N-IbEycTw, accessed on 11 September 2025); Ana Vazquez v Deepika Kumari—Recurve Women Semifinal | Paris 2021 Hyundai Archery World Cup S3 (Available online: https://www.youtube.com/watch?v=keY8ENZzS0c, accessed on 11 September 2025); Recurve Finals | Manila 2018 Asia Cup Stage 2 (Available online: https://www.youtube.com/watch?v=480mHQmWZw8, accessed on 11 September 2025); Korea v USA—Recurve Cadet Mixed Team Gold | World Archery Youth Championships 2019 (Available online: https://www.youtube.com/watch?v=3wLflUeqcQU, accessed on 11 September 2025); Mexico v Indonesia—Recurve Women's Team Quarterfinal | Final Olympic Qualifier 2021 (Available online: https://www.youtube.com/watch?v=YTmDXkHy-9Q, accessed on 11 September 2025); Mackenzie Brown v Ana Vazquez—Recurve Women Bronze | Paris 2021 Hyundai Archery World Cup S3 (Available online: https://www.youtube.com/watch?v=rY-yUd2Grio, accessed on 11 September 2025); and USA v Turkey—Recurve Women's Team Quarterfinal | Final Olympic Qualifier 2021 (Available online: https://www.youtube.com/watch?v=HrmSSlaOZ4A, accessed on 11 September 2025).

**Conflicts of Interest:** The authors declare no conflicts of interest.

## References


1. Wu, Y.C.; Chiu, L.W.; Wu, B.F.; Lin, L.L.C.; Ho, T.H.; Chung, M.L.; Wu, S.F. Motion robust remote photoplethysmography measurement during exercise for contactless physical activity intensity detection. *IEEE Trans. Instrum. Meas.* **2023**, *72*, 2508614. [CrossRef]
2. Jang, P.S.; Kim, Y.H. "[Paris Olympics] How Korea's Archers Managed to Win Olympic Gold, Gold, Gold, Gold." *Hankyoreh English*, 5 August 2024. Available online: https://english.hani.co.kr/arti/english_edition/e_entertainment/1152343.html (accessed on 11 September 2025).
3. Park, K.B. Practice Opponent Is Not a Human but a Robot: The Secret of Archery 'Ten-Ten-Ten' *News1*, 29 July 2024. Available online: https://news.nate.com/view/20240729n10033 (accessed on 11 September 2025). (In Korean)
4. Lu, Y.; Zhong, S. Contactless Real-Time Heart Rate Predicts the Performance of Elite Athletes: Evidence From Tokyo 2020 Olympic Archery Competition. *Psychol. Sci.* **2023**, *34*, 384–393. [CrossRef] [PubMed]
5. Guru, C.S.; Mahajan, U.; Krishnan, A.; Datta, K.; Sharma, D. Can we predict training performance with shooting heart rate in archers?: A machine learning approach. *medRxiv* **2024**. [CrossRef]
6. Battaglini, M.P.; Pessôa Filho, D.M.; Calais, S.L.; Miyazaki, M.C.O.S.; Neiva, C.M.; Espada, M.C.; de Moraes, M.G.; Verardi, C.E.L. Analysis of progressive muscle relaxation on psychophysiological variables in basketball athletes. *Int. J. Environ. Res. Public Health* **2022**, *19*, 17065. [CrossRef] [PubMed]

7. Torun, A.; Kilic, S.; Uzun, M.; Simsek, U.; Aslan, G.Y.; Kahraman, G. Evaluation of high altitude training camps with heart rate recovery and heart rate variability analysis: Beneficial effect in elite swimmers. *J. Sports Med. Phys. Fit.* **2024**, *64*, 1026–1030. [CrossRef] [PubMed]
8. Shinohara, H.; Hosomi, R.; Sakamoto, R.; Urushihata, T.; Yamamoto, S.; Higa, C.; Oyama, S. Effect of exercise devised to reduce arm tremor in the sighting phase of archery. *PLoS ONE* **2023**, *18*, e0285223. [CrossRef] [PubMed]
9. Rusdiawan, A.; Kusuma, D.A.; Rasyid, M.L.S.A.; García-Jiménez, J.V.; Purnomo, M.; Wismanadi, H.; Siantoro, G.; Lani, A.; Irmawati, F.; Ningsih, Y.F. Physical capacity and performance correlation in sub-elite Indonesian archery athletes. *Retos Nuevas Tendencias Educ. Física Deporte Recreación* **2024**, *60*, 1093–1101. [CrossRef]
10. Dal, N.; Tok, S.; Balıkçı, İ.; Yılmaz, S.E.; Binboğa, E. Comparison of Heart Rate Variability Psychological Responses and Performance in Virtual and Real Archery. *Brain Behav.* **2024**, *14*, e70070. [CrossRef] [PubMed]
11. Açıkada, C.; Hazır, T.; Asçı, A.; Aytar, S.H.; Tınazcı, C. Effect of heart rate on shooting performance in elite archers. *Heliyon* **2019**, *5*, e01428. [CrossRef] [PubMed]
12. Vrbik, A.; Bene, R.; Vrbik, I. Heart rate values and levels of attention and relaxation in expert archers during shooting. *Hrvat. Šport. Vjesn.* **2015**, *30*, 21–29.
13. Keast, D.; Elliott, B. Fine body movements and the cardiac cycle in archery. *J. Sports Sci.* **1990**, *8*, 203–213. [CrossRef] [PubMed]
14. Eswaramoorthi, V.; Abdullah, M.R.; Musa, R.M.; Maliki, A.B.H.M.; Kosni, N.A.; Raj, N.B.; Alias, N.; Azahari, H.; Mat-Rashid, S.M.; Juahir, H. A multivariate analysis of cardiopulmonary parameters in archery performance. *Hum. Mov.* **2018**, *19*, 35–41. [CrossRef]
15. Quan, C.; Lee, S. Relationship between aiming patterns and scores in archery shooting. *Korean J. Appl. Biomech.* **2016**, *26*, 353–360. [CrossRef]
16. Ogasawara, T.; Fukamachi, H.; Aoyagi, K.; Kumano, S.; Togo, H.; Oka, K. Archery skill assessment using an acceleration sensor. *IEEE Trans. Hum.-Mach. Syst.* **2021**, *51*, 221–228. [CrossRef]
17. Chai, D.; Bouzerdoum, A. A Bayesian approach to skin color classification in YCbCr color space. In Proceedings of the 2000 TENCON Proceedings. Intelligent Systems and Technologies for the New Millennium (Cat. No. 00CH37119), Kuala Lumpur, Malaysia, 24–27 September 2000; Volume 2, pp. 421–424. [CrossRef]
18. Suh, K.H.; Lee, E.C. Contactless physiological signals extraction based on skin color magnification. *J. Electron. Imaging* **2017**, *26*, 063003. [CrossRef]
19. Sohan, M.; Sai Ram, T.; Reddy, R.; Venkata, C. A review on yolov8 and its advancements. In Proceedings of the International Conference on Data Intelligence and Cognitive Informatics, Tirunelveli, India, 27–28 June 2023; Springer: Singapore, 2024; pp. 529–545. [CrossRef]
20. Jiang, T.; Lu, P.; Zhang, L.; Ma, N.; Han, R.; Lyu, C.; Li, Y.; Chen, K. Rtmpose: Real-time multi-person pose estimation based on mmpose. *arXiv* **2023**, arXiv:2303.07399. [CrossRef]
21. Akinwande, M.O.; Dikko, H.G.; Samson, A.; et al. Variance inflation factor: As a condition for the inclusion of suppressor variable (s) in regression analysis. *Open J. Stat.* **2015**, *5*, 754. [CrossRef]
22. Cohen, I.; Huang, Y.; Chen, J.; Benesty, J.; Benesty, J.; Chen, J.; Huang, Y.; Cohen, I. Pearson correlation coefficient. In *Noise Reduction in Speech Processing*; Springer: Berlin/Heidelberg, Germany, 2009; pp. 1–4. [CrossRef]
23. De Winter, J.C.; Gosling, S.D.; Potter, J. Comparing the Pearson and Spearman correlation coefficients across distributions and sample sizes: A tutorial using simulations and empirical data. *Psychol. Methods* **2016**, *21*, 273. [CrossRef] [PubMed]
24. Gutiérrez, P.A.; Perez-Ortiz, M.; Sanchez-Monedero, J.; Fernandez-Navarro, F.; Hervas-Martinez, C. Ordinal regression methods: Survey and experimental study. *IEEE Trans. Knowl. Data Eng.* **2015**, *28*, 127–146. [CrossRef]

*electronics*

MDPI

*Article*

# Interactive Holographic Display System Based on Emotional Adaptability and CCNN-PCG

**Yu Zhao [1], Zhong Xu [1], Ting-Yu Zhang [1], Meng Xie [1], Bing Han [1] and Ye Liu [2,*]**

[1] College of Information Engineering, Yangzhou University, Yangzhou 225127, China; zhaoyu@yzu.edu.cn (Y.Z.)

[2] Department of Creative Writing, Korea University, Sejong 30019, Republic of Korea

* Correspondence: listenyuran@korea.ac.kr

**Abstract:** Against the backdrop of the rapid advancement of intelligent speech interaction and holographic display technologies, this paper introduces an interactive holographic display system. This paper applies 2D-to-3D technology to acquisition work and uses a Complex-valued Convolutional Neural Network Point Cloud Gridding (CCNN-PCG) algorithm to generate a computer-generated hologram (CGH) with depth information for application in point cloud data. During digital human hologram building, 2D-to-3D conversion yields high-precision point cloud data. The system uses ChatGLM for natural language processing and emotion-adaptive responses, enabling multi-turn voice dialogs and text-driven model generation. The CCNN-PCG algorithm reduces computational complexity and improves display quality. Simulations and experiments show that CCNN-PCG enhances reconstruction quality and speeds up computation by over 2.2 times. This research provides a theoretical framework and practical technology for holographic interactive systems, applicable in virtual assistants, educational displays, and other fields.

**Keywords:** holographic display; color holography; image processing; computer-generated hologram; emotional adaptability

## 1. Introduction

### 1.1. Background

Currently, as technology advances at an unprecedented pace, consumer demand for personalized, intelligent, and immersive experiences continues to escalate. The integration of optical display and artificial intelligence (AI) interaction technologies has emerged as a focal point for both academia and industry. Compared to traditional two-dimensional (2D) display technologies, three-dimensional (3D) display technology has rapidly become a core pillar in domains such as 5G, big data, the metaverse, and the Internet of Things (IoT) [1–4]. Globally, holographic technology is widely recognized as the most promising ultimate solution for true three-dimensional displays. It not only accurately reproduces intricate details such as color and depth but also dynamically adjusts images based on the viewer's perspective, thereby creating an immersive three-dimensional visual experience. Interactive three-dimensional display technology has begun to gain prominence. Building on all the advantages of traditional holographic displays, this innovation allows for real-time interaction between users and three-dimensional images, delivering an unprecedented level of immersion.

Intelligent digital humans, a key application in this field, can replicate the appearance, personality, and behavioral traits of specific individuals based on their personal information


https://doi.org/10.3390/electronics14152981

and preferences. Moreover, through interactive three-dimensional holographic display technology, they enable real-time engagement with users, providing more authentic and deeply immersive experiences [5].

### 1.2. Related Studies

#### 1.2.1. Research on Interactivity of Intelligent Digital Humans

In the landscape of digital transformation, intelligent digital humans have emerged as a novel medium for human–computer interaction, with breakthroughs in their interactive capabilities becoming a shared focus in both academia and industry [6,7]. Early digital human systems, constrained by traditional rule engines, primarily relied on keyword matching and predefined Q & A databases, leading to mechanical dialogs and poor contextual adaptability. With advancements in speech recognition and generative artificial intelligence, intelligent digital humans are gradually overcoming technical barriers, evolving toward multimodal and cognitively robust interaction paradigms.

In voice interaction, speech recognition systems based on HMM-DNN hybrid models and end-to-end deep learning architectures [8,9] equip digital humans with high-precision voiceprint recognition and speech-to-text capabilities. Leveraging breakthroughs in large language models (LLMs) [10], digital humans not only accurately parse voice commands but also acquire human-like interactive abilities—including semantic comprehension, contextual correlation, and creative responses—through training on massive corpora. This technological integration liberates digital humans from scripted dialogs, enabling them to autonomously generate contextually dynamic feedback, which significantly enhances the naturalness and intelligence of interactions.

In visual representation, innovations in 3D reconstruction technology have imbued digital humans with lifelike vitality. Tsinghua University's Unique3D framework [11] achieves precise single-view-to-3D model reconstruction via neural networks, while Nankai University's CAMixer architecture [12] addresses real-time rendering challenges for dynamic expressions and micro-motions.

Although the prior holographic voice interaction system applied [13] used salient object detection algorithms and a distributed computing architecture to achieve preliminary multichannel perception and real-time digital human interaction, current systems remain limited in deeper interactive dimensions such as contextual cognitive transfer and multimodal intent understanding.

#### 1.2.2. Accelerating Computer-Generated Hologram Computation and Enhancing Quality

Significant global research efforts have been directed towards accelerating CGH computation. Initially, to address the slow generation of holograms, hardware acceleration emerged as a primary approach. International research teams explored the potential of graphic processing units (GPUs), leveraging their massive parallel computing capabilities to partition holograms. By assigning the light field computation of each micro-region to individual GPU cores—with one thread precisely managing per-pixel or per-point calculations—the computation time was significantly reduced [14,15].

To optimize memory usage and align with GPU access characteristics, researchers developed enhanced lookup table techniques [16,17], which substantially accelerated hologram computation. Shimobaba et al. introduced the wavefront recording plane (WRP) method [18], which significantly improved the efficiency of 3D scene hologram generation by incorporating virtual diffraction planes. Subsequently, Wang et al. integrated ray tracing with the WRP method for rapid hologram generation [19]. Shi et al. employed convolutional neural networks (CNNs) trained on extensive datasets, reducing computation time to milliseconds—a revolutionary advancement published in *Nature* [20]. Peng et al. utilized camera-in-the-loop optimization, training high-quality holographic neural networks with optical images to simultaneously accelerate generation and enhance reconstruction quality [21]. To enhance the reconstruction quality of convolutional neural network-based methods, Zhong et al. introduced a complex-valued convolutional neural network that directly processes complex amplitudes to generate high-quality holograms while enhancing the network's representational capacity and computational efficiency [22]. Dong et al. developed a cross-domain super-resolution network that inputs low-resolution holograms and extracts inter-pixel information through multi-layer neural operations. This approach triples the speed compared to traditional methods while improving resolution, injecting new vitality into high-quality holographic displays [23]. Despite these algorithmic advancements, the computational speed remains inadequate for practical display applications.

Optimizing hologram generation for real-world objects represents another active research frontier. Li et al. deployed liquid crystal cameras equipped with fast-focusing elastic membrane lenses to capture real 3D scenes and generate holograms in real time [24]. However, as 3D capture technology advances, the demand for the personalized editing and processing of acquired data grows. Salient object detection—which filters out redundant background information and reduces processing complexity—is crucial for handling 3D data in holographic systems [25]. The authors previously proposed deep learning-based point cloud saliency segmentation and point cloud gridding (PCG) algorithms to accelerate CGH generation [26–29]. Nevertheless, challenges persist in real-time data acquisition and computation, along with insufficient reconstruction quality, which hinder practical deployment in intelligent 3D avatar interaction systems.

Substantial progress has also been made in enhancing CGH quality globally [30]. Some researchers have devised a diffraction model based on a split Lohmann lens, which synthesizes 3D holograms through single-step backpropagation. By integrating virtual digital phase modulation, this method significantly enhances the accuracy of 3D scene reconstruction, reduces computational costs, and boosts efficiency [31]. Sun et al. developed a pupil-aware gradient descent algorithm that combines multiple coherent sources and content-adaptive amplitude modulation in Fourier plane hologram spectra. Under the supervision of large-baseline target light fields, this innovation addresses the issues of poor image quality and short lifespan [32]. Despite breakthroughs, chromatic aberration remains a persistent challenge for color holography.

In summary, researchers worldwide have developed sophisticated algorithms addressing core holographic challenges: generation speed, reconstruction quality, and intelligent interaction. However, current computational efficiency and reconstruction quality for real-object holography still fall short of practical requirements for intelligent avatar interaction. To overcome these limitations, this paper presents an emotionally adaptive interactive holographic display system incorporating CCNN-PCG. The system employs 2D-to-3D technology for point cloud data acquisition. Interaction and emotionally adaptive responses are facilitated by ChatGLM. Furthermore, the CCNN-PCG algorithm reduces computational complexity while enhancing display quality. This framework provides a robust technical pathway for holographic intelligent interaction and offers novel perspectives for addressing related challenges.

## 2. Full-Color Holographic System

### 2.1. System Architecture

Building on the foundational research, objectives, and core scientific challenges outlined earlier, this paper delves deeply into optical signal acquisition and processing technologies. It integrates cutting-edge methodologies from multiple domains, including large language models (LLMs), CGH, holographic display technology, image processing algorithms, and holographic encryption strategies, to construct and optimize an interactive 3D holographic display system tailored for intelligent digital humans. The implementation blueprint adheres to the technical pathway illustrated in Figure 1, with the system comprising four core modules:

1. Acquisition and Preprocessing Module: This module utilizes the Unique3D framework and two-dimensional-to-three-dimensional technology to obtain depth multi-view images from single-view input, thereby generating 3D models. It performs point cloud sampling through Poisson sampling to improve the efficiency and accuracy of 3D model construction and point cloud data extraction, laying the foundation for subsequent holographic processing. Its main function is to efficiently build a digital human motion model library.
2. Intelligent Voice Interaction Module: To enable real-time voice interaction in the holographic system, this module integrates the ChatGLM large language model and an emotional adaptability analysis algorithm to improve fluency and accuracy. Utilizing Microsoft's Offline Speech Recognition API, it achieves speech-to-text conversion. The module constructs a point cloud model for digital humans that incorporates interactive textual information, enabling contextually appropriate responses through motion based on dialog content.
3. Hologram Generation Module: This module optimizes computational architecture to achieve high-quality hologram generation with significantly improved computational efficiency by using our proposed CCNN-PCG method. The point cloud data undergoes operations such as point removal, layering, and compression into an image. Subsequently, it is divided into three channels and input into the CCNN to obtain a three-channel output of the CGH. This advancement enables dynamic holographic display capabilities.
4. Reconstruction Module: This module innovatively adopts a double-layer verification mechanism. First, through high-precision numerical simulation, optical wave diffraction theory is used to simulate the hologram encoding data, and algorithms such as Fourier transform are used to verify the imaging effect in advance. Second, the module enters the optical reconstruction stage, relying on core devices such as spatial light modulators and lasers to convert digital signals into actual optical wave interference patterns. Through real-time monitoring and dynamic calibration, it ensures the spatial resolution and depth perception of color holographic images.

### 2.2. High-Quality Digital Human Model Generation and Processing

Automatically generating diverse and high-quality 3D models from single-view images is a fundamental task in 3D computer vision technology, with extensive applications across numerous fields. When collecting human figures with a single-depth camera, there are drawbacks such as insufficient depth accuracy, incomplete 3D information, poor real-time performance, weak anti-interference ability, limited application scenarios, and hardware cost bottlenecks [13]. However, 2D-to-3D conversion combined with Poisson sampling for point cloud collection can complement 3D information through multi-view image fusion, retain details with adaptive Poisson dense sampling, and simultaneously integrate RGB texture and depth data to improve accuracy, dynamically optimize data volume, and feature low hardware cost and strong scene adaptability. Therefore, this paper constructs the character depth information collection component in the intelligent digital avatar interaction and display system based on this technology.

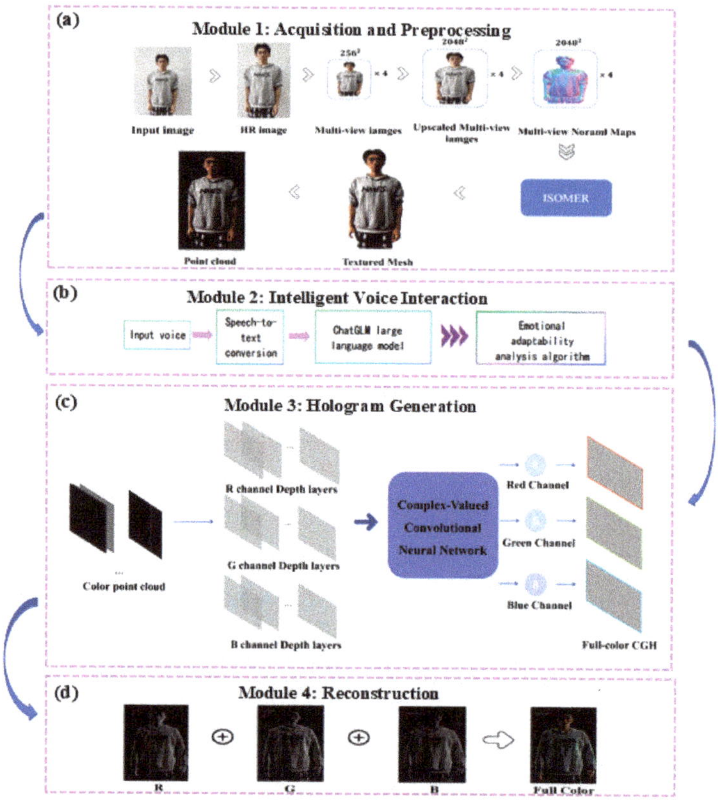


**Figure 1.** Modules of proposed holographic voice interaction system. (**a**) Acquisition and preprocessing module. (**b**) Intelligent voice interaction module. (**c**) Hologram generation module. (**d**) Reconstruction module.

In the acquisition phase, instead of using the depth camera from previous systems to capture character depth information [11], we adopt a method of generating high-quality 3D models from 2D images to further obtain point clouds for acquiring character depth information. In this part, this paper optimizes the process by using the Unique3D framework [9] to achieve the rapid acquisition of character depth information and generate high-quality digital human models.

We then employ a normal diffusion model to predict normal maps corresponding to multi-view color images. This section also adopts a multi-tier generation strategy, using a super-resolution model to increase resolution by 6–8 times. Finally, the normal diffusion model is used to predict normal maps for multi-view color images.

In the multi-view perceptual control mesh algorithm section, the process is divided into three parts: initial mesh estimation; mesh optimization; and explicit target optimization for multi-view inconsistency and geometric refinement. As shown in Figure 2, @ represents matrix multiplication, * represents element-wise multiplication, the initialization model undergoes model refinement to obtain a textured model, then proceeds to model coloring, and finally is converted into a point cloud model.

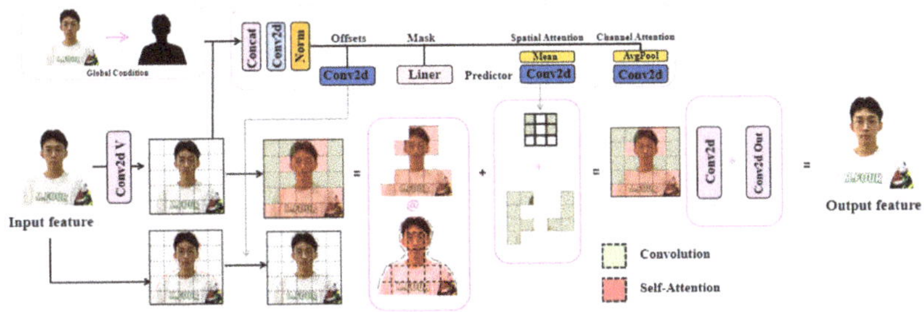


**Figure 2.** Point cloud generation process and single depth camera acquisition.

During initial mesh estimation, front rear views directly estimate the initial mesh. Orthographic maps from the front view are integrated to obtain depth maps (Equation (1)):

$$d(i,j) = \int_0^i \vec{n}(x) \cdot d\vec{x} \approx \sum\nolimits_{t=0}^{i} n_x(t), \quad (1)$$

where $d(i,j)$ is the depth at coordinate $(i,j)$, $\vec{n}(x)$ is a normal vector, and $n_x(t)$ is the x-component normal at time t.

Pseudo-normal maps generated by diffusion cannot form rotation-free true normal fields. To address this, random rotation is introduced into normal maps before integration. This is repeated multiple times, and integration averages are used to calculate depth for reliable estimation. Then, the estimated depth is used to map pixels to spatial positions. Mesh models are created from the front/back views of objects. Next, smooth connections are ensured through Poisson reconstruction, and the models are simplified to less than 2000 faces for initialization. A 3D point cloud model of digital humans is then generated.

To further demonstrate the superiority of this method, we conducted a detailed comparison between this method and the point clouds collected by a single depth camera, as shown in Table 1, and the generation effects are presented in Figure 3.

**Table 1.** Comparison of 3D point cloud model acquisition.

| | Number of Points | Viewing Angle | Point Cloud Distribution |
|---|---|---|---|
| Ours | 200,000–900,000 | 360° | Uniform distribution |
| Depth Camera | 50,000–300,000 | 180° | Concentrated distribution |

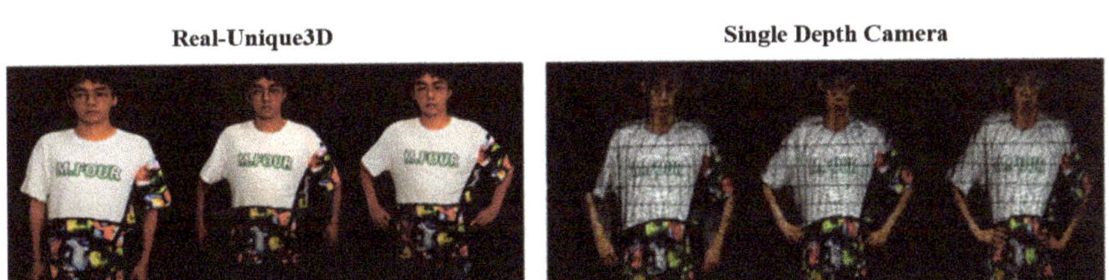


**Figure 3.** Comparison of point cloud generation effects.

The point cloud generation method proposed in this study is capable of acquiring a full-view 3D point cloud model with a point count reaching 900,000, which significantly surpasses the maximum acquisition capacity of depth cameras. Furthermore, through optimized sampling strategies, this method ensures the spatial uniformity of point cloud acquisition, effectively avoiding the problem of uneven data distribution caused by local point cloud aggregation during depth camera acquisition. This eliminates key factors affecting 3D reconstruction accuracy at the data quality level, providing a reliable data foundation for subsequent high-precision model construction.

### 2.3. Emotional Adaptability Analysis

Research indicates significant cognitive and behavioral differences between men and women in intimate relationships. Men and women exhibit distinct preferences in expansive postures: men tend to favor dominant gestures, while women prefer constrictive ones. In emotional expression, female digital characters more frequently adopt closed postures, such as lowering their heads with hunched shoulders, smiling while lowering their heads, or gently twisting their fingers. Male digital characters tend to display expansive and dominant postures, such as standing with their legs apart, clasping their hands behind their back, making outward or upward gestures, or pointing at others to reinforce authority.

Thus, this paper introduces an affective adaptation analysis algorithm module to enhance digital humans' non-verbal behavioral feedback following user emotion recognition. Through this mechanism, digital humans achieve more accurate emotional synchronization during voice interactions.

By pre-categorizing digital human emotions, this algorithm identifies label words in responses generated by large language models (LLMs), determines emotion categories based on recognized label words, triggers corresponding emotional actions, and ultimately generates a point cloud model of interactive movements to form action models incorporating interactive text. As shown in Figure 4, we apply this emotion analysis algorithm to classify the avatar's happiness, sadness, standby state, and other emotions with a classifier. After the LLM generates responses based on the user's vocal queries, this affective adaptation analysis algorithm automatically identifies the generated text content, extracts emotional keywords, and invokes the corresponding emotional interactive action point cloud model based on the emotion category of the keyword. This interactive action point cloud model is output alongside the LLM-generated text content, ultimately producing a digital human action model matching the emotional category of the text.

In the affective adaptation analysis module, we extract key information such as nouns and adjectives from the target domain. Descriptors constitute a set of label words representing high-probability words predicted by the PLM within a given context. Unlike methods relying on external knowledge, we extract domain-specific nouns and adjectives from the target domain using vocabulary annotation tools, avoiding noise and complexity associated with external sources.

Following the final construction of the descriptors, each word is associated with its corresponding token class. Implemented as cross-domain classification, this involves populating the "[MASK]" with each word from the label word space and computing its probability $P$. Subsequently, the predicted probability of each token word is mapped to its corresponding class label, and the average of these predicted probabilities is used for final classification. The predicted probability for the final class label can be expressed as $P([MASK]) = v \in V_t$. This is a function that converts token word probabilities into class label probabilities.

$$P(y|x) = f(P_M|v \in V_t) \quad (2)$$

where $f$ is a function that transforms token probabilities into class label probabilities. In the experiments, the cross-entropy loss function is introduced, updating the parameters of the entire model during training as follows:

$$L = -\frac{1}{N_t}\sum logp(y^*|x) + \alpha||\theta||^2 \tag{3}$$

where $\sum$ represents the sum of losses across all samples, $y^*$ denotes the true label, and $\alpha$ is a parameter regulating the impact of regularization on the total loss.

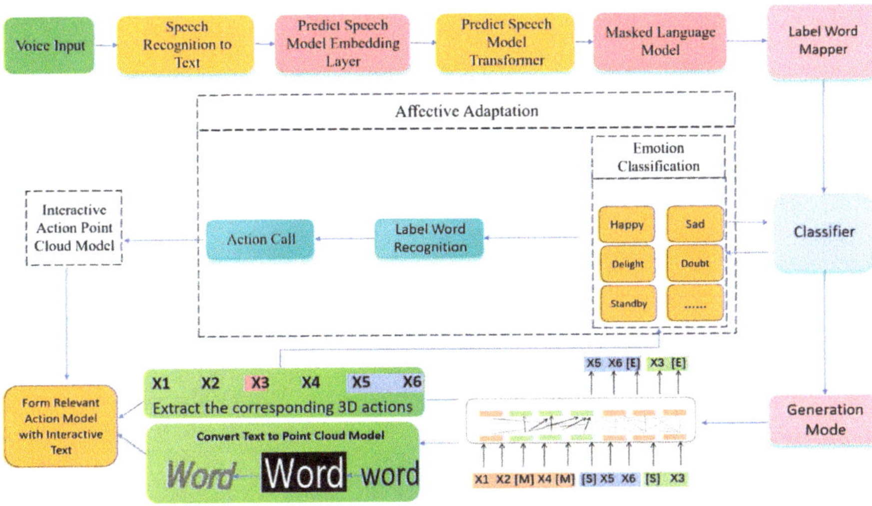


**Figure 4.** The affective adaptation analysis-based voice interaction module. The voice input is first converted to text and processed by the speech model, masked language model, etc. Then it enters affective adaptation, where label words are recognized, and emotions are classified. Combined with the interactive action point cloud model, features are extracted and converted into point clouds and output by the generation mode via the classifier.

As shown in Figure 5, the Speech Recognition and Text Conversion Module can utilize Microsoft's offline speech recognition interface. The system captures user voice input in real time and converts it into text. This process forms the foundation of voice interaction, ensuring the accurate transmission of user instructions. When large language models generate lengthy or complex textual content, the intelligent digital human that utilizes this emotion analysis algorithm can more accurately and effectively identify the emotional intent of the textual response and execute corresponding auxiliary motions.

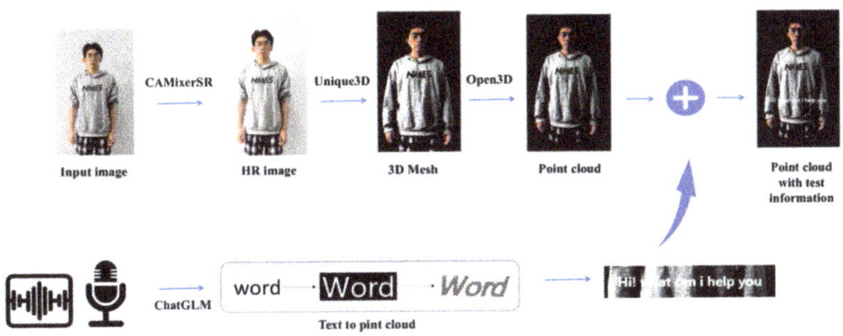


**Figure 5.** Extract corresponding 3D actions from input text.

As shown in Table 2, 14 sets of action modules were collected using our method for generating 3D point clouds from a single view, and an action library was established. Based on the corresponding point cloud modules output by the intelligent voice interaction module, we inserted the answer text point clouds. In small-sample scenarios, traditional algorithms achieved 90% recognition accuracy [13], whereas the emotion-adaptive algorithm proposed in this paper attains 97% accuracy, representing a substantial improvement over conventional methods. This enhancement underscores the algorithm's adaptability to emotional nuances in limited data environments.

**Table 2.** Common action modules for holographic voice interactive system.

| **Number** | **1** | **2** | **3** | **4** | **5** | **6** | **7** |
|---|---|---|---|---|---|---|---|
| Models | Standby1 | Standby2 | Affirmation | Negation | Instructions | Fear | Surprise |
| **Number** | **8** | **9** | **10** | **11** | **12** | **13** | **14** |
| Models | Ponder | Uneasiness | Confidence | Anxiety | Fatigue | Laugh | Cry |

### *2.4. Complex-Valued Convolutional Neural Network Point Cloud Gridding Algorithm*

Currently, in the field of computer-generated holography, numerous methods can achieve hologram generation and enhance quality, but the process of generating high-quality computational holograms is generally time-consuming. In light of this, this study builds upon the point cloud meshing algorithm from the authors' prior research by incorporating a convolutional neural network to accelerate hologram generation and improve reconstruction quality.

The CCNN exhibits unique advantages in holographic phase preservation, which stem from its deep alignment with the physical properties of optical fields. The core of holography lies in the encoding of optical field complex amplitudes, and processes such as light diffraction are inherently complex-domain operations. The CCNN directly uses complex numbers for input, output, and weights, avoiding the information fragmentation caused by real-valued networks splitting complex amplitudes into real and imaginary parts.

This paper proposes a hierarchical computational hologram generation method based on a CCNN. By leveraging learnable initial phases and taking the complex amplitude of the computational hologram plane as input, the method predicts computational holograms, with input depth layers randomly selected during training. The model generates 2D reconstructed computational holograms through different depth layers and synthesizes complex longitudinal magnification to produce layered holograms. The CCNN encodes computational holograms with minimal time consumption and imposes no additional computational burden for multiple layers. Numerical reconstruction and optical experiments demonstrate that this method enables real-time hologram generation for layered scenes. The system generates holograms for the digital human's interactive point cloud model, achieving holographic 3D reconstruction with depth information. The network structure employed is illustrated in Figure 6. The CCNN also incorporates residual skip connections (SCs). The addition of SCs helps mitigate the issues of gradient vanishing and explosion, promotes feature reuse, and simplifies the learning process of the network to accelerate convergence.

Meanwhile, it enhances the model's ability to capture information at different scales and levels, thereby improving the model's representational power, performance, and generalization ability. The input to the complex-valued omni-dimensional dynamic convolution layer is the complex amplitude A of the SLM plane across multiple depth layers. The output is a complex amplitude A that contains more feature information and has a different number of channels, and the phase of this complex amplitude is used as the single-phase CGH.

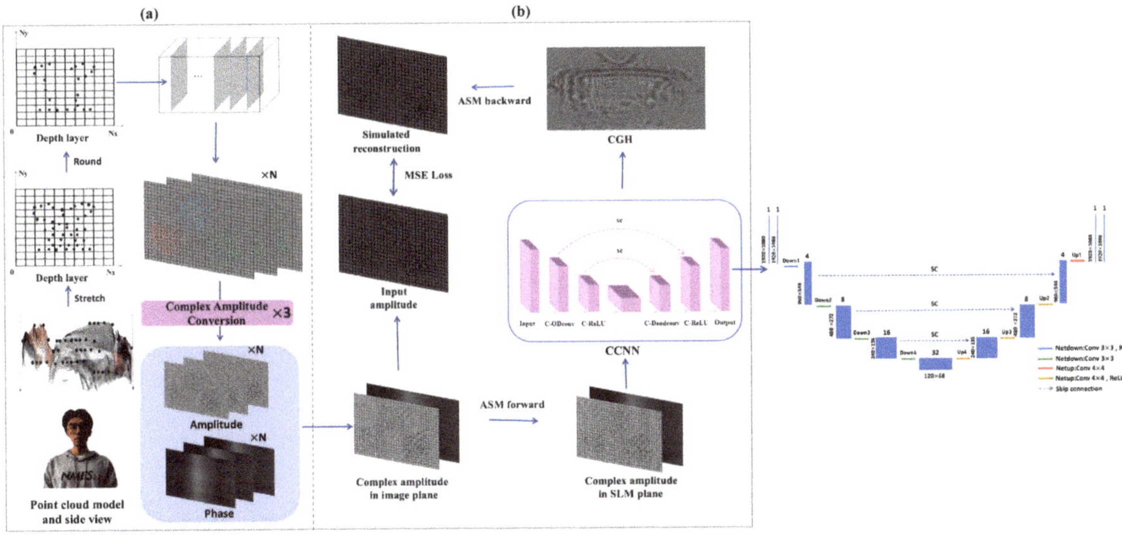


**Figure 6.** The overall process of the CCNN-PCG algorithm. (**a**) Point cloud processing module: The point cloud undergoes sampling, de-pointing, slice compression, and complex amplitude conversion to obtain the complex amplitude of the point cloud slice image. (**b**) The structure of the CCNN algorithm. Finally, the output CGH is obtained.

In this network, the number of point cloud grid layers and the distance between each grid layer must first be configured. For each grid layer, an initial phase set to zero is employed as a learnable parameter during training. For each input amplitude, its depth layer is randomly selected from different target grid layers. The corresponding initial phase is then assigned to the input amplitude. After the system performs segmentation from the image plane to the computational hologram plane using the Angular Spectrum Method (ASM), the CCNN is employed for encoding control. The numerically reconstructed amplitude is subsequently compared with the input amplitude. Within this network, input amplitude $A$ is randomly assigned depth $d$, corresponding phase $\varphi_d$, and complex amplitude $C_d$ as follows:

$$C_d = Aexp(i\varphi_d) \tag{4}$$

Next, the ASM calculates the propagation distance from the image plane to the SLM plane. The complex amplitude at the SLM plane is given by the following:

$$D_d = F^{-1}[F(C_d)\cdot H_d] \tag{5}$$

$$H_d = \begin{cases} exp(ikz_d\sqrt{1-\lambda^2 f_x^2 - \lambda^2 f_y^2}),\ if\sqrt{f_x^2+f_y^2} < \frac{1}{\lambda} \\ 0\ otherwise \end{cases} \tag{6}$$

where $F$ and $F^{-1}$ represent the 2D fast Fourier transform and its inverse, $k$ is the wavenumber, $z_d$ denotes propagation distance, $\lambda$ is the wavelength, and $f_x$ and $f_y$ are spatial frequencies along the x- and y-axes. Zero-padding interpolation and band-limited ASM propagation are applied for enhanced diffraction calculation accuracy. The *loss* function is defined as follows:

$$Loss = \frac{1}{Z}\sum\nolimits_{i=1}^{Z} \|A_{R,i} - A_{T,i}\|^2 \tag{7}$$

where $A_{R,i}$ and $A_{T,i}$ represent the amplitude values of the reconstructed image and the target image at the i-th pixel, respectively, and $Z$ is the total number of pixels. With the addition of the attention mechanism, the network has stronger feature extraction capabilities, which can be reflected in the train loss values during the training process.

The CCNN emphasizes complex-valued operations to preserve phase information and strengthen nonlinear mapping. By integrating PCG with the CCNN, their complementary strengths lead to enhanced feature extraction and processing capabilities, improving point cloud grid hologram generation across multiple dimensions. CCNN-PCG further processes and fuses features in complex-valued space, enabling the network to learn more comprehensive and representative point cloud characteristics. This provides stronger support for generating high-quality mesh holograms.

During training, distinct parameters are set for different channels to optimize output. The processed point cloud data is then separated into three channels (RGB) and fed into the algorithm to generate single-channel holograms. Finally, holograms from all three channels are combined to produce a full-color hologram. In terms of training data, we used 100 layers of point cloud grids and 700 images from the public dataset DIV2K as the training set. In addition, we used 100 images from the DIV2K dataset, excluding the 700 images used for training, as the validation set. Comparisons were made with algorithms such as PCG, the CCNN, and Holo-Encoder under the same testing environment, thereby demonstrating the robustness and universal value of the proposed method.

To enhance the network's performance in generating a CGH from point cloud sliced images, we adopted a multimodal approach for the dataset. Specifically, we incorporated point cloud sliced images into the DIV2K training set, with the ratio of regular images to point cloud sliced images adjusted to 7:1. We set the number of training iterations to 800, the number of validation iterations to 100, the number of training epochs to 50, and the learning rate to 0.08.

## 3. Experiment and Results

### *3.1. Interactive Voice Experiment Verification*

This section presents the digital human point cloud display results based on the emotion analysis algorithm for voice interaction and applies our proposed CCNN-PCG algorithm to generate digital human point cloud holograms. Simulation tests were conducted on a Windows 11 (64-bit) PC equipped with an NVIDIA GeForce RTX 4090 (24GB video memory, Santa Clara, CA, USA) and an Intel Core i9-13900 (32 GB RAM, Santa Clara, CA, USA) using MATLAB R2024a and Python 3.12.

In the human point cloud generation process, Unique3D constructs 3D models from input 2D images; Open3D combined with Poisson disk sampling generates uniformly distributed colored point clouds, with output quality surpassing that of our previous depth camera-based acquisition system. The effect is shown in Figure 7.

During system operation, users can select either a male or female digital human and activate standby motions. As depicted in Figure 8a,b, when a user issues requests for voice input, the system generates inquiry gestures and questions through its emotion analysis-based voice interaction module. When a user asks, "Could you recommend some books?", the system identifies this as a general instruction, performs emotion analysis on the response content, generates recommendation gestures, and provides suggested book titles. As illustrated in Figure 8c,d, our interactive system supports both Chinese and English. The experimental process and results of voice interaction in the color holographic display system demonstrate that the voice interaction system exhibits interactivity.

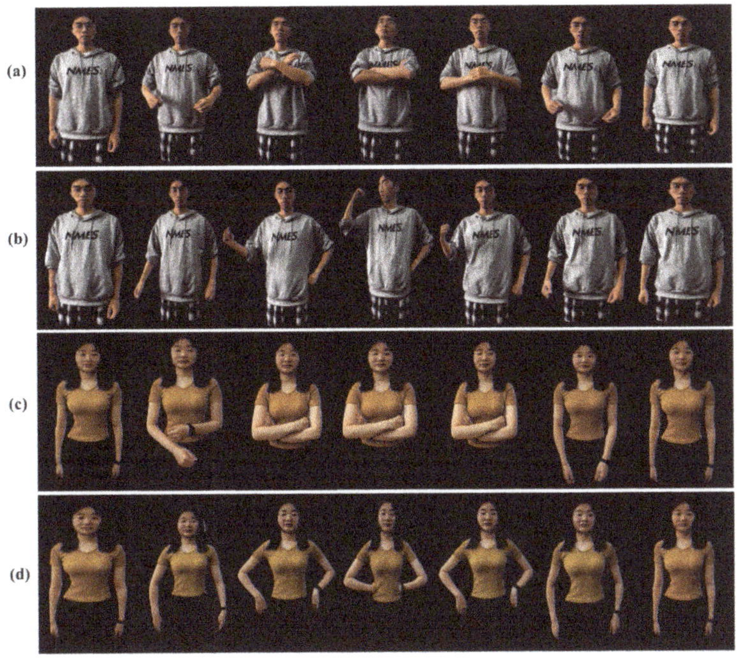

**Figure 7.** Digital human actions by gender: (**a**) male standby, (**b**) male delight, (**c**) female standby, and (**d**) female delight.

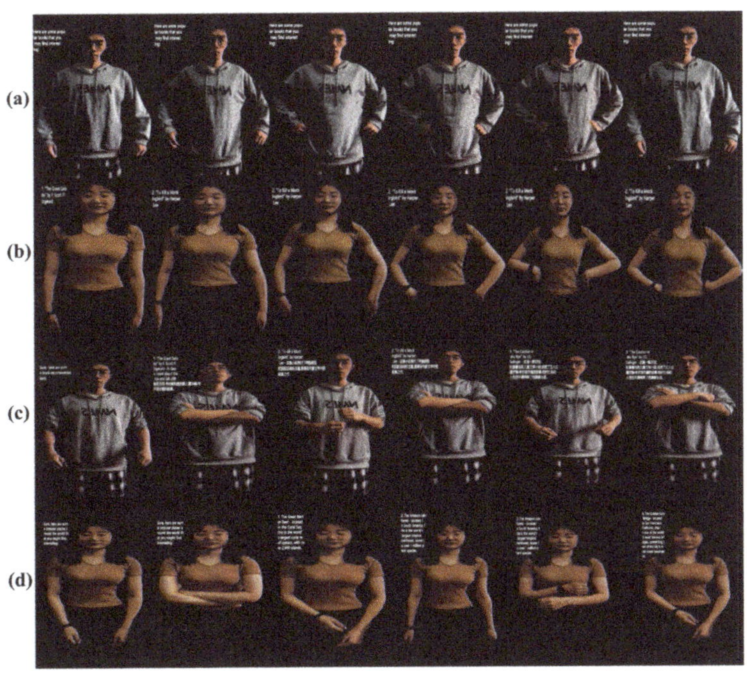

**Figure 8.** Interactive voice experiment verifies results: Voice input requests book recommendations from (**a**) male digital human and (**b**) female digital human. (**c**) Voice input requests book recommendations in Chinese and (**d**) introduction of some travel destinations in English.

*3.2. Generation Speed and Reconstructed Image Quality Enhancement*

To highlight the performance of the CCNN-PCG algorithm in generating 3D point cloud-based holograms, we compared it with the Holo-encoder [20] and PCG [11] algorithms. By comparing layered RGB point cloud images with corresponding simulated reconstruction images, average peak signal-to-noise ratio (PSNR) values were obtained. After dataset modification and network optimization, our method achieved improved PSNR metrics while maintaining generation speed when producing a 1920 × 1080-resolution CGH. Simulated reconstructions of CCNN-PCG, Holo-encoder, and PCG are depicted in Figure 9a–c, respectively. For point cloud-based CGH generation, CCNN-PCG demonstrates significantly superior performance over the CCNN while simultaneously generating R, G, and B channel holograms. Figure 9d,e present comparative reconstructions of CCNN-PCG versus the CCNN without PCG. When GPU memory permits, CCNN-PCG generates full-color 30-layer CGHs in 0.066 s—5% faster than the CCNN (without PCG), 2.32 times faster than PCG, and 3.18 times faster than Holo-encoder. Compared to the CCNN (without PCG), CCNN-PCG achieves a 9% higher PSNR and 50% higher SSIM. The PSNR and generation time comparisons across all methods are shown in Figure 9f,g.

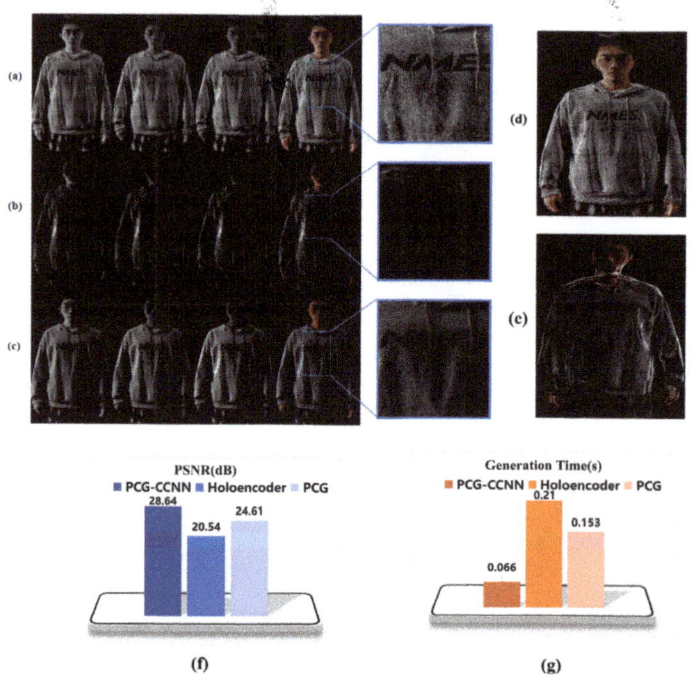


**Figure 9.** Numerical reconstruction in R, G, and B channels, and full-color reconstructed images of (**a**) our proposed CCNN-PCG, (**b**) Holo-encoder, and (**c**) PCG methods. Comparison of simulation reconstruction effects: (**d**) CCNN with PCG and (**e**) CCNN without PCG. Comparison of (**f**) PSNR and (**g**) generation times of holograms.

To more clearly demonstrate the improvements in CCNN-PCG over traditional CNNs, we conducted a structural comparison between CCNN-PCG and the traditional CNN of Holo-encoder, as shown in Table 3.

**Table 3.** Comparison between CCNN-PCG and Holo-Encoder architecture.

| | Network Layers | Arity | Convolution Type | Normalization Module | Activation Function |
|---|---|---|---|---|---|
| CCNN-PCG | 3 | 938 | C-conv | Used | C-Relu |
| Holo-encoder | 8 | Million-level | Conv | Batch Normalization | Relu |

As shown in Table 4, our proposed CCNN-PCG method achieves quality improvements while accelerating CGH generation, and RGB channels can be processed in parallel. When generating holograms over 400,000 point clouds, CCNN-PCG produces a color CGH in 0.063 s, approximately 3.1–3.6 times faster than the Holo-encoder method and 2.2–2.4 times faster than the PCG methods.

**Table 4.** Calculation of generation time of holographic system when resolution is 1920 × 1080.

| Object | | | Generation Time | | |
|---|---|---|---|---|---|
| **Name** | **Points** | **Layers** | **PCG** | **Holo-Encoder** | **CCNN-PCG** |
| Figure 7a—1 | 450,429 | 30 | 0.154 | 0.227 | 0.063 |
| Figure 7a—6 | 423,568 | 30 | 0.157 | 0.214 | 0.068 |
| Figure 7b—1 | 414,298 | 30 | 0.152 | 0.221 | 0.064 |
| Figure 7b—6 | 470,651 | 30 | 0.152 | 0.208 | 0.067 |
| Figure 7c—1 | 438,386 | 30 | 0.153 | 0.231 | 0.064 |
| Figure 7d—1 | 435,582 | 30 | 0.153 | 0.223 | 0.066 |

As shown in Table 5, in terms of reconstruction quality, the Holo-encoder algorithm exhibits insufficient performance in processing point cloud data. Our proposed CCNN-PCG method achieves an approximately 40–44% higher PSNR compared to the Holo-encoder and about a 15–20% higher PSNR than PCG. Additionally, our CCNN-PCG algorithm can encode complex-amplitude holograms with different wavelengths and reconstruction distances, demonstrating stronger adaptability and higher coding efficiency.

**Table 5.** Calculated PSNR of holographic system when resolution is 1920 × 1080.

| Object | | | PSNR | | |
|---|---|---|---|---|---|
| **Name** | **Points** | **Layers** | **PCG** | **Holo-Encoder** | **CCNN-PCG** |
| Figure 7a—1 | 450,429 | 30 | 25.41 | 20.47 | 29.34 |
| Figure 7a—6 | 423,568 | 30 | 24.18 | 20.63 | 29.32 |
| Figure 7b—1 | 414,298 | 30 | 24.22 | 19.98 | 28.95 |
| Figure 7b—6 | 470,651 | 30 | 23.46 | 20.33 | 29.01 |
| Figure 7c—1 | 438,386 | 30 | 23.33 | 21.07 | 28.87 |
| Figure 7d—1 | 435,582 | 30 | 23.74 | 19.54 | 28.28 |

As illustrated in Figure 10, we selected male and female digital humans and conducted diverse interactions to generate corresponding interactive motions and textual responses. This process validated the system's feasibility through both simulated and optical experiments. The optical setup for holographic display is illustrated in Figure 10a. To achieve color holographic display, a time division multiplexing experimental architecture employing RGB laser sources (250 mW, 12 V, 1 A) was implemented: 638 nm red/520 nm green/450 nm blue laser beams were attenuated, expanded, and projected onto a spatial light modulator (SLM). The full-color phase-only SLM (CAS Microstar, Xi'an, China) featured a resolution of 1920 × 1080 with a pixel pitch of 4.5 μm. At a refresh rate of 3 × 60 Hz, three-channel holograms were sequentially loaded onto the SLM. When the refresh rate exceeded the human eye's response time, the reconstructed images were perceived as color images. The reconstructed images of the R, G, and B channels and the color-simulated reconstructed images at different reconstruction distances are shown in Figure 10b–e. The optical reconstruction effects of the R, G, and B channels and the color one are shown in Figure 10f–i.

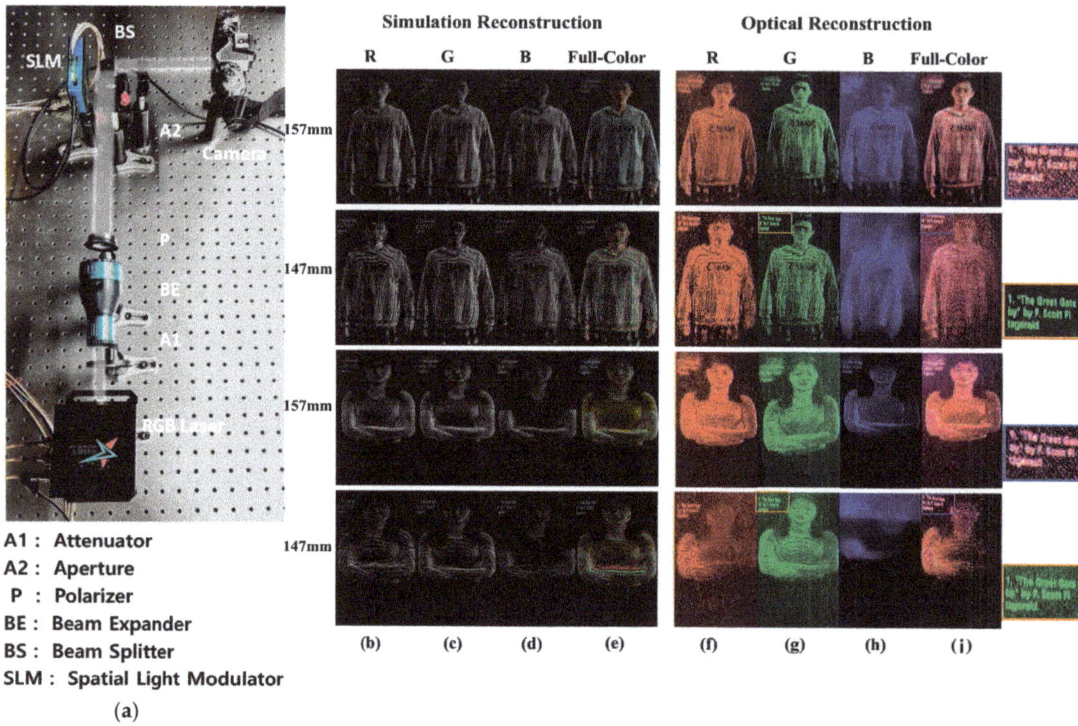


**Figure 10.** (**a**) Optical setup for holographic display, (**b**) red channel, (**c**) green channel, (**d**) blue channel, and (**e**) full-color simulated reconstructed images; (**f**) red channel, (**g**) green channel, (**h**) blue channel, and (**i**) full-color optical reconstructed images.

Optical reconstructed images are presented in Figure 10 f–i. After transmitting phase holograms containing digital human point cloud information and textual interactive information to the SLM, the camera-captured patterns clearly demonstrate the in-focus/out-of-focus effects in optical experiments. When the focusing distance was 147 mm, the textual interactive information in the optical reconstruction was also clearly visible. Both simulated and optical experiments validate the effectiveness of our proposed CCNN-PCG method.

## 4. Conclusions

This paper proposes a holographic voice interactive display system incorporating speech interaction and holographic modules. As the core voice interaction component, the ChatGLM model enables text interaction, emotional adaptation, and digital human motion control within the holographic system. For the holographic module, the CCNN-PCG algorithm is employed to generate a CGH from point clouds with enhanced efficiency and superior quality. The experimental results demonstrate measurable improvements in both generation speed and reconstruction quality compared to the PCG and Holo-encoder methods. This research pioneers approaches for integrating full-color holographic reconstruction with interactive technologies, offering innovative technical pathways and practical references for the advancement of human–computer interaction from 2D screens to 3D holographic environments.

However, since CCNN-PCG requires a large amount of video memory during the training process, this greatly limits the number of depth layers contained in the generated CGH. The maximum number of layers that can be trained with 24 GB of video memory is only about 200, which significantly restricts the demand for generating a CGH with depth information for large scenes. In future research, we will focus on improving the network's feature extraction capability to further increase the number of depth layers generated by the CGH, thereby making the network applicable to more scenarios.

**Author Contributions:** Conceptualization, Y.Z. and Y.L.; Methodology, Y.Z., Z.X. and Y.L.; Software, Y.Z., Z.X., T.-Y.Z. and M.X.; Validation, Z.X. and B.H.; Formal analysis, Z.X., T.-Y.Z. and M.X.; Investigation, Z.X. and B.H.; Resources, Z.X., T.-Y.Z., M.X., B.H. and Y.L.; Data curation, T.-Y.Z., B.H. and Y.L.; Writing—original draft, Y.Z.; Writing—review & editing, Y.L.; Visualization, M.X.; Supervision, Y.L.; Funding acquisition, Y.Z. All authors have read and agreed to the published version of the manuscript.

**Funding:** This research was funded by National Natural Science Foundation of China (No. 62205283) and Natural Science Foundation of Jiangsu Province (No. BE2023340).

**Data Availability Statement:** All data in this manuscript are available from the corresponding author upon reasonable request.

**Conflicts of Interest:** The authors declare no conflicts of interest.

## References

1. Cao, L.C.; He, Z.H.; Liu, K.X.; Sui, X.M. Progress and challenges in dynamic holographic 3D display for the metaverse. *Infrared Laser Eng.* **2022**, *51*, 267–281.
2. Chen, C.P.; Ma, X.; Zou, S.P.; Liu, T.; Chu, Q.; Hu, H.; Cui, Y. Quad-channel waveguide-based near-eye display for metaverse. *Displays* **2023**, *81*, 102582. [CrossRef]
3. Tang, Y.; Yi, J.; Tan, F. Facial micro-expression recognition method based on CNN and transformer mixed model. *Int. J. Biom.* **2024**, *16*, 463–477. [CrossRef]
4. Tan, F.; Zhai, M.; Zhai, C. Foreign object detection in urban rail transit based on deep differentiation segmentation neural network. *Heliyon* **2024**, *10*, e37072. [CrossRef]
5. Nagahama, Y. Interactive zoom display in a smartphone-based digital holographic microscope for 3D imaging. *Appl. Opt.* **2024**, *63*, 6623–6627. [CrossRef]
6. Li, J.; Lai, Y.; Li, W.; Ren, J.Y.; Zhang, M.; Kang, X.H.; Wang, S.Y.; Li, P.; Zhang, Y.Q.; Ma, W.Z.; et al. Agent Hospital: A simulacrum of hospital with evolvable medical agents. *arXiv* **2024**, arXiv:2405.02957. [CrossRef]
7. Durante, Z.; Huang, Q.; Wake, N.; Gong, R.; Park, J.S.; Sarkar, B.; Taori, R.; Noda, Y.; Terzopoulos, D.; Choi, Y.; et al. Agent AI: Surveying the horizons of multimodal interaction. *arXiv* **2024**, arXiv:2401.03568. [CrossRef]
8. Prabhavalkar, R.; Hori, T.; Sainath, T.N.; Schlüter, R.; Watanabe, S. End-to-end speech recognition: A survey. *IEEE/ACM Trans. Audio Speech Lang. Process.* **2024**, *32*, 325–351. [CrossRef]
9. Yang, F.; Yang, M.; Li, X.; Wu, Y.; Zhao, Z.; Raj, B. A closer look at reinforcement learning-based automatic speech recognition. *Comput. Speech Lang.* **2024**, *87*, 101641. [CrossRef]
10. Boisseau, É. Imitation and large language models. *Minds Mach.* **2024**, *34*, 42. [CrossRef]
11. Wu, K.; Liu, F.; Cai, Z.; Yan, R.J.; Wang, H.Y.; Hu, Y.T.; Duan, Y.Q.; Ma, K.S. Unique3D: High-quality and efficient 3D mesh generation from a single image. *arXiv* **2024**, arXiv:2405.20343.
12. Wang, Y.; Zhao, S.J.; Liu, Y.; Li, J.L.; Zhang, L. CAMixerSR: Only Details Need More Attention. *arXiv* **2024**, arXiv:2402.19289. [CrossRef]
13. Zhao, Y.; Huang, Z.; Ji, J.; Xie, M.; Liu, W.; Chen, C.P. Holographic voice-interactive system with Taylor Rayleigh-Sommerfeld based point cloud gridding. *Opt. Lasers Eng.* **2024**, *179*, 108270. [CrossRef]
14. Pan, Y.; Xu, X.; Liang, X. Fast distributed large-pixel count hologram computation using a GPU cluster. *Appl. Opt.* **2023**, *52*, 6562–6571. [CrossRef]
15. Kwon, M.W.; Kim, S.C.; Kim, E.S. Three-directional motion-compensation mask-based novel look-up table on graphics processing units for video-rate generation of digital holographic videos of three-dimensional scenes. *Appl. Opt.* **2016**, *55*, A22–A31. [CrossRef]
16. Pi, D.; Liu, J.; Han, Y.; Khalid, A.; Yu, S. Simple and effective calculation method for computer-generated hologram based on non-uniform sampling using ook-up-table. *Opt. Express* **2019**, *27*, 37337–37348. [CrossRef]

17. Cao, H.K.; Jin, X.; Ai, L.Y.; Kim, E.S. Faster generation of holographic video of 3-D scenes with a Fourier spectrum-based NLUT method. *Opt. Express* **2021**, *29*, 39738–39754. [CrossRef]
18. Shimobaba, T.; Masuda, N.; Ito, T. Simple and fast calculation algorithm for computer- generated hologram with wavefront recording plane. *Opt. Lett.* **2009**, *34*, 3133–3135. [CrossRef]
19. Wang, Y.; Sang, X.; Chen, Z.; Li, H.; Zhao, L. Real-time photorealistic computer-generated holograms based on backward ray tracing and wavefront recording planes. *Opt. Commun.* **2018**, *429*, 12–17. [CrossRef]
20. Shi, L.; Li, B.; Kim, C.; Kellnhofer, P.; Matusik, W. Towards real-time photorealistic 3D holography with deep neural networks. *Nature* **2021**, *591*, 234–239. [CrossRef]
21. Peng, Y.; Choi, S.; Padmanaban, N.; Wetzstein, G. Neural holography with camera-in-the- loop training. *ACM Trans. Graph.* **2020**, *39*, 185. [CrossRef]
22. Zhong, C.L.; Sang, X.Z.; Yan, B.B.; Li, H.; Chen, D.; Qin, X.J. Real-Time High-Quality Computer-Generated Hologram Using Complex-Valued Convolutional Neural Network. *IEEE Trans. Vis. Comput. Graph.* **2024**, *30*, 3709–3718. [CrossRef]
23. Dong, Z.X.; Jia, J.D.; Li, Y.; Ling, Y.Y. Divide-Conquer-and-Merge: Memory-and Time-Efficient Holographic Displays. In Proceedings of the 2024 IEEE Conference Virtual Reality and 3D User Interfaces (VR), Orlando, FL, USA, 16–21 March 2024.
24. Li, Z.S.; Liu, C.; Li, X.W.; Zheng, Y.; Huang, Q.; Zheng, Y.W.; Hou, Y.H.; Chang, C.L.; Zhang, D.W.; Zhuang, S.L.; et al. Real-time holographic camera for obtaining real 3D scene hologram. *Light Sci. Appl.* **2025**, *14*, 74. [CrossRef]
25. Chen, S.; Yu, J.; Xu, X.; Chen, Z.; Lu, L.; Hu, X.; Yang, Y. Split-guidance network for salient object detection. *Vis. Comput.* **2023**, *39*, 1437–1451. [CrossRef]
26. Chen, S.; Tang, H.; Huang, Y.; Zhang, L.; Hu, X. S2dinet: Towards lightweight and fast high-resolution dichotomous image segmentation. *Pattern Recognit.* **2025**, *164*, 111506. [CrossRef]
27. Zhao, Y.; Bu, J.W.; Liu, W.; Ji, J.H.; Yang, Q.H.; Lin, S.F. Implementation of a full-color holographic system using RGB-D salient object detection and divided point cloud gridding. *Opt. Express* **2023**, *31*, 1641–1655. [CrossRef]
28. Bu, J.W.; Zhao, Y.; Ji, J.H. Full-color holographic system featuring three-dimensional salient object detection based on a U2-RAS network. *J. Opt. Soc. Am. A* **2023**, *40*, B1–B7. [CrossRef]
29. Yang, Q.H.; Zhao, Y.; Liu, W.; Bu, J.W.; Ji, J.H. A full-color holographic system based on Taylor Rayleigh-Sommerfeld diffraction point cloud grid algorithm. *Appl. Sci.* **2023**, *13*, 4466. [CrossRef]
30. Sun, X.H.; Mu, X.Y.; Xu, C.; Pang, H.; Deng, Q.L.; Zhang, K.; Jiang, H.B.; Du, J.L.; Yin, S.Y.; Du, C.L. Dual-task convolutional neural network based on the combination of the U-Net and a diffraction propagation model for phase hologram design with suppressed speckle noise. *Opt. Express* **2022**, *30*, 2646–2658. [CrossRef]
31. Chang, C.L.; Ding, X.; Wang, D.; Ren, Z.Z.; Dai, B.; Wang, Q.; Zhuang, S.L.; Zhang, D.W. Split Lohmann computer holography: Fast generation of 3D hologram in single-step diffraction calculation. *Adv. Photonics Nexus* **2024**, *3*, 036001. [CrossRef]
32. Chao, B.; Gopakumar, M.; Choi, S.; Kim, J.; Shi, L.; Wetzstein, G. Large Étendue 3D holographic display with content-adaptive dynamic fourier modulation. In Proceedings of the SIGGRAPH Asia 2024 Conference Paper, Tokyo, Japan, 3–6 December 2024; pp. 1–12.

*electronics*

MDPI

*Article*

# Multiple-Particle Autofocusing Algorithm Using Axial Resolution and Morphological Analyses Based on Digital Holography

**Wei-Na Li *, Yi Zhou, Jiatai Chen, Hongjie Ou and Xiangsheng Xie ***

Physics Department, College of Science, Shantou University, Shantou 515065, China; 22yzhou7@stu.edu.cn (Y.Z.); 22jtchen4@stu.edu.cn (J.C.); 22hjou@stu.edu.cn (H.O.)
* Correspondence: weinali@stu.edu.cn (W.-N.L.); xxs@stu.edu.cn (X.X.)

**Abstract:** We propose an autofocusing algorithm to obtain, relatively accurately, the 3D position of each particle, particularly its axial location, and particle number of a dense transparent particle solution via its hologram. First, morphological analyses and constrained intensity are used on raw reconstructed images to obtain information on candidate focused particles. Second, axial resolution is used to obtain the real focused particles. Based on the mean intensity and equivalent diameter of each candidate focused particle, all focused particles are eventually secured. Our proposed method can rapidly provide relatively accurate ground-truth axial positions to solve the autofocusing problem that occurs with dense particles.

**Keywords:** digital holography; Fresnel diffraction; autofocusing method; axial resolution; particles

## 1. Introduction

Digital holography (DH) is a sophisticated optical technology that specializes in capturing and reconstructing the optical information on three-dimensional (3D) objects. Unlike conventional microscopy, which is limited to imaging a single plane, digital holographic microscopy (DHM) is able to capture an entire volume and reconstruct every plane of this volume. Recently, the challenges of sizing, counting, and locating in situ micro-objects (particles, bubbles, or microorganisms) have garnered significant attention from researchers. This interest has been particularly driven by the development of in-line DH and its potential as an alternative to conventional microscopy [1,2]. In both DH and DHM, autofocusing is a crucial technique used to precisely determine the location of an object. While experimental configurations can achieve autofocusing [3,4], it is more commonly realized through computational algorithms, including the methods based on image sharpness [5,6], structure tensor [7], edge sparsity [8], magnitude differential [9], etc.

A number of researchers [10–13] have employed spherical waves to illuminate particles suspended in water. They determined the position and measured the size of each particle using a captured hologram. The experimental configuration achieved magnification of the target object. However, this approach not only reduces the field of view (FOV), but also significantly impacts the accuracy of both the particle count and their locations along the z-axis, depending on the chosen depth spacing. On the other hand, Tian et al. [14] investigated bubbles in water and employed the minimum intensity as a focus metric to detect the edges of bubbles, thereby accurately determining the location of each bubble, particularly its axial position. However, despite the faster processing speed of their proposed approach, the location information obtained is inaccurate. Moreover, when several bubbles are clustered together, they are mistakenly identified as a single bubble. These conventional methods, which are subject to the diffraction limit, cause severe defocused image problems if the ground-truth z-position of each micro-object is unknown. This ultimately leads to inaccuracies in determining the micro-objects on the mount and their locations. Later on, Lang et al. [15] utilized the Q value as the focus metric to recognize the best axial location for plankton; however, this focus metric is not suitable for numerous particles, especially dense particles in DH.

Compressive models leveraging sparsity have demonstrated remarkable performance in addressing noise and ghost artifacts by reformulating the hologram reconstruction problem as a regularized nonlinear optimization task. Brady et al. [16] introduced a compressive sensing algorithm for DH and showed that decompressive inference can infer multidimensional objects from a single 2D hologram. Liu et al. [17,18] applied compressive holography to object localization, achieving significant improvements in transverse localization accuracy when the solution is sparse in its derivatives. Chen et al. [19] further explored this domain by using a plane wave to illuminate bubbles; however, their method struggled with distinguishing bubbles that were completely or partially overlapped along the z-axis and could not effectively process dense particle fields. A common thread among these studies was the use of total variation regularizers. In contrast, Li et al. [20] applied a 3-D hybrid-Weickert nonlinear diffusion regularizer to DH, which successfully located small-sized transparent scattering particles that overlapped along the z-axis and removed defocused images. As a result, similar autofocusing for multiple micro-objects was achieved while simultaneously eliminating defocused images. Despite these advancements, all of the aforementioned methods have their drawbacks, including slow processing speed, the inability to process dense particles due to a sparse prior, difficulty in fine-tuning the parameters, among others.

With the recent advancements in machine learning, several innovative approaches have been developed to address autofocusing and 3D reconstruction challenges in DH. Ren et al. [21] efficiently employed convolutional neural networks (CNN) to reformulate autofocusing as a classification problem, thereby providing approximations of the focusing distance for each classification. This method is particularly well suited for single large objects, although it does not require reconstructing images. Lee et al. [22] proposed an alternative approach in which the centroid of each particle is first determined and then the cropped hologram of each particle is fed into a CNN to obtain depth information. Shao et al. [23] and Wu et al. [24] utilized a modified U-net network to extract 3D morphological information of all particles, including their 3D positions, sizes, and shapes, primarily from holograms. Li et al. [25] and Hao et al. [26] combined Dense Block and U-net to achieve 3D particle distribution with particle sizes particularly from reconstructed images. Ou et al. [27] employed a modified CNN architecture to predict particle numbers from holograms. However, this approach is incapable of obtaining the 3D positions of particles, especially their axial positions.

In this study, we propose an autofocusing method based on morphological analyses and axial resolution to obtain, relatively accurately, the 3D position of each particle, particularly its axial location, and the particle number of a dense transparent particle solution via a hologram. Our proposed method has two main components. First, morphological analyses and constrained intensity are used on raw reconstructed images, from which information on candidate focused particles is obtained and saved in one matrix. Second, axial resolution is used to obtain the real focused particles from the aforementioned matrix. For the focus metric, we propose using the product of the mean intensity and equivalent diameter of each candidate focused particle. Eventually, we are able to secure all focused particles for one hologram. In our experiments, we used particles located at fixed distances and in a particle solution that was filled in a cuvette to examine and verify the proposed method.

The remainder of this paper is organized as follows. Section 2 introduces the principles. Section 3 presents the methodology, in which the description of the algorithm is a key point. Section 4 discusses the experimental results and analyses. Finally, Section 5 presents the conclusions of our study.

## 2. Principles

Herein, it is assumed there are a large number of transparent particles suspended in Milli-Q water, all with a uniform size (diameter) denoted by $pcle_i(\xi, \eta)$, where $i$ = 1, 2, … $m$. A plane wave with wavelength $\lambda = 532$ nm illuminates these particles, and holograms of the 3D information of all the particles in the entire volume are captured using a complementary metal oxide semiconductor (CMOS) camera, as shown in Figure 1. If each particle is suspended at a distance $z_i$ from the image sensor chip (hologram plane), the Fresnel diffraction [28] for each particle can be mathematically expressed as follows:

$$H_i(x, y, z_i) = FT^{-1}\left\{\exp(jkz_i) \times FT\{pcle_i(\xi, \eta)\} \times \exp\left(-j\pi\lambda z_i\left(f_x^2 + f_y^2\right)\right)\right\} \tag{1}$$

$$H(x, y) = \sum_i^m H_i(x, y, z_i) \tag{2}$$

$$I(x, y) = |R(x, y)|^2 + |H(x, y)|^2 + R^*(x, y)H(x, y) + R(x, y)H^*(x, y) + n \tag{3}$$

$$I_{final}(x, y) = H(x, y) + nse \tag{4}$$

where $\{\xi, \eta\}$ denotes the lateral coordinates of the particle position, $(f_x, f_y)$ signifies the spatial frequency domain, $(x, y)$ denotes the hologram plane, $H(x, y)$ and $H^*(x, y)$ denote the complex amplitude and conjugate, respectively, of the hologram $I(x, y)$, and $n$ indicates the noise induced by the optical system (including high-frequency speckle noise, the diffraction patterns of dust or bubbles in the optical path, among others). Owing to the use of a plane wave as the reference beam, the amplitude of the reference beam $R(x, y) = 1$. Therefore, the hologram can be rewritten as shown in Equation (4), in which $nse = 1 + |H(x, y)|^2 + H^*(x, y) + n$.

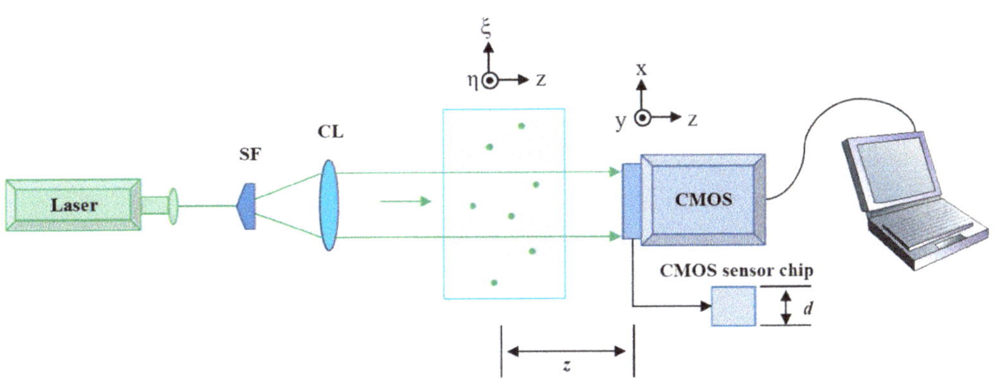


**Figure 1.** Schematic diagram of in-line digital holographic setup for capturing holograms of multiple particles (SF: spatial filter; CL: collimating lens; $z$: transmission distance between object plane and hologram plane; $d$: height of CMOS sensor chip).

# 3. Methodology

## 3.1. Axial Resolution

In a digital holographic system, assume a point light source with a wavelength $\lambda$ is located at a distance $z$ away from the CMOS sensor (hologram plane) whose size is $hy \times hx$ and pixel pitch is $\Delta_{pp}$; therefore, the height of the hologram is $D = hy \cdot \Delta_{pp}$. The schematic diagram is depicted in Figure 2, where $\{\xi, \eta\}$ denote the lateral coordinates of the object's position; $(x, y)$ denote the hologram plane; and $(x', y')$ denote the plane of the reconstructed image. Therefore, the numerical aperture (NA) of the hologram $NA_{holo}$ and sensor $NA_{sensor}$ are given by Equation (5) and Equation (6), respectively. The smaller NA is chosen as the real NA between $NA_{holo}$ and $NA_{sensor}$, and is renamed $NA_{real}$.

$$NA_{holo} = \frac{D}{2z}, \tag{5}$$

$$NA_{sensor} = \frac{0.61\lambda}{2\Delta_{pp}}, \tag{6}$$

$$NA_{dhs} = \mathrm{MIN}(NA_{holo}, NA_{sensor}), \tag{7}$$

where $\mathrm{MIN}(\cdot)$ denotes choosing the minimum one. The lateral resolution $\Delta LR_{dhy}$ of the digital holographic system is given by Equation (8), and the axial resolution $\Delta z'$ of the hologram is presented in Equation (9) [29,30].

$$\Delta LR_{dhs} = \Delta x' = \Delta y' = \frac{\lambda}{NA_{dhs}}, \tag{8}$$

$$\Delta z' = \frac{\lambda}{(NA_{dhs})^2} \tag{9}$$

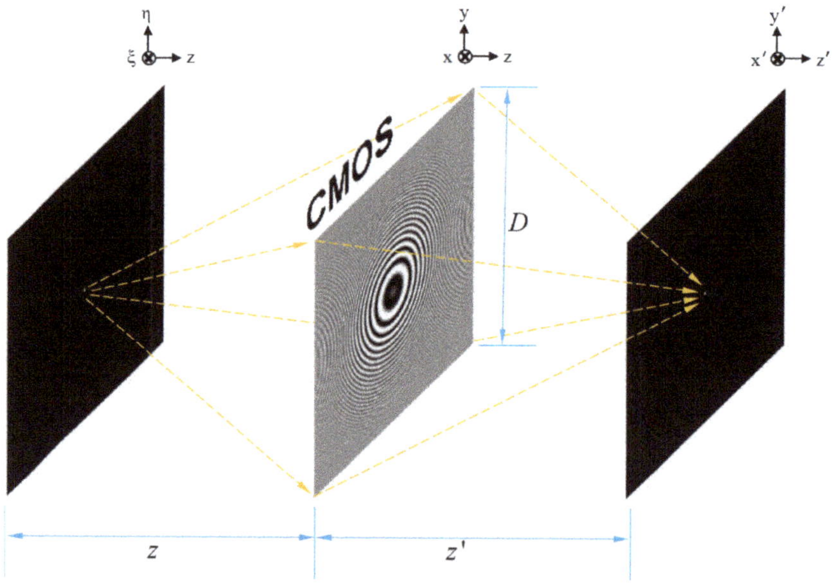


**Figure 2.** Schematic diagram of holographic system for one point.

### *3.2. Constrained Intensity for Each Candidate Focused Particle*

Subsequently, we must find out a suitable threshold value to recognize the candidate focused particles in each raw reconstructed image generated from the hologram, in which there are a large number of transparent particles. A flowchart illustrating the procedure of how to find a suitable constrained intensity is shown in Figure 3. First, a stack of raw reconstructed images $Reim\_all(x, y, n)$ and corresponding gradient images $Reim\_grad\_all(x, y, n)$ is generated. Subsequently, the minimum value along the z-axis is extracted from $Reim\_all(x, y, n)$ to obtain a synthetic minimum intensity image $Reim\_\text{min}(x, y)$. Similarly, the maximum value along the z-axis is extracted from $Reim\_grad\_all(x, y, n)$ to obtain a synthetic maximum gradient image $Reim\_grad\_\text{max}(x, y)$. Then, a threshold in the range of $[v1, v2]$ is sequentially set to binarize $Reim\_\text{min}(x, y)$ to obtain a binarization image $Reim\_\text{min}\_bin(x, y)$. Canny edge detection is applied to obtain the edge of each particle. Afterward, one particle $Pcle(x, y)$ is cropped from $Reim\_\text{min}\_bin(x, y)$, and the corresponding position $Pcle\_grad(x, y)$ in the $Reim\_grad\_\text{max}(x, y)$ is multiplied to obtain the mean value, applying $Grad\_mean = mean(Pcle(x, y). * Pcle\_grad(x, y), \text{"}all\text{"})$. The threshold is considered to be suitable when $Grad\_mean$ reaches the maximum value. Several other particles are similarly chosen, and their corresponding suitable thresholds are similarly calculated. Finally, among these, the minimum threshold is selected; this is the most suitable constrained intensity for the candidate focused particles [31].

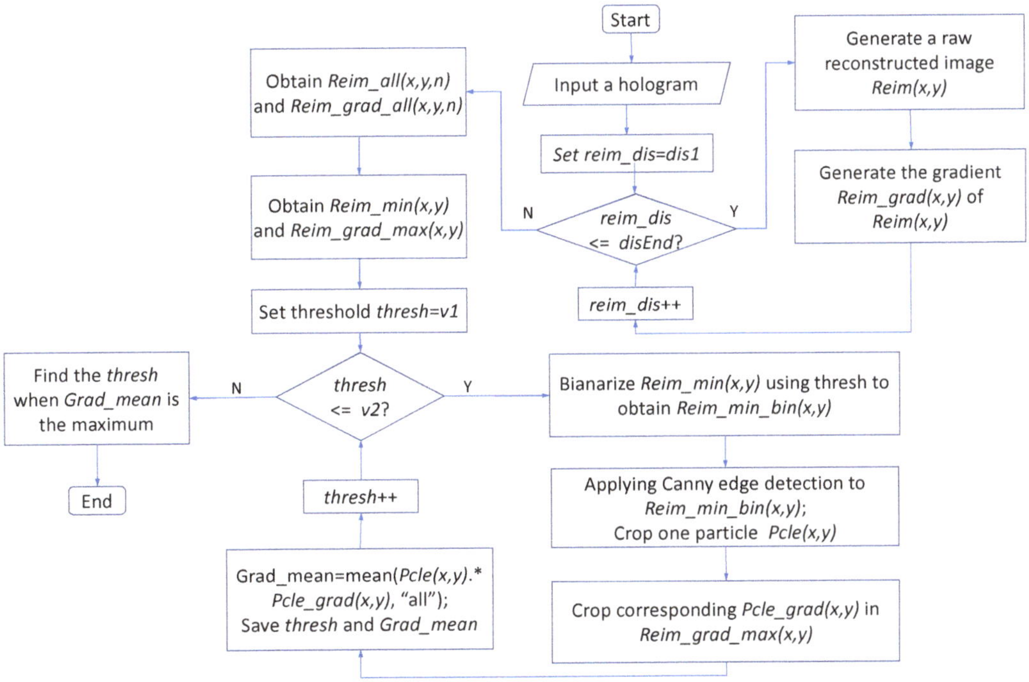


**Figure 3.** Flowchart of procedure to find most suitable constrained intensity for candidate focused particles.

### *3.3. Description of Algorithm*

It is assumed that the hologram is captured using an optical setup, the schematic of which is shown in Figure 1. The axial resolution is obtained as described in Section 3.1 to set the smallest axial distance by which to recognize a focused particle. A flowchart of the overall procedure is shown in Figure 4a, which references process b and process c. Process b, shown in Figure 4b, recognizes and saves the information on each candidate focused particle in matrix $M$, whereas process c, shown in Figure 4c, recognizes the focused particles from matrix $M$ and saves their information in matrix $M\_new$.

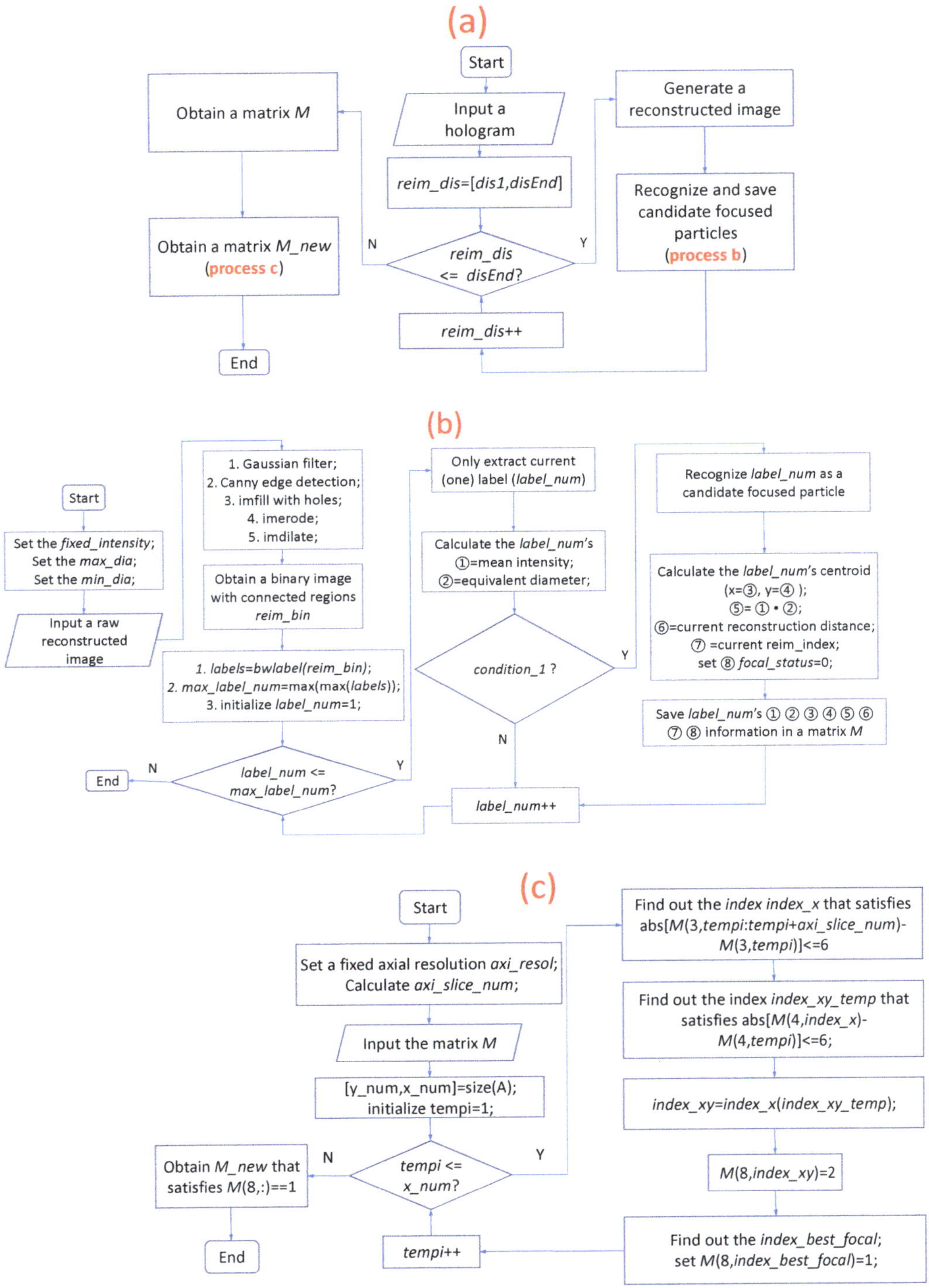


**Figure 4.** Flowcharts of (**a**) overall process to obtain all focused particles' information, (**b**) process to obtain and save all candidate focused particles' information in matrix $M$, and (**c**) process to determine and save the focused particles in matrix $M\_new$.

As depicted in Figure 4a, the reconstruction distance range $[dis1, dis\_End]$ with a fixed reconstruction depth spacing is settled first, and a series of raw reconstructed images are generated using the back Fresnel propagation method. Subsequently, process b is implemented to obtain the matrix *M*, in which the information of all candidate focused particles are saved. Finally, process c is implemented to obtain the matrix *M_new*, in which the informtion of all focused particles are saved. The matrix *M_new* is a subset of the matrix *M*.

In process b, the constrained intensity *fixed_intensity* is calculated as described in Section 3.2 to constrain the intensity of each candidate focused particle. The particle diameters are in the range of $[min\_dia, max\_dia]$ μm, which is known. After Gaussian filtering, Canny edge detection, hole filling, erosion, and dilation of morphological operations are sequentially applied on one raw reconstructed image, a binary image $reim\_bin(x, y)$ with connected regions is obtained. The function *bwlabel* is utilized to extract all of the connected regions (labels), and the number of labels is obtained. Subsequently, all of the labels are traversed. First, the current label *label_num* is extracted in isolation, and its mean intensity (①) and equivalent diameter (②) are calculated using the function regionprops. If ① is smaller than *fixed_intensity* and ② is in the range $[min\_dia, max\_dia]$, which is renamed to 'condition_1' in Figure 4b, *label_num* is recognized as a candidate focused particle. Subsequently, its centroid (*x*, *y*) (③ and ④), and ⑤ $=$ ① $\cdot$ ② are continually calculated; the reconstruction distance (⑥) and *reim_index* (⑦) are saved; and *focal_status* is set to 0 (⑧). Then, for candidate focused particle *label_num*, the values of ①, ②, ③, ④, ⑤, ⑥, ⑦, and ⑧ are all saved in matrix *M*. Eventually, we obtain a matrix *M* containing the information of all candidate focused particles via process b.

In process c, the focused particles from matrix *M* are extracted and the information, ①, ②, ③, ④, ⑤, ⑥, ⑦, and ⑧, of each focused particle are saved into a new matrix *M_new*, except that ⑧ *focal_status* is made equal to 1. The axial resolution *axi_resol* is obtained, as described in Section 3.1, to set the smallest axial distance by which to recognize a focused particle. The corresponding *axi_slice_num* is also calculated. We obtain the number (*x_num*) of all candidate focused particles from matrix *M*. Then, we traverse all of these candidate focused particles. During the process, we set *tempi* = 1:*x_num*, extract the information of particle *tempi*, and find the index *index_xy* in *M* wherein the particles whose *x* and *y* axes of the centroid and the *tempi* particle's *x* and *y* axes of the centroid are both less than six pixels, in a series of the reconstructed images, from *tempi* to $tempi + axia\_slice\_num$. Meanwhile, *focal_status* is set to $M(8, index\_xy) = 2$, to indicate that these candidate focused particles in matrix *M* have already been traversed. Eventually, we find the index *index_best_focal* that satisfies the condition that $M(5, index\_best\_focal)$ is the minimum value in $M(5, index\_xy)$, and *focal_status* (⑧) is set to be equal to $M(8, index\_best\_focal) = 1$. Finally, we obtain a new matrix *M_new* composed of all of the focused particles. As the candidate focused particles in matrix *M* are traversed, *focal_status* is made equal to 2, to indicate that the corresponding particle has already traversed; $focal\_status = 0$ indicates that the corresponding particle has not yet been traversed, whereas $focal\_status = 1$ indicates that the front *axi_slice_num* reconstructed images of the corresponding particle have already been traversed and it is a focused particle, but the rear *axi_slice_num* reconstructed images of the corresponding particle have not yet been traversed. Therefore, if the *focal_status* of particle *tempi* is equal to 0 or 1, the particle should be traversed. After all particles are traversed in matrix *M*, the particles whose *focal_status* are equal to 1 are the focused particles. For the focus metric, we propose using the minimum of product (⑤) of the mean intensity (①) and equivalent diameter (②), which is easier for processing multiple particles in DH, according to the experimental results.

## 4. Experimental Results and Analyses

### *4.1. Particles in Two Layers*

In this experiment, an in-line digital holographic experimental setup, as depicted in Figure 5a, was employed to capture the holograms. The used transparent particles were unibead monodispersed polystyrene microspheres, with diameters of 50 to 62 μm and solid content of 2.5% ($w/v$). First, a coherent (green) light source, with a wavelength of $\lambda = 532$ nm, was utilized to illuminate two layers of particles that were sandwiched between three glass slides; the thickness of each glass slide was about 1 mm. A hologram, which was captured by a CMOS camera with size = 1440 × 1080 and pixel pitch $\Delta_{pp} = 3.45$ μm, is displayed in Figure 5b, and the synthetic minimum intensity image, which was the minimum value along the z-axis of all the raw reconstructed images generated in the distance range of (31, 34) mm with a depth spacing equal to 50 μm from this hologram, is shown in Figure 5c. There were a total of 17 particles in the two layers; the particles enclosed by the red circles were placed in one layer, whereas the particles enclosed by the green circles were placed in the other layer. The particle centroids, *reim_index*, and reconstruction distances are listed in Table 1. We obtained 17 particles when the depth spacing was equal to 50 μm (spent 29.0 s and generated 61 reconstructed images), 100 μm (spent 15.2 s and generated 31 reconstructed images), 150 μm (spent 10.5 s and generated 21 reconstructed images), 200 μm (spent 8.4 s and generated 16 reconstructed images), 250 μm (spent 6.9 s and generated 13 reconstructed images), and 300 μm (spent 6.2 s and generated 11 reconstructed images), respectively. The reconstruction distances of the particles corresponding to these reconstruction depth spacings are depicted in Figure 6. We can observe that these particles were relatively well distributed between the two slices.

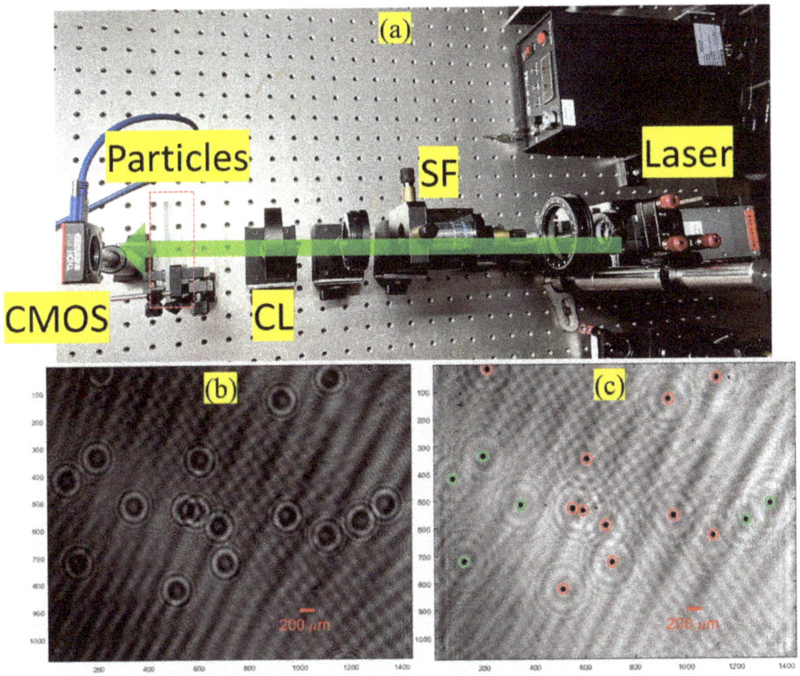


**Figure 5.** (**a**) Experimental setup (SF: spatial filter; CL: collimating lens), (**b**) hologram (size = 1440 × 1080), and (**c**) synthetic minimum intensity image generated from all raw reconstructed images of hologram in (**b**).

**Table 1.** Information for focused particles in Figure 5b's hologram.

| Particle No. | Centroid [x, y] | Reim_Index | Reconstruction Distance (mm) |
|---|---|---|---|
| 1 | [1109, 628] | −43 | 31.85 |
| 2 | [1124, 51] | −42 | 31.90 |
| 3 | [513, 823] | −41 | 31.95 |
| 4 | [684, 590] | −41 | 31.95 |
| 5 | [551, 528] | −40 | 32.00 |
| 6 | [593, 537] | −40 | 32.00 |
| 7 | [609, 348] | −40 | 32.00 |
| 8 | [708, 725] | −40 | 32.00 |
| 9 | [934, 129] | −40 | 32.00 |
| 10 | [952, 555] | −40 | 32.00 |
| 11 | [215, 17] | −35 | 32.25 |
| 12 | [78, 419] | −29 | 32.55 |
| 13 | [197, 336] | −24 | 32.80 |
| 14 | [345, 515] | −22 | 32.90 |
| 15 | [1240, 572] | −22 | 32.90 |
| 16 | [1336, 512] | −22 | 32.90 |
| 17 | [122, 721] | −21 | 32.95 |

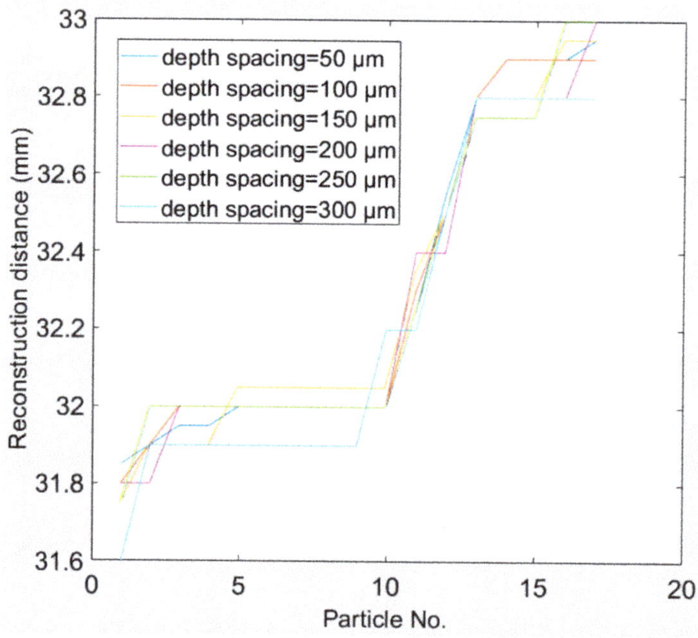


**Figure 6.** Reconstruction distance of each particle corresponding to reconstruction depth spacings equal to 50 μm, 100 μm, 150 μm, 200 μm, 250 μm, and 300 μm, respectively.

*4.2. Particles in Cuvette*

We continually captured holograms of large numbers of particles suspended in Milli-Q water that filled 3-mm (the dimension is $12.5 \times 3 \times 45$ mm$^3$) and 10-mm (the dimension is $12.5 \times 10 \times 45$ mm$^3$) cuvettes, respectively. In this section, only one particle solution, where approximately 3205 particles were seeded per mL, was made. We performed four experiments. In the first one, the 3-mm cuvette filled with the particle solution was placed 30 mm away from the same CMOS camera. While each captured original hologram was cropped into four equal smaller holograms (512 × 512), so each smaller hologram captured a volume of $9.4 \times 10^{-3}$ mL. 16 holograms, each of which approximately contained 30 particles, were collected for this experiment. A hologram sample is shown in Figure 7a. We calculated the axial resolution at the distance of 30 mm to be approximately 2.5 mm, and the constrained intensity for each candidate focused particle must be less than 0.39, according to Section 3.2. Using the proposed method, we counted 498 focused particles from the 16 holograms and obtained a relative error of 3.75%. The particle distribution of the hologram from Figure 7a in 3D space is shown in Figure 8a.

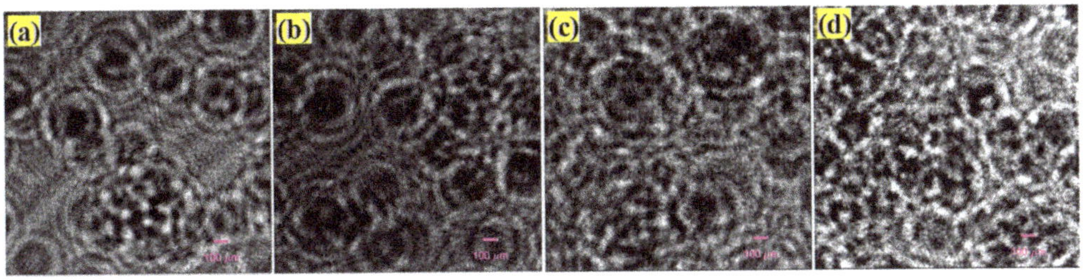


**Figure 7.** Holograms (size = 512 × 512) of same particle solutions in (**a**) 3 mm cuvette placed at 30 mm away, (**b**) 3 mm cuvette placed at 40 mm away, (**c**) 3 mm cuvette placed at 60 mm away, and (**d**) 10 mm cuvette placed at 30 mm away from CMOS, respectively.

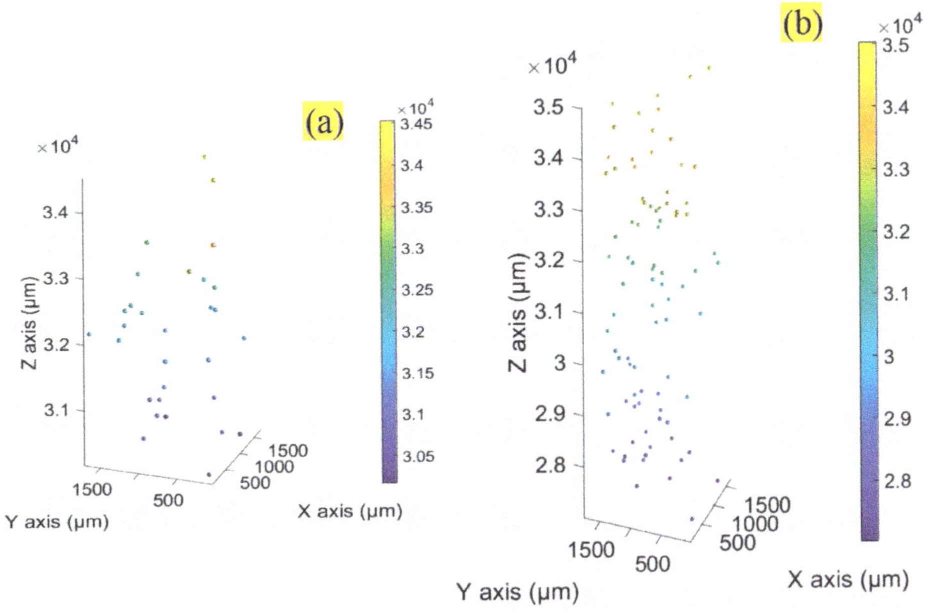


**Figure 8.** (**a**,**b**) are particle distribution of the holograms of Figure 7a (in the 3-mm cuvette) and Figure 7d (in the 10-mm cuvette) in 3D space.

In the second experiment, we placed the same cuvette with the same particle solution 40 mm away from the CMOS camera. A total of 180 holograms with the size of 512 × 512, a hologram sample of which is shown in Figure 7b, were collected for this experiment. We calculated the axial resolution at the distance of 40 mm to be approximately 4.4 mm; however, because the thickness of the cuvette was only 3 mm, we still used the axial resolution of 2.5 mm instead of 4.4 mm, and the same constrained intensity for each candidate focused particle. Using the proposed method, we counted 5796 focused particles from the 180 holograms and obtained a relative error of 7.33%.

In the third experiment, we placed the same cuvette with the same particle solution 60 mm away from the CMOS camera. A total of 160 holograms with sizes of 512 × 512, a hologram sample of which is shown in Figure 7c, were collected for this experiment. We calculated the axial resolution at the distance of 60 mm to be approximately 9.8 mm; however, because the thickness of the cuvette was only 3 mm, we still used the axial resolution of 2.5 mm instead of 9.8 mm, and the same constrained intensity for each candidate focused particle. Using the proposed method, we counted 4841 focused particles from the 160 holograms and obtained a relative error of 0.85%.

In the last experiment, we used a 10 mm cuvette filled with the same particle solution and placed it at 30 mm away from the same CMOS camera. While the original captured holograms were cropped into four equal smaller holograms (512 × 512), so each smaller hologram captured a volume of $31.2 \times 10^{-3}$ mL 200 holograms (512 × 512), a hologram sample of which is displayed in Figure 7d, were collected for this experiment. Since the cuvette was placed 30 mm from the CMOS, we continually set the axial resolution to 2.5 mm and the constrained intensity to be the same as that in the previous experiments. We counted 18851 focused particles from the 200 holograms and obtained a relative error of 5.75%. The particle distribution of the hologram Figure 7d in 3D space is depicted in Figure 8b. The results of the four experiments are presented in detail in Table 2.

**Table 2.** Detailed results of four experiments.

| Experiment No. | 1 | 2 | 3 | 4 |
|---|---|---|---|---|
| Cuvette thickness (mm) | 3 | 3 | 3 | 10 |
| Distance from CMOS (mm) | 30 | 40 | 60 | 30 |
| Axial resolution (mm) | 2.5 | 2.5 | 2.5 | 2.5 |
| Hologram amount | 16 | 180 | 160 | 200 |
| Ground truth of particle amount | 480 | 5400 | 4800 | 20,000 |
| Particle amount recognized by proposed method | 498 | 5796 | 4841 | 18,851 |
| Deviation | 18 | 396 | 41 | 1149 |
| Relative error (%) | 3.75 | 7.33 | 0.85 | 5.75 |

## 5. Conclusions

We propose an autofocusing method based on morphological analyses and axial resolution to obtain, relatively accurately, the 3D position of each particle, particularly its axial location, and the particle number of a dense transparent particle solution via a hologram. Our proposed method has two components. First, morphological analyses and constrained intensity are used on the raw reconstructed images, from which the information on candidate focused particles is then obtained and saved in one matrix. Second, axial resolution is utilized to obtain the real focused particles from the aforementioned matrix. For the focus metrics, we propose using the product of the mean intensity and equivalent diameter of each candidate focused particle. Eventually, we are able to secure all focused particles for one hologram. In our experiments, we used particles located at fixed distances and in a particle solution that was filled in a cuvette to examine and verify the proposed method. The deviations of the recognized axial locations were in the range of ±0.1 mm, and relative errors of the recognized particle numbers were less than 8%. Therefore, the proposed method is able to rapidly provide relatively accurate ground-truth axial positions for machine learning methods to solve the autofocusing problem that occurs with dense particles and makes it convenient to generate ground-truth datasets for these machine learning methods.

**Author Contributions:** Conceptualization, W.-N.L.; methodology, W.-N.L. and X.X.; validation, W.-N.L., Y.Z., J.C. and H.O.; formal analysis, X.X.; investigation, H.O.; data curation, W.-N.L.; writing—original draft preparation, W.-N.L.; writing—review and editing, W.-N.L., Y.Z., J.C., H.O. and X.X.; supervision, W.-N.L.; funding acquisition, W.-N.L. and X.X. All authors have read and agreed to the published version of the manuscript.

**Funding:** This study was supported by the STU Scientific Research Foundation for Talents and Guangdong University Key Platform [No. 2021GCZX009].

**Data Availability Statement:** Data underlying the results presented in this paper are not publicly available at this time but may be obtained from the authors upon reasonable request.

**Conflicts of Interest:** The authors declare no conflicts of interest.

## References

1. Garcla-Sucerqula, J.; Xu, W.; Jericho, S.K.; Klages, P.; Jericho, M.H.; Kreuzer, H.J. Digital in-line holographic microscopy. *Appl. Opt.* **2006**, *45*, 836–850. [CrossRef] [PubMed]
2. Wu, Y.; Yao, L.; Brunel, M.; Coëtmellec, S.; Li, R.; Lebrun, D.; Zhou, H.; Gréhan, G.; Cen, K. Characterizations of transparent particle holography in near-field using Debye series. *Appl. Opt.* **2016**, *55*, A60–A70. [CrossRef] [PubMed]
3. Gao, P.; Yao, B.; Min, J.; Guo, R.; Ma, B.; Zheng, J.; Lei, M.; Yan, S.; Dan, D.; Ye, T. Autofocusing of digital holographic microscopy based on off-axis illuminations. *Opt. Lett.* **2012**, *37*, 3630–3632. [CrossRef] [PubMed]
4. Zheng, J.; Gao, P.; Shao, X. Opposite-view digital holographic microscopy with autofocusing capability. *Sci. Rep.* **2017**, *7*, 4255. [CrossRef]
5. Langehanenberg, P.; von Bally, G.; Kemper, B. Autofocusing in digital holographic microscopy. *3D Res.* **2011**, *2*, 4. [CrossRef]
6. Ilhan, H.A.; Doğar, M.; Özcan, M. Digital holographic microscopy and focusing methods based on image sharpness. *J. Microsc.* **2014**, *255*, 138–149. [CrossRef]
7. Ren, Z.; Chen, N.; Lam, E.Y. Automatic focusing for multisectional objects in digital holography using the structure tensor. *Opt. Lett.* **2017**, *42*, 1720–1723. [CrossRef]
8. Zhang, Y.; Wang, H.; Wu, Y.; Tamamitsu, M.; Ozcan, A. Edge sparsity criterion for robust holographic autofocusing. *Opt. Lett.* **2017**, *42*, 3824–3827. [CrossRef]
9. Lyu, M.; Yuan, C.; Li, D.; Situ, G. Fast autofocusing in digital holography using the magnitude differential. *Appl. Opt.* **2017**, *56*, F152–F157. [CrossRef]
10. Khanam, T.; Darakis, E.; Rajendran, A.; Kariwala, V.; Asundi, A.K.; Naughton, T.J. On-line digital holographic measurement of size and shape of microparticles for crystallization processes. *Proc. SPIE* **2008**, *7155*, 514–523.
11. Darakis, E.; Khanam, T.; Rajendran, A.; Kariwala, V.; Naughton, T.J.; Asundi, A.K. Microparticle characterization using digital holography. *Chem. Eng. Sci.* **2010**, *65*, 1037–1044. [CrossRef]
12. Kempkes, M.; Darakis, E.; Khanam, T.; Rajendran, A.; Kariwala, V.; Mazzotti, M.; Naughton, T.J.; Asundi, A.K. Three dimensional digital holographic profiling of micro-fibers. *Opt. Express* **2009**, *17*, 2938–2943. [CrossRef]
13. Khanam, T.; Rajendran, A.; Kariwala, V.; Asundi, A.K. Measurement of two-dimensional crystal shape using digital holography. *Cryst. Growth Des.* **2013**, *13*, 3969–3975. [CrossRef]
14. Tian, L.; Loomis, N.; Domínguez-Caballero, J.A.; Barbastathis, G. Quantitative measurement of size and three-dimensional position of fast-moving bubbles in air-water mixture flows using digital holography. *Appl. Opt.* **2010**, *49*, 1549–1554. [CrossRef] [PubMed]
15. Lang, K.; Qiang, J.; Qiu, Y.; Wang, X. Autofocusing method for multifocal holograms based on connected domain analysis. *Opt. Lasers Eng.* **2025**, *184*, 108624. [CrossRef]
16. Brady, D.J.; Choi, K.; Marks, D.L.; Horisaki, R.; Lim, S. Compressive holography. *Opt. Express* **2009**, *17*, 13040–13049. [CrossRef]
17. Liu, Y.; Tian, L.; Lee, J.W.; Huang, H.Y.H.; Triantafyllou, M.S.; Barbastathis, G. Scanning-free compressive holography for object localization with subpixel accuracy. *Opt. Lett.* **2012**, *37*, 3357–3359. [CrossRef]
18. Liu, Y.; Tian, L.; Hsieh, C.-H.; Barbastathis, G. Compressive holographic two-dimensional localization with 1/302 subpixel accuracy. *Opt. Express* **2014**, *22*, 9774–9782. [CrossRef]
19. Chen, W.; Tian, L.; Rehman, S.; Zhang, Z.; Lee, H.P.; Barbastathis, G. Empirical concentration bounds for compressive holographic bubble imaging based on a Mie scattering model. *Opt. Express* **2015**, *23*, 4715–4725. [CrossRef]

20. Li, W.-N.; Zhang, Z.; Su, P.; Ma, J.; Wang, X. Removal of defocused images using three- -dimensional nonlinear diffusion based on digital holography. *J. Opt.* **2020**, *22*, 051701. [CrossRef]
21. Ren, Z.; Xu, Z.; Lam, E.Y. Learning-based nonparametric autofocusing for digital holography. *Optica* **2018**, *5*, 337–344. [CrossRef]
22. Lee, S.J.; Yoon, G.Y.; Go, T. Deep learning-based accurate and rapid tracking of 3D positional information of microparticles using digital holographic microscopy. *Exp. Fluids* **2019**, *60*, 170. [CrossRef]
23. Shao, S.; Mallery, K.; Hong, J. Machine learning holography for measuring 3D particle distribution. *Chem. Eng. Sci.* **2020**, *225*, 115830. [CrossRef]
24. Wu, Y.; Wu, J.; Jin, S.; Cao, L.; Jin, G. Dense-U-net: Dense encoder-decoder network for holographic imaging of 3D particle fields. *Opt. Commun.* **2021**, *493*, 126970. [CrossRef]
25. Li, W.-N.; Su, P.; Ma, J.; Wang, X. Short U-net model with average pooling based on in-line digital holography for simultaneous restoration of multiple particles. *Opt. Lasers Eng.* **2021**, *139*, 106449. [CrossRef]
26. Hao, Z.; Li, W.-N.; Hou, B.; Su, P.; Ma, J. Characterization method for particle extraction from raw-reconstructed images using U-net. *Front. Phys.* **2022**, *9*, 816158. [CrossRef]
27. Ou, H.; Lin, W.; Li, W.-N.; Xie, X. Real-time particle concentration measurement from a hologram by deep learning. *Phys. Scr.* **2024**, *99*, 095512. [CrossRef]
28. Goodman, J.W. *Introduction to Fourier Optics*, 4th ed.; W. H. Freeman: New York, NY, USA, 2017.
29. Born, M.; Wolf, E. *Principles of Optics*, 7th ed.; Cambridge University Press: Cambridge, UK, 1999.
30. Meng, H.; Hussain, F. In-line recording and off-axis viewing technique for holographic particle velocimetry. *Appl. Opt.* **1995**, *34*, 1827–1840. [CrossRef]
31. Li, H.; Ji, F.; Li, L.; Li, B.; Ma, F. In lab in-line digital holography for cloud particle measurement experiment. *Proc. SPIE* **2016**, *10156*, 1015618.

*electronics*

MDPI

*Article*

# Design and Optimization of High Performance Multi-Step Separated Trench 4H-SiC JBS Diode

**Jinlan Li [1,*], Ziheng Wu [1], Huaren Sheng [1], Yan Xu [1] and Liming Zhou [2]**

1 College of Information Engineering, Yangzhou University, Yangzhou 225009, China; mz120220965@stu.yzu.edu.cn (Z.W.); mz120230973@stu.yzu.edu.cn (H.S.); mz120230964@stu.yzu.edu.cn (Y.X.)
2 Yangjie Electronic Technology Company Ltd., Yangzhou 225009, China; liming.zhou@21yangjie.com
* Correspondence: jinlanli@yzu.edu.cn

**Abstract:** In this paper, a novel 3300 V/40 A 4H-SiC junction barrier Schottky diode (JBS) with a multi-step separated trench (MST) structure is proposed and thoroughly investigated using TCAD simulations. The results show that the introduction of MST expands the Schottky contact area, resulting in a decrease in the forward voltage drop. Furthermore, the combination of the deep $P^+$ shielded region and the central $P^+$ region effectively reduces the leakage current, leading to a 43.7% increase in the blocking voltage compared to conventional 4H-SiC JBS. The effects of the step depth ($d_s$) and the width of the central $P^+$ region ($w_m$) on the device performance are analyzed in depth. In addition, a multi-step trenched linearly graded field-limiting rings (MTLG-FLR) termination ensures a more uniform electric field distribution, and the terminal protection efficiency reaches up to 90%, which further enhances the reliability of the terminal structure.

**Keywords:** 4H-SiC junction barrier Schottky (JBS); multi-step trench; trench FLR; electric field; blocking voltage

## 1. Introduction

Large-diameter 4H-SiC wafers with low defect density have been commercialized and applied in power devices [1]. Compared with Si-based power devices, SiC power devices have attracted more and more attention in the application market due to their faster switching speeds, better thermal stability and higher efficiency [2]. In particular, SiC power devices show great potential in high-voltage application scenarios such as new energy vehicles, power transmission and electric locomotive traction, etc. However, the current commercial SiC diodes are primarily utilized in the low-to-medium voltage range; the design and development of high-voltage devices still face severe challenges [3–6].

In medium-voltage and high-voltage applications, the balance between the forward voltage drop ($V_F$) and leakage current is critical. For traditional planar junction barrier Schottky (JBS) diodes, the shielding effect of the Schottky barrier region under the reverse voltage depends on the depth of the $P^+$ regions [7–12]. Although narrowing the width of the Schottky region can reduce the leakage current, it leads to an increase in $V_F$ of a diode. Recently, various improved structures based on 4H-SiC JBS diodes have been proposed and studied. The floating junction JBS (FJ-JBS) diode optimizes the reverse electric field distribution and enhances the device breakdown voltage by introducing additional PN junctions within the drift layer, while maintaining low on-state resistance [13]. H. Yuan et al. have optimized the trade-off between breakdown voltage ($V_{BR}$) and specific on-resistance ($R_{on,sp}$) of a 1200 V FJ-JBS diode by simulation, achieving a BFOM (Baliga figure of merit) of up to 8.16 GW/cm$^2$. However, this structure exhibits a high degree of sensitivity to the doping of the epilayer, significantly increasing the difficulty in achieving the desired ion implantation process. The Super Junction JBS (SJ-JBS) diode incorporates a periodic arrangement of P and N layers, offering multiple current conduction pathways during forward biasing, while simultaneously optimizing the electric field distribution under reverse voltage conditions. This approach provides a solution to the trade-off problem between forward and reverse characteristics [14]. B. Wang et al. have successfully prepared a SJ-JBS diode with a $V_{BR}$ of 1920 V and a $R_{on,sp}$ of 1.2 mΩ·cm$^2$ by substrate thinning. The structure still faces many challenges, the most significant of which is its complex manufacturing process and high cost, potentially resulting in reduced yield rates and device reliability. The P-type retrograde-implanted JBS (RP-JBS) diode embeds a lightly doped $P^+$ region beneath the $P^+$ region of the conventional JBS structure. This design deepens the PN junction, reducing the electric field at the Schottky interface and effectively lowering capacitance by widening the space-charge region. Furthermore, Y. L. Zhang et al. have proposed the use of RP-JBS to achieve a leakage current of 0.2 μA at 1200 V [15]. However, although these new structures have improved their performance, they are mainly reported in the medium-voltage field and are limited by high process complexity and poor reliability. In contrast, the trench JBS (TJBS) diode is commercially achievable due to its simple process and excellent performance [16–18]. By flexibly designing the deep $P^+$ region, it can effectively reduce the leakage current and improve the blocking voltage while maintaining a low forward voltage drop. Therefore, the multi-step trench JBS diode could have great potential for high-voltage applications. In addition, an effective edge-termination technique results in electric field distribution that is more uniform at the edge of the device, thereby enabling the device to approach the ideal breakdown voltage capability of the epilayer used. Many researchers have studied edge termination technologies, such as field limiting rings (FLR), field plates, junction termination extensions and some combined structures [19–21]. These techniques help reduce the reverse leakage current and improve the reliability of the device. Therefore, the optimization of terminal technology is also indispensable.

In this paper, the novel MST-JBS diode is proposed; low forward voltage drop and high breakdown voltage are achieved through the optimization of TCAD simulation. Furthermore, the multi-step trenched linearly graded FLR (MTLG-FLR) terminal structure is designed to further enhance the stability and reliability of the device.

## 2. Device Design and Simulation

Figure 1a,b shows a 3D structure of the 4H-SiC JBS and 4H-SiC MST-JBS diodes, respectively. The $P^+$ implanted regions in both JBS and MST-JBS diodes account for 50% of the active area. The anode of both diodes features a Schottky contact with the drift region–SiC interface, as well as an ohmic contact with the $P^+$ interface. The 4H-SiC MST-JBS diode has a three-step trench structure with a central $P^+$ region, forming a Schottky contact with both the trench sidewall and the drift region. The two structures have a width of 7 μm and a substrate doping concentration of 1 × 10$^{18}$ cm$^{-3}$. For 4H-SiC, the epilayer thickness (T) can be expressed as follows:

$$T = \frac{\varepsilon E_c(N_D)}{qE_c} - \sqrt{\left[\frac{\varepsilon E_c(N_D)}{qN_D}\right]^2 - \left[\frac{2\varepsilon V_{BR}}{qN_D}\right]} \quad (1)$$

where $V_{BR}$ represents the breakdown voltage of the device; $q$ denotes the elementary charge; and $\varepsilon$ stands for the dielectric constant of 4H-SiC. The critical electric field ($E_C$) and its relationship with the epilayer doping concentration ($N_D$) can be determined using the following expression

$$E_C = 2.49 \times 10^6 \times \frac{1}{[1 - 0.25\log(N_D \times 10^{-6})]} \quad (2)$$

Based on the Formulas (1) and (2), and assuming a junction terminal efficiency of 70%, the values for $T$ and $N_D$ of the epilayer in the 3300 V MST-JBS diode could be optimally set to 35 μm and 2 × 10$^{15}$ cm$^{-3}$, respectively. In the MST structure, the $P^+$ region has a doping concentration of 1 × 10$^{18}$ cm$^{-3}$, and the width of the central $P^+$ region is 0 to 1 μm.

The width of each step is 0.5 μm; the step depth ($d_s$) is 0.2 to 0.6 μm. In the simulation, the depth of the $P^+$ region is consistent with the step depth. The specific parameters are presented in Table 1.

**Table 1.** Device parameters used in simulation.

| | | |
|---|---|---|
| $N_D$ | Epilayer doping | $2 \times 10^{15}$ cm$^{-3}$ |
| $N_P$ | $P^+$ region doping | $1 \times 10^{18}$ cm$^{-3}$ |
| T | Epilayer thickness | 35 μm |
| $d_s$ | Depth of each step | 0.2–0.6 μm |
| $w_s$ | Width of each step | 0.5 μm |
| $w_m$ | Width of middle $P^+$ region | 0–1 μm |

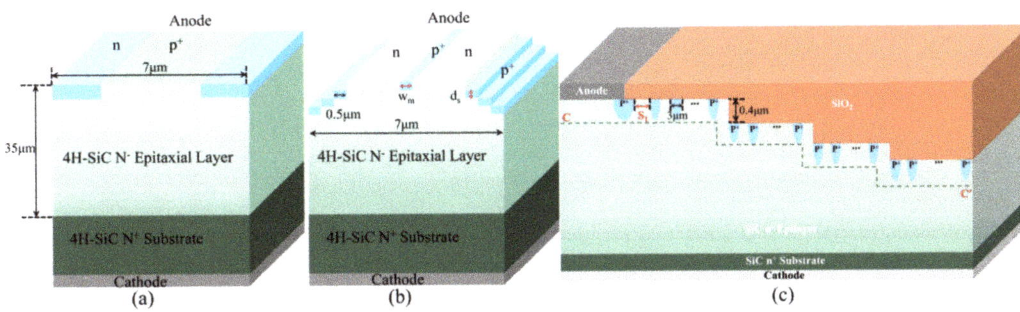


**Figure 1.** The 3D cell structure of (**a**) 4H-SiC JBS, (**b**) 4H-SiC MST-JBS, and (**c**) 4H-SiC MTLG-FLR.

A novel multi-step trenched linearly graded FLR (MTLG-FLR) termination was used, as shown in Figure 1c. The linearly graded FLR structure is formed subsequent to the multi-step trench structure formation to ensure that the MTLG-FLR has a larger junction depth. This edge termination structure combines the strengths of both linearly graded FLR and trench structures, providing more uniform electric field distribution to ensure high breakdown voltages. The terminal structure is set up in three steps, with each step having a depth of 0.4 μm. The depth and width of the $P^+$ rings are 0.4 μm and 3 μm, respectively. The spacing design rule of the MTLG-FLR is described as $S_n = S_1 + 0.1(n-1)$, where $S_1$ is the spacing between the main junction and the first ring. There are five linearly graded $P^+$ rings on each step, totaling 20 rings in all. The 4H-SiC MST-JBS structure design and optimization is conducted using Sentaurus TCAD 2017.

In 4H-polytype SiC materials, the presence of dopant atoms, characterized by their relatively high ionization energies, typically leads to difficulty in achieving complete ionization under room temperature conditions. Thus, the phenomenon of incomplete ionization of impurities must be taken into account during the simulation. The model used in the Sdevice to account for incomplete ionization is as follows:

$$N_D = \frac{N_{D,0}}{1 + G_D(T)\exp\left(\frac{E_{F,n} - E_C}{kT}\right)} \tag{3}$$

$$N_A = \frac{N_{A,0}}{1 + G_A(T)\exp\left(-\frac{E_{F,p} - E_V}{kT}\right)} \tag{4}$$

where $G_D(T)$ and $G_A(T)$ signify the temperature-dependent ionization factors, while $N_{D,0}$ and $N_{A,0}$ denote the concentrations of substitutional donors and acceptors, respectively. $E_{F,n}$ and $E_{F,p}$ correspond to the quasi-Fermi levels associated with electrons and holes, respectively. 4H-SiC exhibits a bandgap width of 3.2 eV, and the variation of the bandgap ($\Delta E_g$) can significantly impact its performance. Therefore, it is essential to incorporate this consideration into the simulations. The physical model integrated into the simulation is addressed as follows:

$$\Delta E_g = E_{ref}\left[\ln\left(\frac{N_D}{N_{ref}}\right) + \sqrt{\left(\ln\left(\frac{N_D}{N_{ref}}\right)\right)^2 + 0.5}\right] \quad (5)$$

where $E_{ref}$ and $N_{ref}$ are $9 \times 10^{-3}$ eV and $1 \times 10^{17}$ cm$^{-3}$, respectively. The fundamental physical models used in the simulation also include effective intrinsic density, models for mobility, impact ionization, barrier tunneling and anisotropic material properties. Recombination models include carrier generation recombination, Auger recombination and Shockley–Read–Hall recombination model. Additionally, the Okuto–Crowell model and Caughey–Thomas model were also considered.

## 3. Results and Discussion

Figure 2a,b shows the influence of varying the width of the central P$^+$ region ($w_m$) on the simulated forward and reverse I–V characteristics of 4H-SiC MST-JBS diodes. The $V_F$ is defined as the voltage drop at the forward-biased current of 40 A, and the $V_{BR}$ defined as the reverse voltage at a current of 10 µA. As illustrated in Figure 2a, when $w_m$ is increased from 0 µm to 1 µm, the reduction of the Schottky contact area leads to an increase in current density at a constant current level of 40 A. This, in turn, causes more collisions between electrons and the lattice, thereby reducing the electron mobility. Consequently, the equivalent resistance of the device increases significantly, leading to the forward voltage drop to rise from 2.0 V to 3.2 V. In Figure 2b, it is worth noting that the leakage current of 4H-SiC MST-JBS, without the central P$^+$ region, rapidly increases with the reverse voltage due to the ineffectiveness of the barrier shielding layer. Conversely, the deep barrier created by the multi-step trench structure, in conjunction with the shielding layer formed by the central P$^+$ region, effectively shields the Schottky junction and reduces the surface electric field. As $w_m$ increases from 0.25 µm to 1 µm, the blocking voltage remains stable, while the leakage current gradually decreases. Consequently, the MST-JBS diode can achieve a higher blocking voltage while maintaining a significantly lower level of leakage current. Therefore, considering the influence of the central P$^+$ region on the forward current and the reverse breakdown voltage, the width is optimized to 0.5 µm. This demonstrates the effectiveness of optimizing the width of the central P$^+$ region as a key parameter for improving MST-JBS diode forward performance.

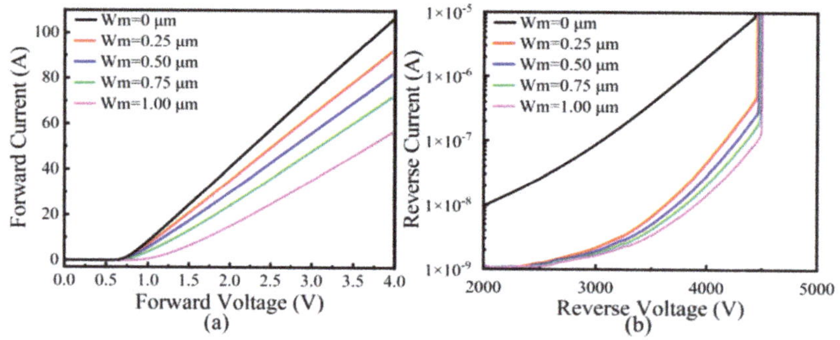


**Figure 2.** The simulated (**a**) forward characteristics and (**b**) reverse leakage current of 4H-SiC MST-JBS diodes as functions of the width of the central P$^+$ region.

Figure 3a shows the simulated $V_F$ and $V_{BR}$ as functions of the step depth of the P$^+$ region of 4H-SiC MST-JBS diodes. The results show that as the $d_s$ increases from 0.2 to 0.6 µm, the $V_F$ exhibits a linear increase from 2.0 V to 2.92 V. Additionally, as illustrated in the inset of Figure 3a, the $R_{on,sp}$ increases correspondingly from 12.8 mΩ·cm$^2$ to 18.7 mΩ·cm$^2$. However, the breakdown voltage exhibits a trend of increasing first and then decreasing. Figure 3b shows the distribution of electric field intensity along AA′ in the 4H-SiC MST-JBS diode in Figure 3d. It is obvious that as the $d_s$ increases, the breakdown voltage is effectively improved due to the notable reduction in the electric field intensity on both sides of the central $P^+$ region. It is indicated that under a high reverse bias, the depletion layer formed by the shallow depth of the $P^+$ region does not effectively shield the Schottky junction, leading to an excessively high surface electric field. Thus, the $d_s$ is 0.2 μm in the 4H-SiC MST-JBS diode, resulting in a breakdown voltage of approximately 2150 V. This is attributed to the increased effect of image forces resulting in a lowering of the effective barrier height, which subsequently promotes more electrons to flow over the lower barrier explained by the thermionic field emission theory. Furthermore, under high electric field conditions, the excessive carriers tunnel through the lowered Schottky barrier. Thus, a combination of thermionic field emission and field emission contributes to reverse leakage currents, which leads to premature breakdown at the central $P^+$ region of the device, as shown in Figure 3e. Figure 3c shows the distribution of electric field intensity along the BB′ as the $d_s$ increases. It is found that as the $d_s$ further increases, the electric field concentration effect gradually shifts from the device surface towards its interior. The intensified effect observed along the lowest edge of the $P^+$ region in the BB′ direction results in device breakdown, as shown in Figure 3f. Furthermore, when the $d_s$ is excessively deep, it causes a decrease in the thickness of the drift layer, which in turn decreases the breakdown voltage. However, when the $d_s$ is 0.4 μm, the deep potential barrier shielding layer plays a crucial role in effectively reducing the high surface electric field. Additionally, this appropriate depth design minimizes the loss of drift layer thickness and significantly alleviates the detrimental impact of the electric field concentration effect on device performance under reverse voltage conditions. Therefore, the uniform distribution of electric field within the active region of the 4H-SiC MST-JBS diode can be achieved by adjusting the $d_s$ as a key parameter. As a result, in order to achieve higher reverse breakdown voltage and lower forward voltage drop requirements, the optimal $d_s$ is determined to be 0.4 μm, resulting in a $V_{BR}$ of 4480 V and a $V_F$ of 2.4 V.

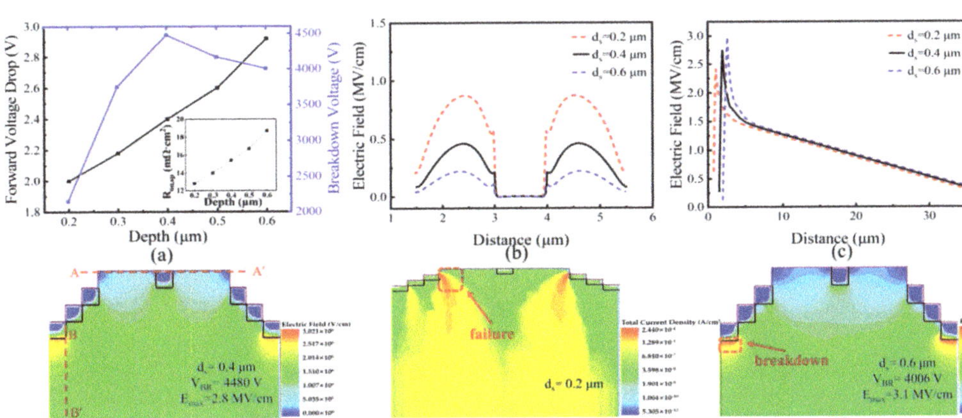


**Figure 3.** (**a**) The simulated forward voltage drop and reverse breakdown voltage of 4H-SiC MST-JBS diodes are functions of the $d_s$. The inset shows the variation of $R_{on,sp}$ with ds. (**b**) Electric field distribution in MST-JBS along A-A′. (**c**) Electric field distribution in MST-JBS along B-B′. (**d**) Schematic of the cross-sectional electric field distribution under reverse voltage condition. (**e**) Current density distribution with $d_s$ = 0.2 μm at breakdown. (**f**) Electric field distribution with $d_s$ = 0.6 μm at breakdown.

Figure 4a shows the simulated forward characteristics of 4H-SiC MST-JBS and conventional 4H-SiC JBS diodes. Both structures have a cell width of 7 μm; all parameters are consistent. It can be observed that under forward bias, the voltage drop of the 4H-SiC MST-JBS diode is 2.4 V, which is slightly lower than that of the 4H-SiC JBS diode. Figure 4b shows the 3D simulation results of the current density distribution for the 4H-SiC MST-JBS, with particular emphasis on the Schottky contact located on the trench sidewall. It can be observed that the forward performance of the device is enhanced by expanding the Schottky contact area, which provides an additional path for current flow and promotes a wider and more uniform current distribution. Therefore, current crowding is minimized, resulting in a decrease in the forward voltage drop and an increase in current-carrying capacity. Figure 4c shows the simulated reverse characteristics of 4H-SiC MST-JBS and conventional 4H-SiC JBS diodes. Under reverse bias conditions, the breakdown voltage of the 4H-SiC MST-JBS diode reaches approximately 4480 V, marking a substantial improvement of approximately 43.7% over the conventional JBS diode. Moreover, the leakage current performance of the 4H-SiC MST-JBS is outstanding, with values several orders of magnitude lower than those of the JBS diode at 3300 V. This is attributed to the multi-step trench $P^+$ region and the central $P^+$ region, which form a PN junction with the N epilayer, effectively shielding the Schottky barrier and significantly suppressing its lowering. In contrast, the JBS diode suffers a shallow $P^+$ region, which contributes to a more rapid deterioration of device performance under high reverse bias conditions. Consequently, the MST-JBS diode exhibits excellent electrical properties under high voltage conditions, rendering it a promising candidate for high-voltage power electronics applications exceeding 3300 V.

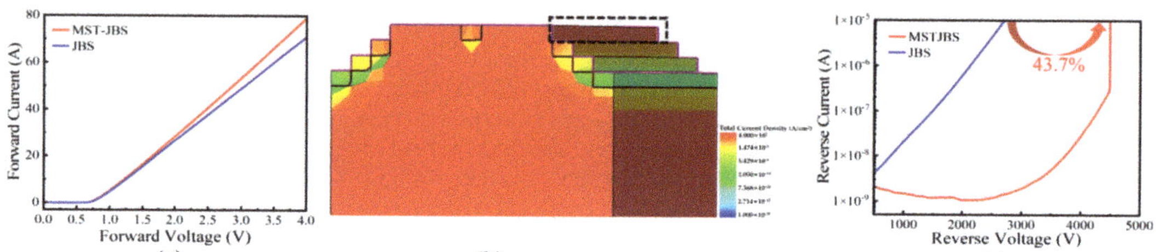


**Figure 4.** (**a**) The simulated forward characteristics of JBS and MST-JBS diodes. (**b**) Current density distribution of a MST-JBS diode. (**c**) Reverse leakage current of JBS and MST-JBS diodes.

## 4. Termination Design and Analyze

A multi-step trenched linearly graded FLR termination structure is designed and optimized based on simulation, as shown in Figure 1c. For the conventional FLR structure, the breakdown voltage of the termination is highly dependent on the size of the ring spacing. More rings are needed to reduce the electric field peak due to the narrow spacing. Similarly, when the spacing is large, the field-limiting rings fail to expand the depletion layer outward. Therefore, the high electric field at the main junction of the device, caused by the curvature effect, is often not effectively mitigated. The introduction of the MTLG-FLR termination structure results in a much higher protection efficiency. Figure 5a shows the comparison of the reverse I-V characteristics between the MTLG-FLR structure and a conventional FLR structure with a uniform spacing of 2.5 μm. The total length of the FLR is consistent with that of the 1.8 μm $S_1$ of the MTLG-FLR structure. The results indicate that the FLR structure exhibits a reverse breakdown voltage of 3380 V. In contrast, the breakdown voltage of the MTLG-FLR structure is increased by 20% ($S_1$ = 1.8 μm). The increase in breakdown voltage observed in the device can be attributed to the combination of two key factors, including the linear variation in the spacing between FLR and the multi-step trench structure of the termination. Thus, the electric field distribution within the MTLG-FLR terminal region is more uniform.

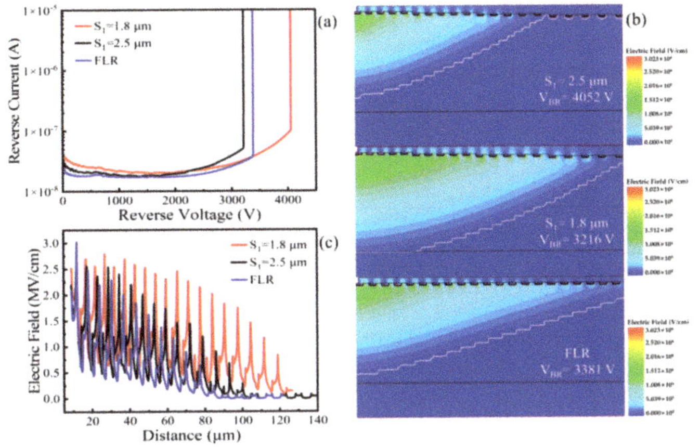

**Figure 5.** (**a**) Simulated reverse I–V characteristics for MTLG-FLR structures and conventional FLR structure. (**b**) Electric field distribution under reverse breakdown of MTLG-FLR structures and conventional FLR structure. (**c**) Electric field distributions along C-C′ for MTLG-FLR structure with $S_1$ = 2.5 μm and $S_1$ = 1.8 μm, respectively, and the conventional FLR structure.

Figure 5b illustrates the electric field distribution under reverse breakdown of the MTLG-FLR structures with different $S_1$ and the conventional FLR structures. As the reverse bias at the main junction increases to a level where the depletion region extends to the first floating limiting ring, holes in the first ring flow out of the main junction by the electric field. Then, the junction surface of the first ring transitions from being electrically neutral to a small amount of negative charge. This accumulation of negative charge generates an electric field at the surface, which is opposite to the electric field that exists between the main junction and the first ring. Thus, the electric field intensity in the region is weakened by reducing the electric field near the main junction. Furthermore, the MTLG-FLR structure is equivalent to modulating the lateral concentration distribution in the terminal region. The device has a high doping concentration internally, which gradually decreases outwards. This effectively reduces the high electric field at the main junction while avoiding electric field peaks at the outer ring. Figure 5c shows the electric field distribution along the CC′ cross-section of the MTLG-FLR structures at breakdown. When $S_1$ is set to 2.5 μm, the MTLG-FLR structure exhibits the highest electric field concentration at the main junction. Due to the large spacing, the external $P^+$ rings fail to play an effective role, ultimately resulting in premature breakdown. On the contrary, when $S_1$ is reduced to 1.8 μm, all the rings of both the MTLG-FLR and conventional FLR structures contribute to the overall performance. The surface electric field distribution of the MTLG-FLR is more uniform compared to that of the conventional FLR. Consequently, the MTLG-FLR structure enhances the effectiveness of the field limiting ring by improving the uniformity of the electric field distribution. This, in turn, leads to an increase in the reliability of the terminal structure.

Figure 6 shows a comprehensive comparison of the specific on-resistance and BFOM (BFOM = $4V_{BR}^2/R_{on\text{-}sp}$) for the device proposed in this paper, as well as the results reported in the references [19,22–27]. The detailed performance parameters are also summarized in Table 2. As illustrated in Figure 6a, at a voltage of 4.48 kV, the $R_{on\text{-}sp}$ obtained from theoretical calculations is approximately 10 mΩ·cm$^2$. The results reveal that the MST-JBS structure exhibits a $R_{on\text{-}sp}$ of 15.4 mΩ·cm$^2$, which is notably closer to this theoretical limit value compared to that of other diodes. This indicates that under forward bias, the MST-JBS has the lowest conduction losses, which can reduce energy losses and enhance the overall efficiency of the system. The BFOM reflects the trade-off between the specific on-resistance of the device and its blocking capability. A higher BFOM value signifies that lower on-resistance can be achieved at a specified voltage. The results indicate that the BFOM of the MST-JBS has achieved 5.21 GW/cm$^2$, which is significantly higher than that of other devices. Combining the above results, it is evident that the MST-JBS structure demonstrates remarkable effectiveness in achieving an optimal balance between forward conduction performance and reverse blocking capability. This balance significantly enhances the overall performance of the device, making it a prominent candidate in the field of high voltage devices.

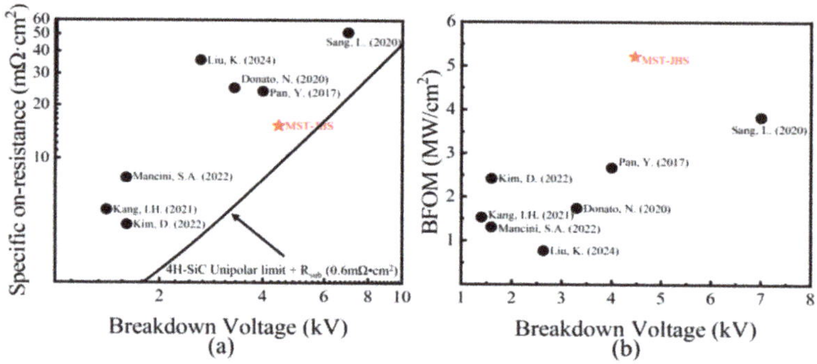


**Figure 6.** (**a**) Trade-off between $V_{BR}$ and $R_{on\text{-}sp}$, as well as (**b**) the trade-off between $V_{BR}$ and the BFOM value of the devices in this paper, as along with the results reported in the references [19,22–27].

**Table 2.** Performance parameters used in Figure 6.

| Reference | Device Structure | $V_F$ (V) | $V_{BR}$ (kV) | $R_{on,sp}$ (mΩ·cm$^2$) | BFOM (GW/cm$^2$) |
|---|---|---|---|---|---|
| [19] | JBS | 1.8 (30 A) | 4 | 23.98 | 2.67 |
| [22] | JBS | 2.0 (20 A) | 3.3 | 25 | 1.74 |
| [23] | JBS | 1.73 (10 A) | 1.59 | 7.79 | 1.31 |
| [24] | PiN | 3.58 (100 A/cm$^2$) | 2.63 | 35.8 | 0.77 |
| [25] | JBS | / | 7 | 51.2 | 3.83 |
| [26] | JBS | 1.9 (370 A/cm$^2$) | 1.4 | 5.14 | 1.53 |
| [27] | JBSFET | / | 1.6 | 4.24 | 2.42 |
| Our work | MST-JBS | 2.4 (40 A) | 4.48 | 15.4 | 5.21 |

## 5. Conclusions

In this paper, a novel 3300 V/40 A MST-JBS diode with MTLG-FLR termination has been designed and thoroughly analyzed. The introduction of the MST structure in the active region has successfully overcome the inherent limitation of P$^+$ region depth in traditional JBS devices. The simulation results demonstrate that the MST-JBS structure utilizes the deep P$^+$ region formed by the multi-step trench structure and tightly connects with the depletion layer of the central P$^+$ region, achieving a more effective electric field shielding effect. Furthermore, the additional Schottky contacts on the sidewalls actively contribute to forward conduction, effectively optimizing the forward current distribution characteristics of the device and further enhancing its overall performance. The optimized MST-JBS diode exhibits superior forward and reverse characteristics, including a forward voltage drop of 2.4 V, a reverse breakdown voltage of 4480 V, which is a significant 47% improvement over conventional JBS diodes, and extremely low leakage current. This structure not only maintains good forward characteristics but also effectively enhances the reverse characteristics, providing a solution to the trade-off issue between the forward and reverse characteristics of medium- and high-voltage devices. Furthermore, the MTLG-FLR termination structure is introduced, which effectively uniformizes the electric field distribution, surpassing that of the FLR structure by 20%. Therefore, an MST-JBS diode with MTLG-FLR termination greatly expands the applicability of the device in high-voltage applications and significantly enhances its stability and durability.

**Author Contributions:** Writing-conceptualization and editing, J.L. and Z.W.; software processing and data collation, Z.W., H.S. and Y.X.; validation, J.L. and Z.W.; funding acquisition and writing-review and editing, J.L., Z.W. and L.Z. All authors have read and agreed to the published version of the manuscript.

**Funding:** This research was funded by the National Natural Science Foundation of China (grant number 62104208 and YZLYJF2020PHD073).

**Data Availability Statement:** Data are included in the article.

**Conflicts of Interest:** Author Liming Zhou was employed by the Yangji Electronic Technology Company Ltd. The remaining authors declare that the research was conducted in the absence of any commercial or financial relationships that could be construed as a potential conflict of interest.

## References

1. Wang, W.; Lu, X.; Wu, X.; Zhang, Y.; Wang, R.; Yang, D.; Pi, X. Chemical–mechanical polishing of 4H silicon carbide wafers. *Adv. Mater. Inter.* **2023**, *10*, 2202369. [CrossRef]
2. Takaya, H.; Misumi, T.; Fujiwara, H.; Ito, T. 4H-SiC Trench MOSFET with low on-resistance at high temperature. In Proceedings of the 2020 32nd International Symposium on Power Semiconductor Devices and ICs (ISPSD), Vienna, Austria, 13–18 September 2020; pp. 118–121.
3. Wu, J.P.; Ren, N.; Sheng, K. Design and experimental study of 1.2 kV 4H-SiC merged PiN Schottky diode. In Proceedings of the 2019 31st International Symposium on Power Semiconductor Devices and ICs(ISPSD), Shanghai, China, 19–23 May 2019; pp. 203–206.
4. Deng, X.; Xu, X.; Li, X.; Li, X.; Wen, Y.; Chen, W. A novel SiC MOSFET embedding low barrier diode with enhanced third quadrant and switching performance. *IEEE Electron. Device Lett.* **2020**, *41*, 1472–1475. [CrossRef]
5. Zhang, Y.L.; Zhang, J.; Ma, H.P.; Chi, Y.Q.; Tian, H.R.; Liu, J.H.; Liu, Q.B.; Chen, Z.G.; Zhang, Q.J. Failure mechanism of 4H-SiC junction barrier Schottky diodes under harsh thermal cycling stress. *Microelectron. Reliab.* **2022**, *136*, 114630. [CrossRef]
6. Yue, Y.; Zhu, H.; Liu, X.; Song, Y.; Zuo, X. First-principles study on non-radiative carrier captures of point defects associated with proton generation in silica. *Aip. Adv.* **2021**, *11*, 015214. [CrossRef]
7. Li, M.B.; Cao, F.; Hu, H.F.; Li, X.J.; Yang, J.Q.; Wang, Y. High single-event burnout resistance 4H-SiC junction barrier Schottky diode. *IEEE J. Electron. Devices Soc.* **2021**, *9*, 591–598. [CrossRef]
8. Meli, A.; Muoio, A.; Trotta, A.; Meda, L.; Parisi, M.; La Via, F. Epitaxial growth and characterization of 4H-SiC for neutron detection applications. *Materials* **2021**, *14*, 976. [CrossRef] [PubMed]
9. Lynch, J.; Yun, N.; Sung, W. Design considerations for high voltage SiC power devices: An experimental investigation into channel pinching of 10kV SiC junction barrier schottky (JBS) diodes. In Proceedings of the 2019 31st International Symposium on Power Semiconductor Devices and ICs(ISPSD), Shanghai, China, 19–23 May 2019; pp. 223–226.
10. Tiwari, A.K.; Antoniou, M.; Lophitis, N.; Perkins, S.; Trajkovic, T.; Udrea, F. Retrograde p-well for 10-kV class SiC IGBTs. *IEEE Trans. Electron. Devices* **2019**, *66*, 3066–3072. [CrossRef]
11. Zhang, Y.L.; Liu, P.; Lei, G.Y.; Zhang, Q.J. 1.2-kV Low-Barrier 4H-SiC JBS Diodes by Virtue of P-Implants Across Dead Field of Current Flow. *IEEE Trans. Electron. Devices* **2023**, *70*, 4293–4302. [CrossRef]
12. Niu, X.; Sang, L.; An, Y.; Wu, P.; Zhang, W.; Liu, R.; Du, Z.; Li, C.; Wei, X.; Yang, Y. Effect of overlap region for schottky metal and field oxide on the electrical characteristics of 6500 V/50A 4H-SiC JBS diodes. *J. Cryst. Growth* **2023**, *603*, 127009. [CrossRef]
13. Yuan, H.; Wang, C.; Tang, X.; Song, Q.; He, Y.; Zhang, Y.; Zhang, Y.; Xiao, L.; Wang, Y.; Wu, Y.; et al. Experimental study of high performance 4H-SiC floating junction jbs diodes. *IEEE Access* **2020**, *8*, 93039–93047. [CrossRef]
14. Wang, B.; Wang, H.; Wang, C.; Ren, N.; Guo, Q.; Sheng, K. Design and fabrication of 1.92 kV 4H-SiC super-junction SBD with wide-trench termination. *IEEE Trans. Electron. Devices* **2021**, *68*, 5674–5681. [CrossRef]
15. Zhang, Y.L.; Liu, P.F.; Zhang, J.; Ma, H.P.; Liu, J.H.; Liu, Q.B.; Chen, Z.G.; Zhang, Q.J. 1.2-kV 4H-SiC JBS diodes engaging p-type retrograde implants. *IEEE Trans. Electron. Devices* **2022**, *69*, 6963–6970. [CrossRef]
16. Yuan, J.; Guo, F.; Wang, K.; Liu, N.; Wu, C.; Yang, B. Demonstration of an 1200V/20A 4H-SiC Multi-Step Trenched Junction Barrier Schottky Diode. In Proceedings of the 19th China International Forum on Solid State Lighting & 2022 8th International Forum on Wide Bandgap Semiconductors (SSLCHINA: IFWS), Suzhou, China, 7–10 February 2023; pp. 1–3.
17. Dou, W.; Song, Q.; Yuan, H.; Tang, X.; Zhang, Y.; Zhang, Y.; Xiao, L.; Wang, L. Design and fabrication of high performance 4H-SiC TJBS diodes. *J. Cryst. Growth* **2020**, *533*, 125421. [CrossRef]
18. Yin, J.; Chen, S.; Chen, H.; Li, S.; Fu, H.; Liu, C. Design space of GaN vertical trench junction barrier schottky diodes: Comprehensive study and analytical modeling. *Electronics* **2022**, *11*, 1972. [CrossRef]
19. Pan, Y.; Tian, L.; Wu, H.; Li, Y.; Yang, F. 3.3 kV 4H-SiC JBS diodes with single-zone JTE termination. *Microelectron. Eng.* **2017**, *181*, 10–15. [CrossRef]
20. Deng, X.; Xu, S.; Zhang, B.; Zeng, L.; Li, C.; Wu, J.; Li, J. A near ideal edge termination technique for ultrahigh-voltage 4H-SiC devices with multi-zone gradient field limiting ring. In Proceedings of the 2018 1st Workshop on Wide Bandgap Power Devices and Applications in Asia (WiPDA Asia), Xi'an, China, 16–18 May 2018; pp. 144–148.

21. Yuan, H.; Liu, Y.; He, Y.; Hu, Y.; Zhang, T.; Tang, X.; Song, Q.; Zhnag, Y.; Zhnag, Y.; He, X.; et al. Characteristic and robustness of trench floating limiting rings for 4H-SiC junction barrier Schottky rectifiers. *IEEE Electron. Device Lett.* **2020**, *41*, 1056–1059. [CrossRef]
22. Donato, N.; Udrea, F.; Mihaila, A.; Knoll, L.; Romano, G.; Kranz, L.; Antoniou, M. Single and repetitive surge current events of 3.3 kV-20 a 4H-SiC JBS rectifiers: The impact of the anode layout. In Proceedings of the 2020 32nd International Symposium on Power Semiconductor Devices and ICs (ISPSD), Vienna, Austria, 13–18 September 2020; pp. 198–201.
23. Mancini, S.A.; Jang, S.Y.; Chen, Z.; Kim, D.; Lynch, J.; Liu, Y.; Raghothamachar, B.; Kang, M.; Agarwal, A.; Mahadik, N.; et al. Static Performance and Reliability of 4H-SiC Diodes with $P^+$ Regions Formed by Various Profiles and Temperatures. In Proceedings of the 2022 IEEE International Reliability Physics Symposium (IRPS), Dallas, TX, USA, 27–31 March 2022; Volume 62.
24. Liu, K.; Zhang, Z.; Tang, X.; Yuan, H.; Zhang, Y.; Liu, Y.; Han, C.; Zhou, Y.; Du, F.; Wang, Z.; et al. Experimental and Simulation Study of Single-Event Leakage Current Degradation and Damage Mechanism in 4H-SiC PiN Diodes. *IEEE Trans. Electron. Devices* **2024**, *71*, 4891–4896. [CrossRef]
25. Sang, L.; Tian, L.; Li, J.; Niu, Y.; Jin, R. Effect of $P^+$ region design on the fabrication of 6500 V 4H-SiC JBS diodes. *J. Cryst. Growth* **2020**, *530*, 125317. [CrossRef]
26. Kang, I.H.; Seok, O.; Moon, J.H.; Na, M.K.; Kim, H.W.; Kim, S.C.; Bahng, W.; Kim, N.K. Design and Fabrication of 1.2 kV/10A 4H-SiC Junction Barrier Schottky Diodes with High Current Density. *Trans. Electr. Electron. Mater.* **2021**, *22*, 115–120. [CrossRef]
27. Kim, D.; Jang, S.Y.; DeBoer, S.; Morgan, A.J.; Sung, W. An optimal design for 1.2 kV 4H-SiC JBSFET (junction barrier Schottky diode integrated MOSFET) with deep P-well. *IEEE Electron. Device Lett.* **2022**, *43*, 785–788. [CrossRef]

MDPI AG
Grosspeteranlage 5
4052 Basel
Switzerland
Tel.: +41 61 683 77 34

*Electronics* Editorial Office
E-mail: electronics@mdpi.com
www.mdpi.com/journal/electronics

www.ingramcontent.com/pod-product-compliance
Lightning Source LLC
Chambersburg PA
CBHW061617210926
51850CB00009B/2357
* 9 7 8 3 7 2 5 8 7 3 0 4 3 *